Black Power U.S.A.

Black Power U S A
The Human Side
of Reconstruction,
1867-1877

LERONE BENNETT JR.

Johnson Publishing Company, Inc.

CHICAGO: 1967

FOR GEORGE, CLARA, THELMA,
AND MILDRED

Preface

$\mathbf{A}$T THE END of the Civil War, America embarked on a racial experiment unprecedented in the inner precincts of the Western world.

In a remarkable turnabout, the former slaves were enfranchised and lifted to a position of real political power vis-à-vis their former masters. And the new national purpose was expressed in the ratification of the Fourteenth and Fifteenth Amendments and passage of the most stringent civil rights legislation ever enacted in America.

It was in this climate that black and white men made the first and, in many ways, the last real attempt to establish an interracial democracy in America. During the heyday of Reconstruction, in the years between 1867 and 1877, black men were elected to the legislatures of every Southern state. Lieutenant governors and other cabinet officers were elected in Mississippi, Louisiana, and South Carolina. Twenty black men were sent to the U. S. House of Representatives from the South, and two black politicians were elected to the U. S. Senate from the state of Mississippi.

Reconstruction in all its various facets was a supreme lesson for America, the right reading of which might still mark a turning point in our history. As a matter of fact, an understanding of the triumphs and failures of this first Reconstruction is indispensable for an understanding of the triumphs and failures of the second Reconstruction we are now undergoing.

The history of this period has been a matter of extreme controversy for several decades. Until quite recently, most white historians denounced the "Africanization" of the South as "a soul-sickening spectacle" of "military despotism," "graft," and "inefficiency." Woodrow Wilson, to cite only one example, was appalled by the whole era and wrote scathingly of the former slaves as "a host of dusky children untimely put out of school."

Within recent years, modern scholars, following the lead of W. E. B. Du Bois and other Negro historians, have proved conclusively that the works of Wilson and other conservative writers were white-oriented distortions of Reconstruction reality. I have attempted in this brief history to give wider currency to the findings of these scholars. I have also made an attempt, based on my own independent research, to give a new dimension to the human conflicts and aspirations of the period.

This book developed over a period of six years. The original research was done for a chapter on Reconstruction, entitled "Black Power in Dixie," which appeared in my history of the Negro, *Before the Mayflower*, published in 1962. The book assumed its present form when I selected the same title, "Black Power," for a study of the Reconstruction period which appeared in *Ebony* magazine from November, 1965 to January, 1967. Since my public use of the title predated the current controversy over Black Power, I have retained it here as an expression of the only period in American history in which black people had real, that is to say effective, power. The original articles have been expanded and rewritten for book publication.

I am grateful to my publisher, John H. Johnson, who made it possible for me to spend two years researching and writing the book. I am also indebted to my editor, Brenda Biram, and to Lucille Phinnie, special librarian at Johnson Publishing Company. I should like to express my appreciation to the personnel of the Newberry Library, the Moorland Library, the Chicago Historical Society and the Hall Branch of the Chicago Public Library. Needless to say, I alone am responsible for whatever shortcomings the book might have.

LERONE BENNETT JR.

Chicago, Illinois

Contents

Illustrations

Black Power U.S.A.
The Human Side of
Reconstruction,
1867-1877

1

Prelude to Power

IT BEGAN HERE in the red blackness of a Friday dawn.

It began out there, on a shoal in the harbor, where, six years ago come April, men mad with passion and fear fired on Fort Sumter and initiated the big war which devoured them and freed their slaves.

And now, after the benediction of blood and steel and the burial of six hundred thousand young men, it is going to end here in Charleston where it all began with a new start the likes of which the world has never seen before. To be precise, it is going to end at the old Charleston Clubhouse on Meeting Street where seventy-six black men, many of them former slaves, and forty-eight white men, some of them former slaveowners, are already gathering to write a new constitution for the state of South Carolina. As these men gather, diffident and somewhat unsure of themselves, their words and gestures are recorded by passels of reporters, drawn here by the spectacle of the first official assembly in the white Western world with a black majority.

Charleston, which has seen many beginnings and many endings, awaits the opening of this extraordinary assemblage, tight with tension. The former masters, expecting riot and disaster, are holed up now in the fine old white mansions near the Battery; and the former slaves, expecting land and retribution, are roaming the streets, giving vent to long-suppressed hopes and emotions.

This day is Tuesday, January 14, 1868; all morning long you meet nothing on the Palmetto-fringed streets but waves of rejoicing blacks. Black people have been pouring into the city since first light; and now, as the historic moment approaches for the noon opening of the assembly, the city is ablaze with the sights and sounds of a world in transition. Black vendors wend their way through the crowds, wooden platters topped with coral-tipped shrimp on their heads, rhythmic cries coming from their lips. Black women, red handkerchiefs covering their heads, carry on a haggling commerce at curb-side stands offering a tempting stock of molasses and benne candy, ground-nut cakes and sassafras beer. Through the narrow streets clatters an extraordinary profusion of wagons and carts of every age and vintage, each one, a visiting reporter notes, "rivalling the other in age, in corners, in shakiness, in protuberance and in general disposition to tumble down and dissolve." Hanging over all, giving a subtle tone and color to all, is the overwhelming presence and reality of blackness. Everywhere one looks on this Tuesday, everywhere one turns — on fashionable King Street, on the Battery, even in the war-singed "Burnt District" — there are black people of all shades and tints: charcoal, chocolate, mahogany, cream.

A mood, frightening in its intensity, oozes up from the restless black people who are moving aimlessly now through the streets. What shall we name this mood? Defiance? Desperation? Joy? The mood is made of all these, but most of all it is made of hope. In their revolutionary innocence, these people actually believe that all things are going to be made new.

Almost all of them are discussing the drama on which the curtain has not yet risen. And some of the elderly men stand somewhat apart on street corners and, from time to time, their eyes move up Meeting Street to the Charleston Clubhouse where the pepper-and-salt assembly is going to convene.

The Charleston Clubhouse is a fine place to make history, for so much history has been made here or near here. Not too far away, in his rooms on Bull Street, Denmark Vesey conceived and almost executed the slave insurrection that terrified the South in 1822. A few blocks away, at Secession Hall on Broad Street, the South Carolina Secession convention took the first step toward Appomattox and Black Power. Now, after hundreds of years of blood and whips and chains, the color of power is changing and black people are scurrying through the white and watchful streets to the fashionable Charleston Clubhouse which has been the scene of so many joyous social events for white-skinned Charlestonians.

It is a matter of grave concern to "proper" Charlestonians that the first meeting of the new regime is to be held in the sacrosanct rooms of this institution. Some aristocrats have charged indignantly that black men of power and their white allies purposely selected the locale in order to humiliate them. Weighed down by the grossness of the thing, the old aristocrats sit now, disconsolate, behind shuttered windows in the quaint, slate-covered houses near St. Michael's. To them and to their allies, this is the first day of hell. Evil men, they say, have taken their power and have given it to their former slaves. An "ignorant and depraved race" has been placed "in power and influence above the virtuous, the educated and the refined." It is an insult, sir, to "Anglo-Saxon race and blood," "to God and to nature." Thus speak the former slaveholders as they contemplate from afar "the maddest, most unscrupulous, and infamous revolution in history." Day and night, the old planters speak of nothing else. And almost all of their anxieties condense themselves in one question, unstated, unasked: "Will black people, now that they have power, do unto us, as we have done unto them?"

Outside the windows of the fashionable white houses, the black crowd eddies, starting, halting, murmuring, singing, shouting, flowing along like black lava to the Charleston Clubhouse where the seventy-six black men and forty-eight white men have gathered to make law for South Carolina's black majority and its white minority.

Before following the crowd, let us pause for a moment to get our bearings. The drama we are about to witness is the symbolic peak of a nationwide struggle which has raged in America since the end of the war. Two years ago, President Andrew Johnson made a hurried and unsuccessful attempt to settle the war issues and reconstruct the late rebel states on the basis of the white electorate. This attempt was foiled by Congress, which passed the Fourteenth Amendment and enfranchised the freedmen who compose a majority of the registered voters in five states—South Carolina, Mississippi, Alabama, Florida, and Louisiana—and the balance of power in the remaining states of the old Confederacy. Beginning last year, the freedmen embarked on a career of power by organizing political parties and trooping in large numbers to the polls. Now, after a turbulent period of riots and church burnings and whippings and demonstrations, the black harvest is about to begin.

At this very moment, in capitals all over the South, black and white men are rewriting the basic law of the South in constitutional conventions. Only in South Carolina, however, do black delegates comprise a majority. Hence the excitement and intensity that pulsate through the Charleston Clubhouse where a huge crowd, including many Northern reporters, is now gathering. Let us join the crowd, noting with the *New York Times* correspondent that the black spectators seem perfectly at home and that they are spitting around "as naturally as any white native."

The large room in which we find ourselves was made for lighter, whiter pleasures. It is, in fact, a ballroom, and about a third of the floor has been railed off for the public. This space is filled now by an integrated crowd, predominantly black. The reporters occupy the bar, on both sides of the president's platform, facing the delegates.

Viewed collectively, the delegates are impressive, presenting in their frock coats, side whiskers and beards, the same picture as similar bodies in the North. Indeed, the "get-up" of the convention, as a Northern reporter phrases it, "is so respectable that the Charleston journals" cannot help remarking it, pointing out that "many of the colored delegates [are] intelligent and respectable-looking." One ought to note, however, that a great controversy is raging outside these walls over one black delegate who showed up today in a gray Confederate overcoat. Local pundits are interpreting this as a studied political insult to the Confederate dead.

We can discern three distinct groups among the delegates before us: (1) the black group, itself divided into former slaves, roughly fifty-seven of the seventy-six, and men who were free before the war; (2) the twenty-seven native white Southerners who have abandoned white supremacy with varying degrees of sincerity in order to create a new social order in South Carolina; (3) Northern-born white men who settled in the state after the war, as missionaries, planters, or businessmen. There is, of course, considerable speculation about the white Southerners. Some of them are former slaveholders, some are former Confederate soldiers. What are they doing here? Some are here out of hope of gain, some out of zeal, some out of a dim appreciation of the possibilities of bridging the gap between the races. Solomon George Washington Dill of Kershaw, for example, is a poor white who believes that the salvation of the poor white and of the South lies in a coalition of poor whites and poor blacks.

It is being said outside this hall that the first group, the dominant black group, is singularly deficient in the skills of government and that former slaves, fresh from the cottonfields, have taken over the state. Is this true? Let us consult the official roster which indicates that the black men of power are, as one scholar later notes, "anything but ex-field hands." The leading black delegates are, in fact, lawyers, ministers, businessmen, teachers, former Union soldiers.

What of the former slaves? Surely, the critics are right about them. Let us see. Eight of the former slaves are ministers, two are businessmen, one is a former captain in the U.S. Navy. The rest are carpenters, blacksmiths, shoemakers, coachmen, barbers, teachers, carriage-makers, waiters. Most of these men are literate. Only a few are without the rudiments of education, and even they are wise in the ways of the world. To understand what follows, however, one must remember that training is not education and that literacy is not wisdom. The race in affairs of power is not always to the A.B. degree, nor is the battle to the learned. Beverly Nash, six feet two inches, exquisitely black, an ex-waiter and bootblack, is a living example of this fact. It is said hereabouts that this former slave has a razor-sharp mind and quotes Shakespeare with ease and eloquence.

Lifting our eyes from the roster to the scene before us, we perceive immediately that the men in this hall are adequate to the demands of the hour. Already, they have assumed the air and address of power. Some are whispering in ears, preparing deals and booby traps. Standing somewhat apart, taking the measure of their colleagues, are the managers, the men—black and white—who will end up on top. Here, for example, is Franklin J. Moses Jr., a Charleston bluebood who helped pull down the U.S. flag at Fort Sumter and later leaped, with extraordinary agility, to the side of the freedmen. Though he kisses black babies with practiced skill and speeds through the streets of Charleston with sumptuously gowned black belles, it is said in the corridors that he bears watching. And what is being said is perfectly true. Magnetic, charming, unscrupulous,

Franklin J. Moses Jr., South Carolina's native son, is something of an archetype of the age's opportunists.

Another man who will go far, a completely different type, comes into our view. As he moves through the crowd, shaking hands here, bowing there, eyes follow him. This is Robert Brown Elliott, twenty-five, a graduate of England's Eton, black, clean-shaven, commanding. He will sit in this convention for fourteen days without opening his mouth. Then, speaking, he will establish himself as one of the South's greatest orators. Let us mark Elliott well. He is a brilliant man, an ambitious man. We shall hear more of him. Even now, he is dreaming of the governor's chair. Another man, of similar educational attainments but of a different color, stands somewhat apart, looking more like a professor than a politician. This is Daniel Henry Chamberlain, a Northern-born white man who is a graduate of Harvard and Yale. Chamberlain, who is thirty-two, is also aiming for the governor's chair.

Three men now, standing on the edge of the group, whispering. The man in the middle, fair of skin with luxuriant side whiskers, is Francis Louis Cardozo, the son of a Charleston Jewish economist and a black woman, a Presbyterian minister, a school principal and a graduate of the University of Glasgow. Cardozo is thirty. On his left, listening intently, is a war hero, Robert Smalls, late captain in the U.S. Navy, a bold former slave who electrified the North by sailing the steamer "Planter" out of the Charleston harbor under the guns of the Confederate fleet. Smalls, who is now twenty-eight, is also the son of a Jew and a black woman. The third man, *the man talking*, is Richard Harvey Cain who is, in some respects, a prototype of Adam Clayton Powell. He is in his early forties, somewhat older than his colleagues, most of whom are in their twenties and thirties. Born free, Cain is eloquent, shrewd, enterprising. He heads the huge Emanuel AME Church of Charleston and it is said here that his church is "one of the strongest political organizations in the state." As Cain whispers, laying the foundations of power,

Thomas J. Robertson, a former slaveowner and one of the wealthiest men in the state, mounts the flag-draped platform between the two bars. The talk dies down. The delegates take their seats. There is a moment of electric silence. Then Robertson, fully conscious of the eyes of history, brings the gavel down with a flourish. The convention called "for the purpose of framing a constitutional and civil government" for the state of South Carolina is in session.

THUS BEGAN the first and last real attempt to establish a truly interracial society in the white-obsessed regions of the Western world. Members of the convention, aware of the gravity of the occasion, moved cautiously at first. Northern friends had told black delegates that it would be imprudent for them to use their power directly in the first innings of the game. They had advised black leaders to work through sympathetic white men. This advice, which would have disastrous consequences, was followed, and Albert Gallatin Mackey, a native white South Carolinian and a nationally known expert on Masonry, was elected permanent president of the convention. A full slate of subsidiary officers, including two black vice-presidents, was also elected.

The organizing over, the first fateful words said, the delegates adjourned to the hotel lobbies and the drawing rooms of the large and well-to-do free Negro colony of Charleston. One can readily imagine the leading members of the convention bowing deep in one of these rooms, kissing the hands of the Rollin sisters, five dazzlingly beautiful daughters of a Frenchman and a black woman. Some delegates doubtless gathered around the sisters—Katherine, Charlotte, Louise, Florence, Marie—and discussed Byron, an especial favorite of the *café au lait* beauties. Other delegates—less literary perhaps, certainly more practical—huddled in darker rooms and discussed the advisability of confiscating the white man's land and dividing it among poor whites and poor blacks.

Outside the rooms of power, the streets pulsated with wispy rumors of the impending confiscation and distribution of land. The mood of the people in the streets was avowedly revolutionary. The black people of South Carolina had been deeply stirred by the day's events, and they expected great deeds from the assembled delegates. Most of all, they expected land, and the Revolution would be judged by its success in meeting that basic demand. Farther away, in the charming old houses of the old aristocrats, all was silence and gloom, and the windows were dark.

Such was the spirit of Charleston, South Carolina, on Tuesday, January 14, 1868, the first day of a constitutional convention which symbolized in its sweep and promise the beginning of America's Second Revolution.

To understand that revolution and why it failed, to relate the Revolution to the central issues of that day and of this one, to understand how black men attained the palm of power and why it drooped and died in their hands, it is necessary to go back now and examine the forces that paradoxically midwifed the Revolution and dug its grave at the same time.

At the war's end, nobody thought it would come to this—with black men and their white allies making and administrating laws for black and white people. Back there, at the end of the war, men in the North and South were overwhelmed by the gravity of a situation without precedent in American law and history. Eleven states were out of the Union. Four million black people, neither slaves nor free men, were tramping the roads, restless and discontented; and their former masters, impoverished and embittered, were cowering in shuttered rooms, fearing a Southwide insurrection. This situation presented grave problems of power and statesmanship. How and under what conditions were the rebel states to be readmitted to the Union? What was to be done to the former Confederate leaders, many of whom had violated federal and state oaths in a revolutionary attempt to rend the Union? Above all else, what was to be done *to, for* and *with* the former slaves? The status of the more than one hundred thousand Southern slaves who had enlisted in the Union Army was particularly delicate. Could the nation, would the nation, refuse ballots to men who had helped to save the nation while extending ballots to Confederate veterans who had tried to destroy the nation?

There were no clear answers to these questions in the North at the end of the war because there had been no clear purpose in the North at the beginning of the war. Deeply divided against itself, cleft by conflicting tendencies and purposes, the North had never really decided what it was fighting for. And since one man who knows what he is fighting for is a match for ten who don't, the North was at a distinct disadvantage, particularly in the opening rounds, against a smaller and materially weaker opponent. The South was fighting for slavery, a name that stands here for a whole way of life, *a whole way of organizing white men as well as black men.* With the South fighting for slavery, the North was in the enviable position of appropriating the alternative slogan — freedom. What is truly astonishing is that the North resisted this boon, preferring in the early stages to define the war narrowly as a war for Union, a legalistically abstract notion of the perpetual adherence of abstract unities. The North's reluctance to take an open stand on the issue of freedom and its subsequent vacillation in defining its war aims explain much that would otherwise be incomprehensible in the Reconstruction period. For the war one fights is a reflection of the peace one seeks. What peace did the North seek? Or better still: What did the North want? Northerners never answered these questions or, to be more precise, they answered them in different ways at different times. And this confusion of will and direction was manifested in the fumbling of Northern generals, many of whom were half-convinced of the soundness of the Southern idea, and the ambivalence of Northern soldiers, many of whom believed that the great evil of slavery was that its benefits were restricted to too small a circle.

The Hamlet-like indecision of the generals, the ambivalence of the foot soldiers, and the resistance and defiance of white workers who saw the war as a struggle for "rich white folks and poor niggers"—all these currents reflected the agonies of a society in transit from the Jeffersonian Eden (which had never really existed) to a vague and threatening world with undefined shadows and contours.

Under the impact of slavery and the industrial revolution, the Northern social structure had been pushed into strange and disturbing shapes, and the old political rhetoric of a society of independent farmers and artisans directly participating in power was no longer relevant to the new world of cities and machines. More sinister yet was the erosion of the Revolutionary faith. By the time of the Civil War, America had drifted so far away from the ideals of the original American Revolution that the vocabulary of that epoch seemed strange, even menacing, to many. Hence the embarrassment of Northerners in the face of abolitionist demands for a crusade of freedom against slavery. Hence Northern groping and fumbling for a counter-ideal in the face of the Confederates who openly proclaimed their willingness to fight and die for human slavery and the rule of the many by the few. Northerners were helpless against this antidemocratic idea for the very simple reason that the anti-democratic idea had penetrated deeply into the tissue of Northern society.

Throughout this period—and on into the Reconstruction period that followed—a small band of abolitionists, based primarily in New England, railed against the flaccidity of the Northern soul. But the abolitionists occupied a position in the nineteenth century roughly comparable to the civil rights and peace activists of the twentieth century. They were, in short, a small and despised minority, regarded by their contemporaries as eccentric troublemakers. It was not until the abolitionists touched that great bedrock of social change — Yankee self-inter-est — that the North roused itself for a life-and-death struggle against slavery. In the decade before the Civil War rising concern over the free lands of the West (which were coveted by the slaveowners) and demands for government protection of the expanding industrial empire (which were opposed by the slaveowners) pushed Northerners closer to the abolitionist movement. Out of this extraordinary miscegenation of Puritan idealism and Yankee self-interest came the Free Soil party, the Republican party, and Abraham Lincoln.

Abraham Lincoln was the agony of the North made flesh.

A conservative Illinois railroad lawyer, born in Kentucky and raised in Southern Illinois, Lincoln was neither an aboli-tionist nor a racial liberal; and few American Presidents have been more averse to sudden social change or large-scale social experiments. The man's character, his way with words, and his assassination, together with the psychological needs of a racist society, have obscured these contradictions under a mountain of myths which undoubtedly would have amused Lincoln, who had a wonderful sense of the ridiculous and the ironic. The qualities Lincoln didn't have were the qualities the North didn't have, and it would be interesting to speculate on the dark — the precise word — urges that drove Americans to invest Lincoln with precisely the qualities that he and they lacked.

Like most white men of his section and station, Lincoln had deep-seated fears and phobias on the race question. It appears from the record that he had profound doubts about the possi-bility of realizing the Declaration of Independence on this soil. And until his death he believed that black Americans and white Americans would be much better off separated — preferably with the Atlantic Ocean or some other large body of water between them.

Lincoln grew during the war — but he didn't grow much. On every issue relating to the black man — on Emancipation, on the use and protection of black soldiers, on the confiscation and distribution of rebel property — he was vague, dilatory, contradictory. It was left to a runaway Congress, paced by Charles Sumner and Thaddeus Stevens, to define the issues of the war by authorizing the employment of black soldiers, the emancipation of the slaves and the confiscation of rebel property. Lincoln followed Congress' lead slowly and cautiously, moving to the high ground of the Emancipation Proclamation under persistent pressure from powerful segments of Northern public opinion. Nothing better illustrates Lincoln's ambivalence than the Emancipation Proclamation which was as dry as a real estate brief and contained none of the sonorous rhetoric of which Lincoln was capable when his emotions and principles were engaged. Moreover, the document didn't free a single slave. Lincoln "freed" the slaves where he had no power (in the Confederacy) and left them in chains where he had power (in the Border States and areas under federal control in the South). The theory behind the Proclamation, an English paper noted tartly, "is not that a human being cannot justly own another, but that he cannot own him unless he is loyal to the United States."

In peace, as in war, Lincoln's policy on the black man was to have no policy. In the beginning, he defined the war as a struggle for the preservation of the Union, a struggle in no way related to the black man or the issue of freedom. After issuing the Emancipation Proclamation, Lincoln shifted gears and announced a new policy of liberation and social renovation. At Gettysburg, on November 19, 1863, he said America was engaged in a great war testing whether it or any other nation "conceived in liberty and dedicated to the proposition that all men are created equal" could long endure. The war would decide whether "government of the people, by the people, for the people" would perish from the earth. It was a war to give America "a new birth of freedom." But how was all this to be done? How was America to be given a new birth of freedom?

More concretely, what did the phrase "government of the people, by the people, for the people" mean in the context, say, of South Carolina where the overwhelming majority of the people were black?

Lincoln was silent on these questions. When he unveiled his postwar program, he repudiated Gettysburg and went back to the war aims of 1861 with yet another oratorical flourish: "With malice toward none, with charity for all." What did this mean? How could one be charitable to both the former slave-owner, who was determined to keep his former slaves as close to slavery as possible and the former slave, who was determined to have all the rights enunciated in the Declaration of Independence and the U.S. Constitution? The claims of the unrepentant slaveholder and the resistant freedman were mutually exclusive. They could not be bridged by eloquent perorations. Nor did Lincoln try to bridge them. When he left the realm of rhetoric and got down to the grubby specifics, it was evident that *all* meant the same thing to Lincoln that it had always meant: all white people. In his Proclamation of Amnesty and Reconstruction, issued on December 8, 1863, Lincoln placed under the ban of proscription all high-ranking Confederate military officers and all persons who had held state or federal offices and had abandoned them to support the Confederacy. As for the rest of the white population, Lincoln was willing to forgive and forget. He would recognize any rebel state in which one-tenth of the white voters of 1860 took an oath of allegiance to the United States and organized a government which renounced slavery. What of the black people? Slavery apart, Lincoln ignored them. Incredibly, the commander-in-chief of the U.S. Army abandoned his black soldiers to the passions of Confederate veterans who feared and hated them. Lincoln barely suggested "privately" that it would be a good thing for Southern states to extend the ballot "to the very intelligent" [Negroes], and especially those who have fought gallantly in our ranks." But these were private sentiments, not public acts, and they were expressed in an extremely hesitant manner at that. Lincoln didn't require fair or equal treatment of the freedmen. In fact, he didn't make any demands at all. Reconstruction Lincoln style was going to be a reconstruction of the white people, by the white people, for the white people. It was also going to be a reconstruction dominated by the President, though this was hotly and immediately contested by Congress, which reflected the new militancy of Northerners educated by six hundred thousand casualties. Benjamin Franklin Wade, the astringently brilliant senator from Ohio, and Henry Winter Davis, the radical Maryland representative, challenged Lincoln with a counter-plan which claimed the whole issue for Congress and required the participation of a majority, instead of one-tenth, of the white electorate. The Wade-Davis Bill also demanded what became known as "the iron-clad oath" — an oath which stipulated that the person had never *voluntarily* borne arms against the United States of America.

When Lincoln pocket-vetoed the Wade-Davis Bill, blandly observing that he was unwilling to commit himself to any one plan of reconstruction, Wade and Davis issued a manifesto which marked a new plateau in public denunciation of a U.S. President. Not long after that, Congress added repudiation to insult by refusing to recognize the newly organized "Lincoln states" of Arkansas, Tennessee, and Louisiana. Charles Sumner of Massachusetts led this revolt, filibustering until the Senate dropped "the pretended state government" of Louisiana which Sumner grandiloquently called "a mere seven-months abortion, begotten by the bayonet in criminal conjunction with the spirit of caste, and born before its time, rickety, unformed, unfinished — whose continued existence will be a burden, a reproach and a wrong." Sumner was also in the forefront of the congressional forces which created on March 3, 1865, the Bureau of Refugees, Freedmen, and Abandoned Lands (the Freedmen's Bureau).

In the deepening political crisis, some men spoke openly of

the impeachment and trial of Abraham Lincoln. George Washington Julian, the radical representative from Indiana, set the stage for legal action in a remarkable House speech which called Lincoln to account for "the blunders, proceeding from a feeble, timid, ambidextrous policy, resulting in great sacrifices of life and treasure, and perilling the priceless interests at stake." Lincoln, Julian said, had moved to a policy of emancipation after "much hesitation and apparent reluctance ... great deliberation, and many misgivings," stemming apparently from a dislike of "radical and extreme measures" and fear of "a revolutionary conflict." Should the President back down now, Julian said, should "he now place himself in the people's way, by reviving the old policy of tenderness to the rebels," he would be called to account.

Lincoln refused to answer in kind. To visitors, he explained that he was doing the best he could and that he didn't intend to be hurried into precipitate action. At the same time he maneuvered skillfully to avoid answering the question of whether the rebel states were in or out of the Union. This question, which was argued with metaphysical passion by opponents and proponents of a hard peace, was a mask for questions of substance and style. If the states were still in the Union, it would be impossible to reorder their domestic institutions without a Constitutional amendment. But if they were out of the Union, Congress could work its will, imposing standards of racial equality and confiscating land. Congress, focusing on the end, argued that the states were out of the Union. Lincoln, who said he sympathized with the end of racial equality, opposed the only means that could lead to that end. In his view, the states were merely out of their proper relation with the Union. As for the complex racial question, he said he was concerned to spare the races the "evils of sudden derangement." He was searching, or so he said, for some arrangement "by which the two races could gradually live themselves out of their old relations to each other." He hoped, moreover, to send some or perhaps all of the freedmen to Africa or South America. A few days before his death, he called Benjamin Butler, the radical Union general and Massachusetts politician, to the White House and inquired about the possiblities of "sending the blacks away." According to Butler, Lincoln said "I wish you would examine the question and give me your views upon it and go into the figures as you did before in some degree so as to show whether the Negroes can be exported." Butler went away and came back two days later with a sad story. "Mr. President," he said, "I have gone very carefully over my calculation as to the power of the country to export the Negroes of the South and I assure you that, using all your naval vessels and all the merchant marine fit to cross the seas with safety, it will be impossible for you to transport to the nearest place that can be found fit for them—and that is the Island of San Domingo, half as fast as Negro children will be born here."

The confusion of purpose in Washington at this moment had the most serious consequences, for the time for imposing a lasting solution was at the end of the war when the opposition was weak and disorganized. The South at this plastic moment was dazed by the trauma of defeat. Most Confederate leaders expected imprisonment, confiscation, perhaps even banishment. Expecting the worst, they were willing to give up many things in order to keep some. If there was ever a moment for imposing a lasting solution to the American racial problem, this was it. But the North dawdled and the moment passed. When the Confederates realized that the North was divided and unsure, hope returned. And with hope came a revival of the spirit of rebellion. Charles Sumner, Carl Schurz and other Radical leaders were to point out later that this was one of the greatest political blunders in American history.

The implications of this political failure have never been adequately analysed. Nor has adequate attention been given to Lincoln's role in the failure. If Lincoln had a plan for giving

America a new birth of freedom, he never unveiled it. Nor did
he use the powers of his office to educate the public. Even
worse, he and his successor let one of those moments which are
decades in preparation slip by without indicating that they
understood that the war had released forces that made possible
a great leap forward. Good faith and largeness of character
apart, it would not be ungenerous to say that Lincoln either
misunderstood the nature of the struggle or lacked the will and
vision to give America a new birth of freedom. This was
evident in the way he conducted the war, in his unwillingness
to evoke the dynamic of democracy as a fighting faith. It was
evident, too, in his attempt to make peace by ignoring the
forces that caused the war. He didn't see in the concluded
struggle new and immense possibilities. He thought of a Union
preserved instead of a Union to be created. And if Lincoln,
with his social gifts, overlooked the plastic possibilities of the
moment, it is hardly surprising that his successor took a narrow
view.

    While Lincoln and the North thrashed about in the agony of
indecision, History decided. Lincoln went to Ford's Theater,
John Wilkes Booth shot him, and Andrew Johnson became the
seventeenth President of the United States. Almost everyone
was shocked by Lincoln's assassination, but "the feeling [in the
Radical camp]," Julian reported, "was nearly universal that the
accession of Johnson would prove a Godsend to our cause."
After all, Johnson was reputed to be something of a social
revolutionary. And it was of record that he had advocated
confiscation of rebel property and punishment of the architects
of the rebellion. In the weeks that followed his accession to
power, Johnson's statement that "treason must be made odious
and the traitors must be punished and impoverished" was
recalled with appreciation in many Washington drawing rooms.
Reviewing Johnson's record, recalling his blunt views on the

major issues of the day, Radicals convinced themselves that
their cause was safe. This was a classic example of men seeing
what they wanted to see. For Johnson's rhetoric, like Lincoln's,
was misleading, as the Radicals would have discovered had
they probed in the tangled skein of his life.

An Andrew Jackson Democrat, a Southern Loyalist and a
former slaveholder, Johnson had clawed his way from the
mudsills of the poor white communities of North Carolina and
Tennessee to the summit of power, and the marks of passage
were graven on his skin. Deeply sensitive to nuances of place
and position, envious of the rich whites above him and suspicious of the poor blacks beneath, he was a dark-haired man of
medium height, physically powerful and personally courageous, but somewhat unsure of himself and therefore vain,
disputatious, graceless. He had been born in poverty in North
Carolina in 1808 and was thus fifty-six when he became
President and fifty-nine when Congress came within one vote
of dismissing him from office. At an early age, he removed to
Tennessee where he mastered the trade of tailoring, married,
and learned the ABC's—in that order. He then branched out
into politics, serving as U.S. representative, governor, and U.S.
senator. As a senator, he authored the Homestead Bill and
opposed the encroachments of what he called the Northern
"money power." When the war came, he chose the Union
instead of the Confederacy and Lincoln made him military
governor of Tennessee. In 1864, in a gesture of national unity,
Lincoln selected him as his running mate on the National
Union ticket.

Johnson came on the national scene with a social philosophy
that was confused and chaotic. He was for the poor man, but
against the black man, who was the poorest of all men. He was
against slavery, but he had owned eight slaves. He had
promised in a speech in Nashville to assume the mantle of
Moses and lead black people "through the Red Sea of war and
bondage to a fairer future of liberty and peace," but he had said

in the same speech that "this is a white man's government."

Politically, Johnson was an archetypal example of a classical American political type, the poor boy who hacks his way upwards and arrives at the top enchanted by the company he is keeping and forgetful of what it was he originally wanted and what he intended to do once he got there. The Radical Republicans were wrong: Johnson was no social revolutionary. His radicalism didn't go beyond a sentimental and somewhat demagogic concern over the plight of poor whites. And his defiance, far from expressing an authenic vision of social change, was the obverse side of his yearning for respectablitiy and acceptance within the system. Told once that abolitionists were fighting to free the black man and change the American social structure, Johnson exploded: "Damn the Negroes. I am fighting those traitorous aristocrats, their masters."

Johnson opposed slavery, not because it was wrong, but because it degraded poor whites. On this issue, as on others, he was much closer to Lincoln than to Radical Republicans. Like Lincoln, he had grave doubts about the possibility of black and white Americans living together in peace. Like Lincoln, he was obsessed by fears of a race war. Where the two men differed was in their reading of the motives and aims of Southern aristocrats. Johnson, who had lived in a primary relationship with planter scorn and pretensions, had no illusions about the political imperatives of peace. The first requirement, he said, was the destruction of the social power of the aristocrats. It would be necessary to seize the great plantations, divide them into small farms and sell them to "honest, industrious men." When the war ended, Johnson thanked God, saying that the conflict had freed "more whites than blacks."

Radical Republicans who called on Johnson after his inauguration found him strong in the Radical faith and eager to please. Charles Sumner reported that Johnson's "sympathy was entirely different from his predecessor." Sumner understood Johnson to say that black people were to have the ballot and that the rebel states would have to undergo a period of probation before being readmitted to the Union. Sumner was so impressed by Johnson's grasp of the realities of the hour that he left the White House feeling that the great battle of his life was nearing a successful conclusion.

While the Radical Republicans congratulated themselves on the impending end of the struggle for equal rights, President Johnson turned his mind to the specifics, sending emissaries to the South for hard facts on which to base a policy.

The South to which Johnson's emissaries went in the hot, dry summer of 1865 was in the throes of a tumultuous social upheaval. Moving across the South on a Johnson mission, General Carl Schurz, a Radical Republican who had participated in the Revolution of 1848 in Germany, saw a land that "looked for many miles like a broad black streak of ruin and desolation—the fences all gone; lonesome smoke stacks, surrounded by dark heaps of ashes and cinders, marking the spots where human habitations had stood; the fields along the roads wildly overgrown by weeds, with here and there a sickly patch of cotton and corn cultivated by Negro squatters." Once proud cities, like Columbia, South Carolina, were "a wilderness of crumbling walls, naked chimneys and trees killed by flames." The social system had collapsed. Production was virtually at a standstill and white refugees and black freedmen were crowding into villages and cities, turning them into slums.

Anarchy threatened. General Oliver Otis Howard, the new commissioner of the Freedmen's Bureau, said the sudden collapse of the rebellion shook the South like an earthquake, "shattering the previously existing social system," breaking up "the old industries" and threatening "a reign of anarchy." The old planters, he said, were demoralized, without any knowledge of free labor or any hope that their former slaves would work for them without physical complusion. As for the freedmen, they were in "a state of great excitement and uncertainty. They could hardly believe that the liberty proclaimed was real and permanent. Many were afraid to remain on the same soil that they had tilled as slaves lest by some trick they might find themselves again in bondage."

What did freedom mean to the freedman? The answer, if one can credit contemporary reports, is that it meant different things to different freedmen, as it meant different things to different white people. To some freedmen, it meant power over their own lives, a say-so in the things that concerned them most. To others it meant unfettered movement, a chance to be better, a chance to learn, to have, to grow. More than that: freedom meant land, for the freedmen had never heard of power except in relation to the land. No hope was more compelling or more enduring to the freedmen than the hope that the government would give each freedman "forty acres of land and a mule." In this summer and in the summer that followed, many freedmen bought halters for the promised mules and colorful pegs to mark off the promised land.

The joyful and the tragic, the noble and the ignoble: all were grotesquely confused in this strange hot summer in which the freedmen reached out tentatively for the fruits of freedom. It had been against the law for slaves to wear hats, carry canes or stand up straight and look other people in the eyes. Now, in the whirlwind of change, the freedmen put on hats, twirled canes, married and added family names. A white South Carolinian noted that black people no longer yielded the sidewalks to white people. Black people, he said, were shoving white people off sidewalks and black women were dressing "in the most outré style, all with veils and parasols for which they have an especial fancy." In what was probably a deliberate testing of the boundaries of freedom, some black workers refused to answer the old slave bells and gave notice that they would no longer work in gangs under overseers. Some said openly that they didn't intend to work "for any rebel son-of-a-bitch." The general feeling of whites, in the face of defiance, was expressed by a South Carolina white who said: "All [former slaves] have turned fool together."

Having regarded blacks for so long as *things*, most white Southerners found it impossible now to see them as *men*. Although most Southern whites agreed reluctantly that black people no longer belonged to individual white men, most Southern whites still believed that black people in general belonged to white people in general. Some of the traveling experts said the South was reconciled to black emancipation and would extend to black people the amenities of social intercourse. But the weight of the evidence, as well as the subsequent behavior of Southerners, contradict that view. Nothing is clearer than the fact that Schurz spoke the truth when he said: "The emancipation of the slave is submitted to only in so far as chattel slavery in the old form could not be kept up. But although the freedman is no longer considered the property of the individual master, he is considered the slave of society, and all independent state legislation will share in the tendency to make him such. . . ."

One did not have to travel far to find corroboration. In the first few months after the war, murders, shootings, and whippings were reported from all sections of the South. Vigilante groups, composed for the most part of former Confederate soldiers, cropped up in many areas and assumed the task of keeping black people in their old places. Such a group, called "the Regulators," caught the attention of a *New York Herald* reporter who said: "It is needless to say that their attention is largely directed to maintaining quiet and submission among the blacks. *The shooting or stringing up of some obstreperous 'nigger' by the 'regulators' is so common an occurrence as to excite little remark. Nor is the work of proscription confined to the freedmen.* The 'regulators' go to the bottom of the matter, and strive to make it uncomfortably warm for any new settler with demoralizing innovations of wages for 'niggers.' "

With the South teetering on the brink of anarchy, the Union
Army, including eighty-five thousand black troops, assumed
many of the functions of government. Union soldiers, black and
white, were also active in the Freedmen's Bureau, which had
virtually unlimited authority over all matters relating to white
refugees and former slaves. Armed with legislative, judicial and
executive powers, the Bureau combined the governmental functions of the WPA, the Office of Economic Opportunity, and
Medicare with the defensive functions of the NAACP and the
National Urban League. It made laws and executed them; it
established courts, schools, asylums, hospitals; and it assumed
full jurisdiction in the economic field, instituting a system of
written contracts, transporting freedmen to jobs and supervising the terms of their employment. Despite its vast powers, the
Bureau operated on a miserly budget. In 1865 and 1866, it
relied mainly on funds which came from the sweat and blood
of the freedmen themselves. Regular government appropriations were authorized later and the Bureau received eighteen
million dollars before going out of exisence in 1872.

Under the leadership of Commissioner Oliver Otis Howard,
an imaginative one-armed general from Maine, the vague congressional mandate was soon translated into a formidable
Southwide apparatus with state bureaus headed by assistant
commissioners. As the directors of the government's first welfare agency, Howard and his assistants entered an uncharted
realm with inadequate funds and few guidelines. Under these
circumstances, it is not surprising that mistakes were made.
What is amazing really and worthy of note is the rapidity with
which the organization was organized and the extent of the aid
it rendered in the face of methodical hostility from white
Southerners and the President of the United States. The
Bureau issued more than twenty-one million food rations to
whites and blacks and provided medical service to more than a
million persons. Between June, 1865, and September, 1871, it
spent more than five million dollars on day schools, night

schools, grammar schools, and colleges. Many of the best known black colleges, including Howard, Fisk, Morehouse, Talladega and Atlanta University, were founded or aided in their early days by the Freedmen's Bureau.

No less important, though far less successful, were the Bureau's first tentative steps in land reform. Under the original provisions of the Freedmen's Bureau Act, agents were authorized to lease forty-acre plots to freedmen with an option to buy the land at a reasonable price. Proceeding under this provision, Bureau agents settled hundreds of thousands of freedmen on abandoned and confiscated plantations. In some states, freedmen were paid regular wages for harvesting corn and cotton, and special taxes were levied on their wages to support the community and care for the sick and infirm. Provocative attempts were also made to found self-supporting black colonies with black sheriffs, judges, and other officials.

The most important experiment in land reform was made in South Carolina, where General William T. Sherman's celebrated Field Order No. 15 of January 15, 1865, had set aside for exclusive settlement by black people all the Sea Islands from Charleston to Port Royal and considerable chunks of the adjoining land for thirty miles inland. Some forty thousand freedmen colonized this area and staked out forty-acre plots on the basis of "possessory titles" issued by General Rufus Saxton, the brilliant and compassionate South Carolina Bureau chief.

While the freedmen were painfully stitching together new relations of work and culture, men and forces of which they had little understanding were pushing to decisions that would reverse their strides toward liberation. Even as the freedmen cleared away the brush on their Sea Island enclaves, Andrew Johnson came to a momentous decision that boded ill for democracy in America. On Monday, May 29, a bare seven weeks after Lincoln's death, Johnson announced a Reconstruction plan that was, in some respects, more liberal than Lincoln's. Johnson's plan, unlike the Lincoln and Wade-Davis plans, required the participation of neither 10 per cent nor a majority of the white voters. He proposed instead to recognize rebel states as soon as an indeterminate number of whites took the oath of allegiance and organized state governments which accepted the Thirteenth Amendment. To the class of rebels proscribed by Lincoln, Johnson added an additional group: all persons with property worth $20,000 or more. Of his old plan for confiscating rebel property and reordering the social relations of the South to the advantage of the small farmer, Johnson said not a word. Nor did he mention the idea, reported by Sumner, that "all loyal people, without distinction of color, must be treated as citizens and must take part in any proceedings of reorganization."

Obviously, Johnson had changed. But what was behind the change and what did it portend? In June and July, Radical Republicans surveyed the situation and came up with a variety of answers. Some, eyeing the growing influence of Secretary of State William H. Seward, expressed the opinion that Lincoln's conservative cabinet, which Johnson had retained, was responsible. Others gave chief importance to Southern aristocrats who flocked to the White House with pleas for clemency and amnesty. Carl Schurz said he had been told that "the White House had been fairly besieged by Southern men and women of high social standing...." Now, Schurz continued, "it was thought that Mr. Johnson, the plebeian who before the war had been treated with undisguised contempt by the slave-holding aristocracy, could not withstand the subtle flattery of the same aristocracy when they flocked around him as humble suppliants cajoling his vanity."

But the core of Johnson's tragedy lay deeper than this. The prototype of the poor white in power, Johnson epitomized the tragedy of that cushion class which has been forced repeatedly to deny itself in order to deny black people. It appears that

Johnson scuttled his own Reconstruction plan when he realized that the residuary legatees of economic reform in the South would be black people. He was not the first poor white leader—nor would he be the last—to abandon poor whites after discovering that there was no way to help poor whites without helping poor blacks. Nothing indicates this more clearly than Johnson's new land policy. Reversing Freedmen's Bureau policy, he ordered the immediate return of confiscated and abandoned land to prewar owners. Whatever his intent, this act returned economic power to the prewar aristocrats and insured a continuation of the antagonism between poor whites and poor blacks who could neither love nor understand each other as long as they were forced to fight each other in order to eat.

All this was pure windfall to diehard Southerners who speedily called constitutional conventions and began what Professor John Hope Franklin has accurately called "Reconstruction Confederate Style." By late summer, white Southerners, under the leadership of Confederate colonels and brigadiers, had ratified the Thirteenth Amendment and were preparing a new Southern structure based on the forced labor of black peons.

With Congress in recess, Radical Republicans were powerless to check this development. But they had resources and skills which it was ill-advised for Johnson and white Southerners to ignore. In August and September, as white Southerners dug their own social graves by electing scores of proscribed Confederates to their lily-white legislatures, the Radical core of the Republican party mobilized for a counterthrust. Always a minority in the Republican party, forced by the exigencies of the situation to rely on moderate to conservative politicians serving, with varying degrees of consciousness, business and commercial interests, the Radical core consisted of idealistic leaders of the old middle class like Charles Sumner, a handful of radical congressmen like Thaddeus Stevens, and leaders of the old abolitionist movement like Frederick Douglass and

Wendell Phillips. These men will repay some study, for they and the forces they represented were responsible for the Reconstruction acts, the Fourteenth and Fifteenth Amendments, and the most radical civil rights legislation ever passed in America.

Of the men cited, it is best perhaps to begin with Wendell Phillips, who represented that strain of indigenous radicalism which claims such diverse American activists as Samuel Adams, Thomas Paine, Eugene Debs and the white and black radicals of the New Left movement of the twentieth century. What makes this all the more remarkable is the fact that Phillips was a certified product of the American Establishment. He had been born in 1811 on Boston's Beacon Street and he was a graduate of Harvard College and the Harvard Law School. But Puritan idealism and a chance recounter with a proslavery mob led him to renounce Beacon Street and all it stood for. Taking his stand with downtrodden Irish workers and the disinherited slaves of the South, Phillips became one of the leaders of the abolitionist movement, refusing to vote, practice law or perform any function under the U.S. Constitution until the emancipation of the slave.

With William Lloyd Garrison, the Boston journalist, Phillips helped educate the American public to a policy of emancipation. Garrison and Phillips had much in common but differed considerably in their goals and styles. Garrison was an idealistic reformer who believed one renovation—the abolition of slavery—would change the whole social structure. Phillips, on the other hand, was a social revolutionary who directed his blows at the entire social system. When Garrison faltered and endorsed Lincoln's conservative Reconstruction plan, Phillips seized leadership of the abolitionist movement and articulated an advanced program of land and ballots for the freedmen. He was contemptuous of Lincoln's Reconstruction plan which, he said, made "the freedom of the Negro a sham," and perpetuated slavery under another name. As for Lincoln's motives, Phillips said: "He may wish the end—peace and freedom—but is wholly unwilling to use the means which can secure that end." Phillips was willing to use the available means—the Union Army and a plastic situation created by war—to achieve his fundamental goal: "the safety beyond peril and the equality without a doubt of the colored race in this country." He demanded justice for the black man—"not charity, not patronage, but justice." And what was justice for the black man? The Ballot, Phillips replied, Education and, above all, Land. Confiscate the land, he demanded, and divide it among the freedmen and the poor whites. "Confiscation," he said, "is mere naked justice to the former slave. Who brought the land into cultivation? Whose sweat and toil are mixed with it forever? Who cleared those forests? Who made those roads? Whose hand reared those houses? Whose wages are invested in those warehouses and towns? Of course, the Negro's. . . . Why should he not have a share of his inheritance?" As Johnson's Reconstruction plan unfolded, Phillips warned his colleagues to prepare for a long and bitter struggle. To Sumner, he wrote: "Remember these are not times of *ordinary* politics: they are formative hours: the national purpose and thought grows and ripens in thirty days as much as ordinary years bring it forward. We radicals have all the elements of national education in our hands—pressure of vast debt—uncertainty of it—capital unwilling to risk itself in the South but longing to do so—vigilant masses—every returned soldier a witness—every defeated emigrant to the South a witness and weight." This was not the time, he said, to consult harmony. "Harmony purchased at any sacrifice of the absolute need of the hour is dangerous. To do nothing is infinitely better and safer than to do half what we need." And what did the hour require? "Plant yourselves on the bare claim: no state readmitted without impartial suffrage—live and die by that vote alone, if necessary, against everything short of it."

Allied with Phillips in the prewar and postwar campaigns

was Frederick Douglass, the bearded black abolitionist who had also participated in the struggles that led to the Liberty, Free Soil, and Republican parties. Now, at forty-eight years of age, Douglass was a striking figure—over six feet tall, with a vast, well-proportioned head and a great shock of *au naturel* hair. Unlike other advocates of the black man, Douglass embodied the agonizing issues confronting the nation. Did someone say that the black man was a savage, impervious to education and the higher flights of logic? Douglass' words, Douglass' acts, Douglass' life contradicted him. Did someone say that the black man didn't want freedom, that he was content to raise corn and cotton and wait tables forever? Douglass stood athwart the proposition. He was a living refutation of every thing most Americans believed and said about black Americans.

Born in slavery on the Eastern Shore of Maryland, Douglass had educated himself and posessed a keen and inquiring mind that ranged over the whole ideological landscape. Moreover, he had extraordinary gifts of oratory which he used to condemn a system of slavery which he knew at first hand. As a slave, he had known brutality, want, and humiliation. And he, like tens of thousands of slaves, had escaped to tell the world what the slave system had wrought. From the time of his escape in 1838 until emancipation, he was in the advance guard of the abolitionist ranks, speaking, editing, acting.

During the Civil War, Douglass criss-crossed the land, denouncing the President's "vacillation, doubt, uncertainty and hesitation." Lincoln said he was fighting for the Union. Douglass replied that the old Union was dead. "We are fighting," he said, "for something incomparably better than the old Union. We are fighting for unity; unity of idea, unity of sentiment, unity of object, unity of institutions, in which there shall be no North, no South, no East, no West, no black, no white, but a solidarity of the nation, making every slave free, and every free man a voter." This idea formed the spine of Douglass' postwar program. His major theme, thundered from hundreds of platforms, was "the immediate, complete, and universal enfranchisement of the colored people of the whole country.

It was fashionable then to say that the antagonism between the poor whites and poor blacks precluded any possibility of racial justice in America. Douglass, more farsighted than his contemporaries, identified this antagonism as an effect of the race problem, not the cause. The main problem, he said, was the aristocratic elite which fostered division at the bottom of the ladder to maintain its place at the top of the ladder. Legal emancipation alone, he said, would not free the Negro. To do that, it would be necessary to annihilate a whole social system. The whole South would have to become a missionary area. The work before America, he said, was nothing less than "National Regeneration" — "nothing less than radical revolution in all the modes of thought which have flourished under the blighting slave system."

Douglass' importance at this juncture can be gauged by an interesting Presidential maneuver that backfired. In an inept attempt to divide the Radical movement, the White House offered Douglass the position of commissioner of the Freedmen's Bureau. No black man had ever held a job of comparable importance in America, and Douglass, an ambitious man, was sorely tempted. In the end, he declined the offer, and the *Independent* said: "The greatest black man in the nation did not become the tool of the meanest white."

Douglass and Phillips worked on the sideline of power, mobilizing supporting forces, leading the cheering and booing and sometimes calling the plays. Charles Sumner and Thaddeus Stevens were in the infield of power, throwing the ball and batting. Of the men who realized that the war had released forces that would make it possible to realize, at least in part, the promises of the Declaration of Independence, none were more perceptive or more daring than these two men who were so different in their conceptions of power and yet so similar in their ideas of the uses to which power should be put. Sumner,

who represented Massachusetts in the Senate, was that rarity in
American politics, a politician with the instincts and the tough-
ness of a radical reformer. "I am in morals," he used to say,
"not politics."

Tall, handsome, something of a dandy in his dress, Sumner
was born in Boston in the same year as Phillips, and he, like
Phillips, was a graduate of Harvard College and the Harvard
Law School. As a young lawyer, he argued and won what was
probably the first suit against the separate-but-equal school
doctrine. But law bored him and he soon drifted into "legal
literature." He went to the U.S. Senate in 1851 and rapidly
earned an international reputation as an advocate of the slave.
In May, 1856, in a famous Senate speech, he denounced the
Kansas-Nebraska Act and heaped abuse on the heads of its
authors, Stephen Douglas of Illinois and Andrew P. Butler of
South Carolina. Two days later, Preston Brooks, a South
Carolina congressman and a relative of Senator Butler, attacked
Sumner at his Senate seat and rained blows on his head until
he collapsed. This assault, which figured largely in the events
that inflamed the prewar political climate, sidelined Sumner for
three years. But it didn't daunt his ardor for the slave. Returning to the Senate in 1859, he helped prepare the high ground of
emancipation which Lincoln later occupied.

A perennial bachelor who married late and was soon
divorced, Sumner lived for his principles. The dominant conviction of his life was that arbitrary and artificial distinctions
between men were socially destructive. There was, he said, no
substitute for equality. "It is not enough to provide separate
accommodations for colored citizens, even if they are in all
respects as good as those of other persons. Equality is not
founded in any pretended equivalent, but only in equality." As
chairman of the Senate Foreign Relations Committee and as a
sleepless sentinel of the equal rights brigade, Sumner proposed
and carried legislation that almost made that principle an
operating idea in American law. Every major bill of the

period — the Thirteenth, Fourteenth, and Fifteenth Amendments, the Freedmen's Bureau Act and the Reconstruction acts — bore the imprint of this zealous reformer who believed that "anything for human rights is constitutional."

Sumner, who was the first major American politician to advocate ballots for African-Americans, insisted that the rebel states couldn't come back "except on the footing of the Declaration of Independence and the complete recognition of human rights." He demanded not only ballots for the freedmen but land, homes and a federally sponsored program of education and social welfare. When Johnson reversed himself, going back on what Sumner considered a solemn promise, the elegantly dressed Massachusetts senator flung himself into such a frenzied round of agitation that friends feared for his sanity. All summer long, he pressed the freedmen's cause, thinking of nothing else, speaking of nothing else, bringing the subject up at dinner tables and in posh salons, writing and distributing hundreds of letters and pamphlets. This, clearly, was a dangerous man in an ideological struggle, as Andrew Johnson soon discovered.

Even more dangerous in a real political dogfight — which this was clearly going to be — was wily old Thaddeus Stevens, the Pennsylvania representative who was the virtual boss of the House of Representatives and the dominant force in the dominant political party of the land. If, as Harold Laski said, great leadership is the ability to make the possible inevitable, then Thaddeus Stevens was the greatest parliamentary leader in American history. Even, today, even after Kennedy and Lyndon Johnson, it is difficult to grasp the meaning of this strange, brilliant man who was the best friend black people have ever had in power. The *New York Herald*, an anti-Negro journal, said Stevens had "the boldness of Danton, the bitterness and hatred of Marat and the unscrupulousness of Robespierre." Pejoratives apart, the names, at least, suggest the mettle of the man. For what made him memorable — and ultimately unforgetta-

Thaddeus Stevens, leader of Radical Republican
forces in Congress, demanded impeachment of
President Andrew Johnson in a speech in the
House of Representatives.

Frederick Douglass, black
abolitionist, was in the
forefront of the Radical
Reconstruction movement.

Riots and political massacres punctuated political
debate in the postwar period. In the infamous
New Orleans riot, a mob of whites attacked
black and white Republicans.

ble — was the fact that he was a real social revolutionary. In fact, he was the first — and last — real radical to gain real public power in the American republic.

A tall, thin, striking figure, with a face of sharp angles and wrinkles framed by an ill-fitting black wig, Stevens was always a loner, separated by many walls from other men. The clubfoot with which he was born set him apart somehow and gave him a sense of comradeship with the separated, the reviled, the damned. He was born in poverty on April 4, 1792, in Danville, Vermont. Though poor, he managed to graduate from Dartmouth College and migrated to Pennsylvania where he became a lawyer, practicing first in Gettysburg and then in Lancaster, accumulating in the process a tidy fortune in real estate and the iron industry. But money was a means, not an end, to Stevens, who was soon a major power in Pennsylvania politics. In 1848, at the age of fifty-six, he was elected to Congress as a Free Soil Whig. For the next four years, he was in the front ranks of the fight against the extension of slavery. When the Compromise of 1850 shut off debate on slavery, Stevens tired of the pettifogging debates on the tariff and returned to his Lancaster home. The Kansas-Nebraska Act, which opened the free lands of the West to slaveowners, brought him out of retirement and set the stage for the last and greatest phase of his career. When he returned to Congress in 1859 at the age of sixty-seven, he immediately moved into the small circle of men who control all such bodies, becoming chairman of the House Ways and Means Committee.

As a politician, Stevens never hesitated to take positions far in advance of his constituents. Lincoln was always "dragging the anchor of public opinion," to use John F. Kennedy's felicitous phrase. Stevens was his own anchor. Unlike Lincoln, who followed public opinion, Stevens made public opinion. But he didn't on that account disdain the ways public opinion is made. Coldly unsentimental, he took his colleagues as he found them, using their passions, phobias, and interests to advance his own purposes. He despised hypocrisy and delighted in shocking Pharisees by calling things by their right names. There was the day, for example, that he entered the House in the midst of balloting on candidates for a disputed House seat. A colleague told him that it was merely a contest between "two damned rascals." Grabbing a ballot, Stevens asked: "Which is *our* damned rascal?"

It was said openly and libelously that Stevens not only preached equality but that he lived it. This was a veiled allusion to Stevens' household arrangements. A lifelong bachelor with no real social life apart from all-night sessions at the poker table, Stevens employed Lydia Hamilton Smith, an attractive and efficient African-American widow, who ran his house in the Capital and his home in Lancaster. Stevens' enemies suggested that there was more to the arrangement than met the eye. There was no evidence to support this theory, which was circulated widely by American newspapers. Stevens, who cared nothing for public gossip, maintained a withering silence in the face of a whispering campaign that reached scandalous proportions.

People who accused Stevens of believing the radical doctrines he espoused were wrong in this instance, but they were right in general. His was not a rhetorical posture. He believed what he said, and his passion for the poor and the disadvantaged was manifested not only in politics but in his private life. The story is told of the morning Stevens met a black preacher after a profitable all-night session at the poker table. When the preacher asked for a donation for his church, Stevens handed him fifty dollars of his poker winnings, remarking to a friend: "God moves in a mysterious way His wonders to perform."

Sardonic, daring, brilliant, driving: such was the man Andrew Johnson baited with his proposal to run Reconstruction from the White House. As Johnson knew, Stevens believed that Reconstruction was a matter only Congress could decide. More concretely, Stevens believed, as Johnson had once believed, that a root-and-branch destruction of the Southern aristocracy was necessary for the preservation of democracy in America. Far in advance of his time, he argued that economic emancipation was a precondition of political and social emancipation. He had the vision to see that black liberation could not be made real unless it was grounded on economic independence. Unlike Sumner, who said the ballot was "the essence — the great essential," Stevens placed primary stress on economic reform. "Forty acres of land and a hut," he said, "would be more valuable [to the freedman] than the immediate right to vote." Failure to give it, he said, "would invite the censure of mankind and the curse of heaven." Like Sumner, Stevens was greatly impressed by the contemporary example of the Czar of Russia who freed Russian serfs and settled them on the land they had tilled for generations. Citing that precedent, Stevens suggested a policy of "complete confiscation and thorough redistribution of the land." "The South," he said, "has called for war and we have given it to her. We will fix the terms of peace ourselves and we will teach the South that Christ is disguised in a dusky race."

Stevens opened the fight for Radical Reconstruction with a slashing speech at Lancaster on Wednesday, September 6, 1865. In great form, holding his audience by the grimness of his manner and the revolutionary implications of his proposals, he asked: "Is this great conquest to be in vain?" And he answered: "That will depend upon . . . the next Congress" for "to Congress alone belongs the power of Reconstruction, of giving law to the vanquished." As for the principles that should govern Reconstruction, Stevens took his stand on one word, *reformation:* "the foundation of their institutions, both political, municipal, and social, *must* be broken up and *relaid*, or all our blood and treasure have been spent in vain." Why was this necessary? It was necessary to pursue such a course "as to exclude from those Governments every vestige of human bondage; and render the same forever impossible in this nation. . . ." It was

the duty of the federal government "to inflict condign punishment on the rebel belligerents, and so weaken their hands that
they can never again endanger the Union." More than
that—"The whole fabric of Southern society must be changed,
and it never can be done if this opportunity is lost." How could
all this be done? Confiscate the land of the chief rebels, Stevens
said, and allocate forty acres of land to each adult male freedman.

All this was premature in the climate of contemporary public
opinion. No one knew this better than Stevens. He was staking
out a position, planting seeds—he could wait for the harvest.
Besides, a plan—stunningly simple in outline but devastatingly
effective in execution—was already germinating in his mind;
and when the members of the Thirty-ninth Congress poured
into the muddy little village that was the Washington of
December, 1865, Stevens was ready. On the Friday night
before the opening of Congress, he called a small group of
supporters to his house on "B" Street and outlined his plan. A
super-committee, composed of nine members of the House and
six members of the Senate, would be created with the power to
examine all aspects of Reconstruction and recommend legislation. No members from the late rebel states would be accepted
by either house of Congress until this committee had made its
report. Nor could either house debate Reconstruction proposals
without first referring them to the select committee. The
revolutionary implications of this proposal were not immediately recognized by conservative supporters of the President,
for on the next night, Saturday, December 2, it was approved
by the Republican caucus with barely a dissenting voice.

With his trap set, Stevens walked into the House on Monday, December 4, and sprang it, barring all representatives
from "the Johnson states" and referring all legislation on
Reconstruction to the Joint Congressional Committee of Fifteen, a new and revolutionary grouping which shifted the
balance of power from the President to a congressional commit-

tee with the power to propose and dispose. Fourteen days later, Stevens rose in the House and laid out the field of battle. His words were harsh: "The future condition of the conquered power depends on the will of the conqueror." Having laid down that principle, he at once deduced its consequences. "The rebel states must come in as new states or remain as conquered provinces." Since there were no signs that the people of these "provinces" would be prepared to participate in constitutional government "for some years," he knew of no arrangement so proper for them as territorial governments. "There they can learn the principles of freedom and eat the fruit of foul rebellion." The rebel states "ought never to be recognized as capable of acting in the Union, or of being counted as valid States, until the Constitution shall have been so amended as to make it what its framers intended; and so as to secure perpetual ascendancy to the party of the Union; and so as to render our republican Government firm and stable for ever."

The men before Stevens weren't interested in black people—they were interested in power. Stevens talked to them where they were. Under the old Constitution, three-fifths of the slaves had been counted in determining the number of representatives from the Southern states. But with the adoption of the Thirteenth Amendment, all black people would be counted, whether they voted or not. And what this meant was that the South would return to the Union with more power than it had when it left. Was this what the North fought for? Did Congress want to reward rebellion? "With the basis unchanged," Stevens said, "the 83 Southern members, with the Democrats that will in the best times be elected from the North, will always give them a majority in Congress and in the Electoral College." Stevens paused and then dropped his bombshell: "I need not depict the ruin that would follow."

The old man, his wig awry and his black eyes burning, had everybody's attention now and he hurried on to his main point—the Negro. "We have turned, or are about to turn, loose four million slaves without a hut to shelter them or a cent in their pockets. The infernal laws of slavery have prevented them from acquiring an education, understanding the common laws of contract, or of managing the ordinary business of life. This Congress is bound to provide for them until they can take care of themselves. If we do not furnish them with homesteads, and hedge them around with protective laws; if we leave them to the legislation of their late master, we had better have left them in bondage." Then, with great passion, Stevens elaborated a vision of total democracy that startled his auditors:

Governor Perry of South Carolina and other provisional governors and orators proclaim that 'this is the white man's government.' ... Demagogues of all parties, even some in high authority, gravely shout, 'This is the white man's government.' What is implied by this? That one race of men are to have the exclusive rights forever to rule this nation, and to exercise all acts of sovereignty, while all other races and nations and colors are to be their subjects, and have no voice in making the laws and choosing the rulers by whom they are to be governed....

Our fathers repudiated the whole doctrine of the legal superiority of families or races, and proclaimed the equality of men before the law. Upon that they created a revolution and built a Republic. They were prevented by slavery from perfecting the superstructure whose foundation they had thus broadly laid....

The time to which they looked forward with anxiety has come. It is our duty to complete their work. If this Republic is not now made to stand on their great principles, it has no honest foundation, and the Father of all men will still shake it to its center. If we have not yet been sufficiently scourged for our national sin to teach us to do justice to all God's creatures, without distinction of race or color, we must expect the still more heavy vengeance of an offended Father....

This is not a white man's Government, in the exclusive sense in which it is used. To say so is political blasphemy, for it violates the fundamental principles of our gospel of liberty. This is Man's Government, the Government of all men alike; not that all men will have equal power and sway within it. Accidental circumstances, natural and acquired endowment and ability, will vary their fortunes. But equal rights to all the privileges of the Government is innate in every immortal being, no matter what the shape or color of the tabernacle which it inhabits....

Rhetoric apart, Stevens was saying one thing: that the issue was justice for the black man or political and economic ruin for the Northern white man. What could be more simple or more persuasive? And when Stevens sat down, he had planted seeds of doubt, his praise of democracy apart, in the minds of both moderate and conservative Republicans. As 1865 ended and 1866 began, these seeds grew, watered by the prodigious efforts of Charles Sumner, Wendell Phillips, Frederick Douglass, and the forces they represented.

It became evident early in the national debate that there were, in fact, only three alternatives:

1. **The Johnson-Lincoln-Southern Plan** which envisioned the reconstruction of the states by white voters with no federal requirements for black suffrage or civil rights. Proponents of this view said the states had never been out of the Union and that the Constitution prohibited Congress or the President from interfering in their domestic affairs without a constitutional amendment. As for black suffrage and civil rights, it was said that these goals, however desirable, were estopped by the doctrine of states rights.

2. **The Territorial Plan,** a loosely structured idea, never fully defined or debated, which required rebel states to undergo a long period of probation, perhaps as long as a generation, with territorial governments and assemblies. Under this plan, which was backed initially by Stevens, territorial governments would have continued in the South until new civil institutions were established and an interracial society had been created in the minds of men. Some modern scholars, like W. E. B. Du Bois, and some contemporary politicians, like Albion Tourgee, believed that "Regeneration before Reconstruction" was "by far the best and safest plan." Tourgee maintained presciently that any other mode of reconstruction was doomed to failure.

3. **The Congressional Consensus Plan,** eventually adopted, which called for immediate Reconstruction with black suffrage and federally guaranteed civil rights. Proponents of this plan said black suffrage was necessary to endow black people with power so they could protect themselves against oppressive class legislation and private persecution. It was also said that black suffrage was necessary to protect Southern white Loyalists, who couldn't organize without a black power base, and to defend vital national interest (the national debt, tariff and fiscal policies), which were

threatened by the resurgence of planter power. As for arguments based on the illiteracy of the slaves, Radicals said the ballot itself was a school. "Practical liberty," Schurz argued, "is a good school, and, besides, if any qualifications can be found, applicable to both races, which does not interfere with the attainment of the main object, such qualification would in that respect be unobjectionable. But it is idle to say that it will be time to speak of Negro suffrage when the whole colored race will be educated, for the ballot may be necessary for him to secure his education. It is also idle to say that ignorance is the prinicipal ground upon which Southern men object to Negro suffrage, for if it were that numerous class of colored people in Louisiana who are as highly educated, as intelligent, and as wealthy as any corresponding class of whites, would have been enfranchised long ago."

From the beginning of the Thirty-ninth Congress it was clear that the game was going to be played within the boundaries of these three plans and within a context that reduced the options to two: (1) white supremacy and political autocracy in its most virulent form, or (2) democracy in a form that the North had never dared to implement for poor whites, not to speak of free Negroes who were generally barred from the ballot box and the public schools in Northern states.

At this point it was still possible for President Johnson and the South to control events by making a token gesture of a selective franchise for literate Negroes and Union Army veterans coupled with a sincere gesture of patriotic repentance (rejection of former Confederate leadership) and a massive educational program for the freed slaves. But it is hard, habits being what they are, to see how the South could have made these gestures. Perhaps there was no way out of the historical dilemma, given the unrepentant attitude of Southerners and the increasingly militant attitude of Northerners traumatized by Lincoln's assassination and Northern war casualties. At any rate, no one has ever suggested how black emancipation could have been made more than nominal by any means short of Plan 2 or Plan 3. What is usually overlooked is that the North had shown unexampled clemency to its vanquished foes. There had been no firing squads, no mass imprisonments, no harsh or humiliating occupation. Northerners only asked a token gesture from the South. The South refused to make that gesture and thereby made Black Power inevitable.

But inevitability comes not from the sky but from the purposes of real men with interests that run with the grain of history. There were men in America at that moment with viable purposes and it was these men who capitalized on the incredible blunders of the South and made what was merely possible necessary and even inevitable.

Foremost among these men were the freedmen who filled the land with laments and pleas. Far from being the passive and inert tools of designing demagogues, as they are usually pictured, the freedmen vibrated with the issues of the day. They staged demonstrations and parades and bombarded legislatures and the U.S. Congress with petitions and resolutions. These petitions usually cited the services black people rendered during the war and demanded ballots, fair wages, and land. In tones reminiscent of the twentieth-century freedom struggle, the *New Orleans Tribune*, the first Negro daily newspaper in America, said: "We want to ride on any conveyance, to travel on any steamboat, dine at any restaurant, or educate our children at any school."

The freedmen also formed independent political organizations. In Louisiana and Florida, freedmen organized Freedom Republican parties similar to the Freedom Democratic parties organized by Mississippi civil rights workers in 1964. In 1865, Florida freedmen assembled in a Methodist church in Tallahassee and selected a congressman. The same year, in November, black people in Louisiana appointed election officials, printed ballots, and elected a slate of officers.

No less audible in these years were the voices of white allies, particularly white missionaries—ministers, teachers, doctors, New England schoolmarms—who flocked to the South to help build bridges from slavery to freedom. Even more significant, however, were the voices of indigenous white radicals who

joined black people in a demand for a basic social revolution in
the South. James W. Hunnicutt, a fiery Virginia radical and a
former slaveowner, said: "If the next Congress does not give us
universal suffrage, we will roll up our sleeves, pitch in and have
the damndest revolution the world ever saw."

As various voices swelled the fast-rising chorus of Freedom
Now! the Radical core seized control of Reconstruction and
cemented an alliance between the Freedom movement and the
growing forces of rampant industrialism. The first fruits of the
alliance were the permanent Freedmen's Bureau Bill and a
Civil Rights Bill which extended citizenship to African-Americans. President Johnson unwisely vetoed these measures, which
were moderate responses to the pressing necessities of the hour.
In so doing, he alienated moderate and conservative Republicans and strengthened the Radical coalition. Worse yet, Johnson came down hard on the side of the America-for-white-folks
contingent. The proposed acts, he said, discriminated against
white people in that they established "for the security of the
colored race safeguards which go infinitely beyond any that the
General Government have ever provided for the white race." In
a later message, the President admitted that black people were
entitled "to be well and humanely governed" and to have the
protection of just laws. "If it were practicable," he said, "at this
time to give them a Government exclusively their own, under
which they might manage their own affairs in their own way, it
would become a grave question whether we ought to do so, or
whether common humanity would not require us to save them
from themselves." But it was "worse than madness" to make
black people the arbiters of the fate of white men—to give
them power to "rule the white race, make and administer State
laws, elect Presidents and members of Congress, and shape to a
greater or less extent the future destiny of the whole country."
Such a course would be monstrous, Johnson said, adding: "It is
the glory of white men to know that they have had these
qualities in sufficient measure to build upon this continent a

great political fabric and to preserve its stability for more than ninety years, while in every part of the world all similar experiments have failed. But if anything can be proved by known facts, if all reasoning upon evidence is not abandoned, it must be acknowledged that in the progress of nations Negroes have shown less capacity for government than any other race of people. No independent government of any form has ever been successful in their hands. On the contrary, wherever they have been left to their own devices they have shown a constant tendency to relapse into barbarism." Unimpressed by Johnson's logic, Congress passed the Civil Rights Bill over his veto and the issue was joined. Both sides hurried now to the people, seeking vindication in the congressional elections of 1866.

The North to which the politicians hurried had changed enormously. In the North, as in the South, the Emancipation Proclamation had freed more white people than black people. As a direct result of the war, the lands of the West had been opened to poor whites and rich white railroad operators, and the hot hands of planter agrarians had been removed from the tariff and fiscal machinery. The grand outcome was the emergence of the nation's first millionaire class and the development of a new ethos of possessive individualism. This ethos, a distillate of steel, iron tracks, and stocks and bonds, spread in ever widening circles, making everything over in its own image. President Johnson saw it and cried out against the "money power" which had supplanted the old slave power. Some of the Radicals, notably Wendell Phillips and George W. Julian, saw it, too. But how to combat it? How to create a countervailing power — that was the question. Johnson's solution, self-contradictory and inherently implausible, was a coalition of the lords of the land of the South and the yeomen of the West. Phillips and Julian, on the other hand, argued for a coalition of the middle and bottom, based on structural reforms in the South.

The fundamental question here was: Whither America? Or better still: What was America? These were the real issues in the 1866 election, perhaps one of the most significant in the whole of American history, and they were never explicitly formulated by either side. It was, in fact, impossible to formulate the real questions, for both sides consisted of self-contradictory elements, with wealthy Republicans fighting for the poor black laborers of the South, and the poor white laborers of the North and West fighting for the aristocrats of the South. The Democratic party was composed, the *New York Herald* said, of merchants opposed to the tariff, the unemployed, foreign-born immigrants, Roman Catholics, and workers. The Republican party, on the other hand, was based primarily on the old middle class, western farmers, the emerging industrial and fiscal elite, and the old abolitionists. Republicans were also helped by abolitionist societies, Union Leagues and liberal whites who organized one of the most effective public education campaigns in American history. Using funds provided by wealthy industrialists, these groups flooded the country with pamphlets, speeches, and broadsides.

It would not be unjust to say that in this campaign black people were helped more by the blunders of their enemies than by the passions of their friends. No one helped more than Andrew Johnson, who toured the country in a canvass that would have been brilliant for a stump speaker in Tennessee but was disastrous for the President of the United States in Illinois and Ohio.

Like his namesake of the twentieth century, who also inherited power in the midst of a racial maelstrom after an assassination which deified his predecessor, Johnson had massive image problems. Many voters considered him rude, vulgar and totally self-centered. It was also said that he was a drunkard. (It appears from the evidence that Johnson was not a drunkard, though on some days he did take "two or three or four glasses of Robertson's County Whiskey.") More damaging were the persistent but groundless rumors that Johnson was involved in the assassination of his predecessor. These rumors and the

President's tactlessness and monumental vanity siphoned away hundreds of thousands of votes.

Additional help came from the South, which didn't realize until it was too late that the name of the game had changed. The South had always won its way by covering its cards and calling the North's bluff. This tactic, which worked so well in the old days, fell flat in the postwar world for the North now had all the trumps—the banking capital, the industrial machinery and army to boot. The new leaders of the North—the Rockefellers, the Goulds, the Carnegies, the Armours—controlled or saw a way to control resources that made the South's prewar game seem child's play. And what this meant in terms of *realpolitik* was that the South was going to play by the North's rules or it wasn't going to play at all.

Disregarding indices which were clearly visible on Wall Street, the South embarked for the second time in a decade on a suicidally disastrous course. Having riled Northern sensibilities by sending the vice-president of the Confederacy, four Confederate generals, five Confederate colonels, six Confederate cabinet members and fifty-eight Confederate congressmen to the Thirty-ninth Congress, the South now proceeded to enact legislation that virtually re-enslaved the Negro. In the infamous Black Codes, enacted by the lily-white legislatures of the Johnson states, Southerners unwittingly brought about a situation that was finally to destroy them.

These codes gave freedmen the right to marry, hold property, and initiate court suits, but these "rights" were hedged about with a formidable array of prohibitions and proscriptions. It was a crime under these laws for black people to be idle. A Mississippi law required every black man to have a lawful home and employer and written evidence thereof from the mayor or a member of the police force. A Louisiana law required every agricultural laborer to sign a contract embracing all members of his family and such contracts were binding on children yet to be born. Laborers, so bound, could not leave their places of employment until the fulfillment of the contract. In some states, any white person could arrest any black person. In other states, minor officials could arrest black vagrants and "refractory and rebellious Negroes" and force them to work on roads, levees, and other public work without pay. Specifically designated as black vagrants were prostitutes, fortune tellers, beggars, drunkards, hunters, gamblers, "the idle and disobedient," "persons wandering from place to place and selling without license," and "all persons able to work and having no visible and known means to a fair, honest, and respectable livelihood."

"Servants" in South Carolina were required to work from sunrise to sunset, to be quiet and orderly, and to go to bed at "reasonable hours." It was illegal for laborers to receive visitors during work hours and, in some cases, "bad work" was against the law. The South Carolina Black Code gave "masters" the right to whip "servants" moderately. Florida forbade "colored and white persons respectively from intruding upon each other's public assemblies, religious or other, or public vehicle set apart for their exclusive use, under punishment of pillory or stripes, or both." Special provisions in other states forbade or limited the black man's right to own firearms. It was a crime in Mississippi for Negroes to own farm land and in South Carolina Negroes had to get a special license to work outside the domestic and farm laborer fields. Local codes were even more restrictive. The Black Code of Opelousas, Louisiana, made it a crime for unattached African-Americans to live in that city. Nor could an African-American visit Opelousas "without special permission from his employer, specifying the object of his visit and the time necessary for the accomplishing of the same."

If the Black Codes disconcerted the North, the wave of violence that followed cauterized it. On Monday, April 16, 1866, Norfolk freedmen, celebrating passage of the Civil Rights Act, were attacked by white supremacists, and two whites and two freedmen were killed. Fourteen days later, a white mob, led by policemen, attacked the black community of Memphis, Tennessee. Forty-six freedmen were killed and seventy-five were wounded, including a black woman who was robbed and raped by white hoodlums. At least ninety homes, twelve schools, and four churches were burned to the ground. The shock waves of the Memphis massacre were still echoing in the nation when the "St. Bartholomew's Day Massacre" erupted in New Orleans. This massacre grew out of an attempt by black and white radicals to reconvene the controversial constitutional convention of 1864. When the delegates convened in Mechanics Institute on Monday, April 30, a white mob, composed largely of policemen, opened fire on the building. More than forty persons were killed, and some one hundred and fifty were wounded. General Phillip H. Sheridan, military commander of the state, said: "It was no riot; it was an absolute massacre . . . a murder which the mayor and the police of the city perpetrated without the shadow of a necessity."

All this—the Black Codes, the Johnson image, the massacres and riots—was grist for the Radical mill. Convinced that their own interests were threatened and that the Bourbons of the South had learned nothing and forgotten nothing, powerful interests in the North began to march by the sound of the Radicals' drummer. After passage of the Mississippi Black Code, the *Chicago Tribune* said: "We tell the white men of Mississippi that the men of the North will convert the state of Mississippi into a frog pond before they will allow such laws to disgrace one foot of soil in which the bones of our soldiers sleep and over which the flag of freedom waves." More persuasive was the argument of businessman Elizur Wright who said Negro enfranchisement was the only way to "make our victory immediately fruitful." Wright wasn't interested in race. He wasn't "disputing about tastes. A Negro's ballot may be more vulgar than his bullet. Being already in for it, the question with me is, how the one or the other can be made to protect my property from taxation...." Wright went on to say that he "could easily convince any man, who does not allow his prejudices to stand in the way of his interests that it will probably make a difference of a least $1,000,000,000 in the development of the national debt, whether we reconstruct on the basis of loyal white and black voters, or on white votes exclusively, and that he can better afford to give the government at least one-quarter of his estate than have it try the latter experiment."

Put that way, the argument for black suffrage proved irresistible, as the results of the congressional election indicated. The Radical Republicans swept the North and won two-thirds majorities in the House and Senate.

Stevens had his mandate. What was he going to do with it? He was going to do precisely what he said he was going to do: drive the aristocrats from power and create the conditions for a real democracy in the South. If these goals were not accomplished, it was not Stevens' fault. During the second session of the Thirty-ninth Congress, he focused all his dwindling energy and hurled it against the bastion of privilege. In constant pain, expecting death daily, often fainting in the House anterooms, the acerbic old commoner spared neither himself nor his foes. Nothing but passion—his enemies called it hate—kept him alive now. It was during this time that a reporter saw him "feeble and tottering on his cane or crawling from desk to desk, apparently in the last stages of debility." Stevens was fighting not only the clock but the conservatism, opportunism, and love of ease of his colleagues. "Some members," he told a reporter, "had their wives in Washington and their women at home, and others had their women in Washington and their wives at home, and it was impossible to keep them together."

With the help of the Radical core, Stevens kept the congressmen together long enough to pass the Fourteenth Amendment

Gardane Casanave, a wealthy black undertaker, was
a member of the Louisiana Returning Board. Union
military commanders appointed black men to first
political posts in the South.

Black men voted for the first time in
the South in 1867. Reconstruction acts
of Congress enfranchised freedmen
who constituted the majority of
voters in five states.

and a series of Reconstruction acts which called for a reconstruction of the Southern states on the basis of the loyal black
and white population. In a related development, Stevens and
his colleagues humiliated President Johnson by stripping him
of much of his power and patronage.

Even so, the Radical Republicans didn't get all they wanted.
The story of their failure is the story of the failure of Reconstruction, for the end of Reconstruction was implicit in the
beginning of Reconstruction which was timid, inadequate and
entirely disproportionate to the questions put by history. With
the aid of hindsight we can see quite clearly now that land
reform was an absolute prerequisite for a just and lasting peace.
The failure of Radical Republicans to achieve this basic objective doomed Reconstruction from the start and paved the way
for one hundred years of tragedy and terror.

The freedmen saw this. They saw clearly the close connection between politics and economics and they realized, better
than some of their leaders, that it was necessary to ground
political freedom on economic freedom. When Andrew Johnson ordered the return of confiscated rebel plantations, the
freedmen armed themselves and fought federal soldiers who
tried to drive them from the land. Johnson resorted to guile,
sending General O. O. Howard to South Carolina to pacify the
rebellious freedmen. Howard, who had no stomach for the
mission, called a huge assembly on Edisto Island, but the words
wouldn't come. How does one tell a people who have known
nothing but betrayals, that they have been betrayed again?
Howard couldn't say it; and he asked the freedmen to sing one
of the good old Negro spirituals. The freedmen *knew*. They
sang *Nobody Knows The Trouble I've Seen* and Oliver Otis Howard broke down and wept.

In the weeks that followed, the freedmen fought a rearguard
action against the Freedmen's Bureau and the U.S. Army.
Defeated finally by hunger and superior firepower, they surged
forward on the political front, eagerly grasping for ballots in the

vain hope of converting political power into social and economic power. Only the very cynical and the very radical knew that this effort was doomed to failure.

The grand outcome of the failure of the Radical land reform proposals was the perpetuation of the power of the lords of the land and the elimination of any possibility of sustained cooperation between poor whites and poor blacks. As for the freedmen, they had been made dependent on their enemies for the necessities of life. Beyond all that, the failure of land reform closed certain democratic alternatives in American life and culture. As Du Bois noted, the allocation of forty acres of land to every adult freedman would have created a democratic infrastructure that would have changed the course of American democracy. Failure to allocate that land led inexorably to a totalitarian South which foreclosed the possibility of creating a democratic North.

Stevens and Sumner seemed to have glimpsed more clearly than any other politicians the dangers that America then faced. And they made repeated attempts to give the Radical program the economic thrust it lacked. Three days after the opening of the Fortieth Congress, Sumner reopened the question by demanding homes and a permanent policy of federal aid to education. Congress refused and Sumner tried again in July, 1867. When Congress again balked, Sumner, the eloquent, elegant Puritan, fled the Senate, blinded by tears of remorse.

Stevens pressed a similar fight in the House, where he tried unsuccessfully to amend the Freedmen's Bureau act to include provisions for allocating forty acres to freedmen and loyal white refugees. He later introduced resolutions providing for the immediate enforcement of the Confiscation Act of July, 1862. These resolutions provided that "the land so seized and condemned should be distributed among the slaves who had been made free by the war and constitutional amendments, and who were residing on said land on the 4th of March, 1861, or since; to each head of a family 40 acres; to each adult male whether head of a family or not, 40 acres; to each widow, head of a family, 40 acres; to be held by them in fee simple, but to be inalienable for ten years after they should become so seized thereof. . . ."

This proposal and others of similar depth failed because most Republicans lacked the inclination to grapple with the political imperatives of Reconstruction. Most of Stevens' colleagues were more interested in securing the industrial supremacy of the North than in creating democracy in the South. Other Republicans, while sincere, lacked an understanding of the price of reform. They were blinded, moreover, by the concept-tools of the time. These concepts condemned government subsidies for anyone except large corporations. Although America later gave away an empire of land larger than the whole of Western Europe to railroad promoters and corporations, it was considered gauche to give land or anything else, except charity, to the poor.

But there was a more important reason for the Radicals' legislative difficulties—a reason that reflected the strategic weakness of the whole Reconstruction program. Many, perhaps most, Republicans never intended to transform American society. They never intended to give black people any more power than was necessary to check Southern planters. This group instinctively recoiled from measures which would have given black men a measure of economic security still denied the white workers of the North. They had never admitted the full logic of the democratic idea for poor whites; it was unthinkable that they would countenance it for poor blacks, especially since wholesale confiscation of property in the South would have set a bad example for the restless workers of the North and West.

Stevens saw this. Rising in the House after passage of the Fourteenth Amendment, Stevens announced that the dream was stillborn. He was seventy-four years old then, and he had been long in the field, tilling. In his youth, in his manhood, in his old age, he had "fondly dreamed that when any fortunate chance should have broken up for a while the foundations of our institutions, and released us from obligations the most tyrannical that ever man imposed in the name of freedom," that American institutions would be so remodeled "as to have freed them from every vestige of human oppression, of inequality of rights, of recognized degradation of the poor, and the superior caste of the rich." He had hoped, in short, that "no distinction would be tolerated in this purified Republic but what arose from merit and conduct." But, alas, he said, this "bright dream has vanished like the baseless fabric of a vision. I find that we shall be obliged to be content with patching up the worst portions of the ancient edifice, and leaving it, in many of its parts, to be swept through by the tempests, the frosts, and the storms of despotism."

Always a realist, Stevens took what he could get — which was considerable. The Reconstruction acts — passed in March and July of 1867 over the President's veto — divided the South into five military districts and authorized military commanders to enroll male voters irrespective of race or previous condition of servitude. All voters were required to take an "iron clad" oath of loyalty to America and some white males, particularly former Confederates who had violated oaths of loyalty to the United States, were deprived temporarily of the ballot. The implications of all this were revolutionary, for black people outnumbered white people in Mississippi, South Carolina, and Louisiana and held majorities of seven, eight, and ten to one in some Black Belt counties. As details of the plan filtered South, blacks and whites began to gird themselves for what a French reporter called "the beginning of America's Second Revolution." Before detailing that Revolution, let us take a hasty survey of the ground on which the battle would be fought.

Power in the South grew out of and reflected the land, which was black. The rich black soil which was the setting and the

stake of the struggle dropped down from Tidewater Virginia
into eastern North Carolina and then zig-zagged across the
South, covering the low country of South Carolina, the central
section of Georgia, northern Florida, south central Alabama,
western Mississippi, east central Louisiana, eastern Arkansas
and eastern Texas. This was the Black Belt. It was inhabited by
black men who coaxed wealth from the black soil and by rich
white men who appropriated that wealth and kept the black
men poor. It was the Black Belt which entranced Union
soldiers as they fought their way across the South and it was to
the Black Belt that many of them returned, once the victory
was won. On the outside looking in were the poor whites who
inhabited the hills and Piedmont areas fringing the Black Belt.

The struggle for control of Reconstruction unfolded against
this sharply etched background of rich land and poor land with
three groups—freedmen, Southern whites and Northern
whites—competing for place and power. Of these three groups
none commanded more attention than the freedmen who had
moved from the depths of the most tyrannical form of slavery
ever organized into the cockpit of the most daring social
experiment the white Western world had ever attempted.

As a group, the new citizens were prototypes of what Arnold
Toynbee calls the internal proletariat of the Western world. In
other words, they were *in* but not *of* a society to which they had
been forcibly transported and reduced to the level of subhuman
labor machines for the money and comfort of their captors.
They were descendants of Africans, but they were also, as their
skin colors indicated, descendants of Englishmen, Irishmen,
Jews, Chinese, and Indians.

Not biology but ideology distinguished this group which had
been artifically impoverished by men who used force to keep
them from blending with their environment. It was the idea of
race—the idea that nonwhite peoples are irremediably and
irredeemably inferior—that separated these citizens from their
fellow men. That idea had been invented by men who found it

economically profitable, and it persisted in the postwar world because men realized dimly that it served their purse and their psyche.

The freedmen were what history and the white men had made them. Since it had been a criminal offense for the black man to read and write and hold property; since, in fact, black people had been property, most of the new citizens were propertyless and could not read and write. Most were agrarian laborers, but many were skilled artisans. In fact, there were more black skilled artisans in the South at that time than white skilled artisans.

Power in a democracy is made of three things: numbers, resources, and organization. The freedmen lacked resources and organizations, but they were abundantly endowed in the first department. The black population enfranchised by the Reconstruction acts was larger by at least a million than the whole population at the time of the Revolutionary War. At that time, 92 per cent of all African-Americans lived in the South. Of the 4,500,000 African-Americans, 4,000,000 were former slaves and 500,000 were of that twilight class called "free persons of color," a phrase that designated black men who had been neither free men nor slaves in the ante bellum period.

The new citizens were by no means unprepared for the boons of power. If, as a result of slavery, most of the freedmen could not read or write, perhaps as many as 200,000, more than is generally recognized, were literate. Though unlettered in the main, the new citizens had a thorough understanding of the political landscape and of the interests at stake. Many, moreover, possessed gifts of mother wit and imagination that would tell in the dangerous days ahead.

Turning from the freedmen to the half million free Negroes we find additional social assets. Among the free Negro colonies of Charleston, Richmond, New Orleans, Washington and other cities, there were wealthy and talented black men — doctors, lawyers, artists, preachers, teachers, architects. The ten thousand free men in South Carolina were, in the main, literate, and some were well-to-do. The eighteen thousand free Negroes in New Orleans owned twenty million dollars in taxable property and many of them were blood relatives of the South's first families. The free Negro colonies would contribute substantially to the skill banks of the new power group. But so also would the plantations, which began in 1867 to yield a large crop of indigenous leaders. Some of these men moved into politics after serving apprenticeships to power as preachers. Others, who had studied the style of local white politicians, not always to their advantage, would go straight from the cottonfields to power. It would be said later that the freedmen showed a real genius for the game of politics, picking up rules and methods "like a flash."

Numerical strength assured black people of a large voice in Southern life, but it didn't assure them of power. So long as they voted, nothing real could be done in the South without them. But it remained to be seen whether they themselves could do anything real with the power that the ballot promised. As a marginal minority in the total American population, the freedmen could not operate without national allies. Allies were necessary even in the South where a second group occupied all the trenches of power.

History, geography and economics — not biology — separated the freedmen from this second group, which was made up of about seven million whites with a Southern background and an identification, real or remote, with slavery and the Lost Cause. Socially, this group was divided into planters and poor whites. The planters constituted a tiny minority of the white group, for only two million whites had owned slaves. And of this number, eight thousand had owned most of the slaves and most of the land. This oligarchy of planters had ruled Southern society with a thoroughness unknown in the modern world until the rise of the totalitarian states. In defense of this antidemocratic society, the planters had risked all and had lost all and now, in

the wake of a catastrophic defeat, they constituted an unemployed power elite.

The planters were an unemployed elite, but they were far
from powerless. They still owned the land and in the South
that was half the game. Defeat had shaken but hadn't destroyed
their social prestige; and in their long years of political domi-
nance they had acquired political skills and a mode of address
that made them dangerous foes, as the Andrew Johnson epi-
sode indicated. Moreover, slavery as the dominant institution of
the section had created attitudes and institutions that perpetuated the planter myth, even in the minds of the planter's
victims. But the skills and attitudes that made the planters
omnipotent in the old world made them vulnerable in the new.
The planters' milieu was feudal, not democratic. Begging black
people and poor whites for votes was demeaning. They
believed poor whites were inherently unequal. How could they
feign sympathy for Negro equality?

The planters were doomed as a class, but individual planters
who loved money more than the planter myth survived in the
new world by capitulating to the money-making ethos they had
unsuccessfully contested on the battlefield. Business-oriented
planters had been slowly ripening in the planter class for years.
The emancipation of the slaves freed them, too; and they were
soon deeply immersed in stocks, bonds, insurance companies,
and railroads.

It is the new planter-capitalist wing that concerns us
here—for, as the curtain rose on the campaign of 1867, it was
these men who created a New South power structure on the
ruins of the old. The embryonic elements of the New South
power structure were planter-capitalists, bankers, merchants,
corporation lawyers, and poor whites who had distinguished
themselves as Confederate brigadiers and colonels. In every
state it was organized around major newspapers, (the *Charleston Courier*, the *Floridian*, the *Jackson Clarion*, the *New Orleans
Times*), which championed diversification, industrialization, sub-

sidies to railroads, and a minimum of social experimentation. Never a stable entity, composed of old planters looking backward and business-oriented types looking northward, the New South Bridge Group tried in the first years of Reconstruction to form a counter power structure to the new power structure of black men, poor whites, and Northern immigrants. Initially, at any rate, it moved cautiously toward an acceptance of token black participation with the hope of retaining the power of Black Belt counties as a counterweight against the emerging poor white group. This strategy never got off the ground, partly because of the limitations of the time, partly because of the limitations of the planters who never realized, until it was too late, that security on the old terms was no longer available to them. There remained, in fact, only three ways for them to salvage a modicum of control. They could have sought an accommodation with Northern capital which would have given them proconsul power under the general authority of the colonial North; or they could have allied with either the freedmen or their ancient enemies, the poor whites.

It was the poor white class that Robespierre had in mind when he said, "Men would rather submit to chains themselves than see the number of their equals multiply." In all respects, save color, the poor whites were Negroes, if we understand by that vague word a social rather than a biological condition. To be sure, poor whites owned more land than Negroes; and they certainly had greater freedom of movement. But this only meant that their cage was larger, not that they were free. The poor whites were exploited as savagely as Negroes, and they lived in equal misery, without even the excuse of slavery to explain their poverty and general illiteracy.

The name was accurate. Poor whites were poor people who called themselves white. The category included at the very least the five million whites who had never owned a slave and who blamed both the slave and the slaveowners for their plight. Unable to compete with the planters for the rich bottom land, they had retreated to the hills and piedmont areas where they eked out a scrubby existence on land no one else wanted. They were, as Charles Nordhoff said later, a peculiar people—settled "upon a thin and infertile soil; long and constantly neglected before the war; living still in backwoods country, and in true backwoods style, without schools, with few churches, and given to rude sports and a rude agriculture."

The dominant characteristics of this group were envy-hatred of the planters and fear-hatred of the blacks. It was from this group that the aristocrats had recruited slave overseers and slave drivers and it was this group that the aristocrats had ordained to stand in the middle as a cushion between rich whites and poor blacks. Now, as the black man reached out for political power, the poor whites were terrified by the possibility of being forced into direct social and economic competition with the freedmen. And, of course, they hated black people, largely because they had been taught to hate black people but also because hate dignified and gave meaning to their lives.

If the poor whites hated black people, they didn't on that account love the planters. They knew that the planters looked down on them as "white niggers," and they realized dimly that they were paying in the flesh for planter opulence and planter power. The resentment was there, but poor whites didn't know what to do about it, for they had never developed or found a leadership of their own. During the Civil War, most poor whites followed Confederate leadership, but there was strong pro-Union sentiment in the poor white enclaves of the upcountry. In northern Alabama and western North Carolina, poor whites organized open resistance and fought guerilla actions against Confederate soldiers. During the latter stages of the war, poor whites deserted the Confederate Army in droves.

When Andrew Johnson said the Emancipation Proclamation freed more whites than blacks, he was thinking specifically of poor whites. The emancipation of the slave emancipated poor whites from the domination of the slave-rich planters and created conditions which permitted them to compete for economic power. But the poor whites, like the slaves, lacked capital and access to credit. Even worse, poor whites lacked social and political focus. Remarkably, the freedmen seem to have had a higher level of consciousness at this point than the poor whites. In the first few years of freedom, the freedmen produced scores of major political leaders. Poor white leadership, on the other hand, was hesitant and did not reach full consciousness until the Populist movement a generation after the war.

The themes of this later revolt were present, though in muted form, in the Reconstruction period. The fundamental interests of poor whites were land and wider social opportunities. Tentative Republican efforts in these directions attracted an astonishingly large group of poor whites. Indeed, it has been estimated that more than one-third of the poor whites of the hill country supported Radical Reconstruction in 1867 and 1868. In some cases, poor white zeal outstripped the Radical Republican programs. The movement to place greater restrictions on the political activities of Confederate leaders was generally led by poor white loyalists. These same politicians were in the forefront of the movement to confiscate and distribute the land.

The alliance of poor whites and poor blacks, which contained so many pregnant possibilites for the development of a New South, was checked by the failure of land reform and the development of the Ku Klux Klan movement. One of the major reasons for the development of the Ku Klux Klan movement was the determination of powerful white Southerners to arrest the defections of poor whites.

A third and complicating factor in the Reconstruction equation was the presence in the South of a large number of white men and women with Northern backgrounds. Many of the Northerners were Union Veterans who had returned to the South, "some to run plantations, some to open mines of coal and iron, some to build railroads, others to establish hotels, and all to give a grand impulse to Southern progress, and show the 'old fogies' in the South how to do it." By 1867, there were at least ten thousand Northern men in Louisiana alone and tens of thousands were sending down roots in South Carolina, North Carolina, Florida, and other Southern states. During this same period, there was a large in-migration of white professionals, many of them New England schoolmarms who established Peace Corps-type colonies.

The Northerners were no more homogenous than the freedmen or the Southern whites. There were at least two subgroups or factions: (1) hard-nosed stalwarts, primarily business-oriented Union veterans, and federal officeholders on the make; (2) idealistic humanitarians, generally ministers, teachers, and missionaries. Each faction had its own traits. The stalwarts were in the main opportunists, deeply influenced by the planter ideal, with little interest in either Negroes or causes. The second faction, more complex, included men with a deep strain of idealism and others, less idealistic, who were motivated primarily by a desire to make the South over in the North's image. Despite differences in tone and style, members of both groups shared the same basic orientation. They believed, as most men of that day believed, in the supremacy of the Puritan code—thrift, hard work, individualism. So believing, most of them opposed massive government aid to the freedmen as an unwarranted intrusion that would harm the initiative and thrift of the freedmen. Others were elitists with grave doubts about the possibilities of poor people—black or white—governing themselves. Most, it seems, were white supremacists in a paternalistic sort of way. Like modern missionaries, they usually defined their mission as the elevation of a benighted race to the standards of white civilization. To this picture one should add in all fairness that the white newcomers were limited by the idea-forces of their time. They were typical products of a system most of them could not surmount. It should also be said that their help, at least in the initial stages, was indispensable and that many of them paid a high price in terms of social ostracism, proscription, and violence.

It is against this background that we must view the billows
of hope that rolled over the South as the campaign of 1867
opened. This was a campaign of a tone and type unparalleled in
American history. The campaign had passion in it; it pulled
people out of themselves and sent them marching across the
Southern landscape. Midsummer days in this long hot summer—the first of many long hot summers—saw thick black
lines snaking across the land, trumpets blaring, drums sound-
ing, men, women, and children weeping and shouting:

> *The bottom rail is on top*
> *And we gonna keep it there.*

Away from the roads and parades, in small rooms, black and
white men laid the foundations of power, organizing Republican state organizations and auxiliary groupings, Loyal Leagues,
Reconstruction clubs, and "Companies of the Grand Army."
At a People's Convention in March, a North Carolina state
organization was formed. The next month a Republican state
convention met in Virginia with 210 delegates, 160 of them
black. In July, a Republican state organization was effected at a
meeting in Columbia, South Carolina. In the interest of
"harmony" and "fair play," it was suggested that the overwhelmingly black convention name a white president. This
suggestion was hooted down, and R.H. Gleaves, a black businessman from Pennsylvania, was elected. The South Carolina
convention adopted a "one man, one vote" platform and recommended the division and sale of unoccupied land to poor
people. On a resolution of J. J. Wright, who would soon be
elected to the state supreme court, it was declared that the
African-American should "be represented by one of his own
race [as vice president] on the next Presidential ticket of the
Republican party."

After the state Republican meetings, leaders organized in
every district and precinct, and commissioned "organizers" to
go into the back counties to rouse the faithful. Black ministers

from the North and black and white agents of the national Republican organization supplemented state "organizers" in a door-to-door and cottonfield-to-cottonfield campaign. Soon black people had formed a chain of organizations that extended across the Black Belt areas of the South.

None of these organizations was more important than the controversial Loyal League which transformed the political consciousness of the most underprivileged segment of Southern society. Organized in the North during the war to combat defeatism, the League followed the Union Army into the South and organized poor white Loyalists in the Piedmont areas. After the War, the Northern and Southern branches moved in different directions, the Northern branches (usually called Union Leagues) becoming elite social clubs and the Southern branches becoming radical cells for the politicizing of the poor. By 1867, Loyal Leagues were organized in most Black Belt and Piedmont areas with a blatantly interracial membership of freedmen, Northern immigrants, and Southern Loyalists.

The purpose of the League, according to a contemporary pamphlet, was "to secure the complete ascendancy of the true principles of popular government — equal liberty, education, and the elevation of the working men of the Nation, and the security of all by means of the elective franchise." In pursuit of this purpose, Republican politicians organized Loyal League cells in each precinct of the Black Belt counties. Local councils held frequent meetings and elected delegates to the state councils which met annually in most states. State and local councils pushed an aggressive program aimed at the aorta: political and economic power. Holding meetings in churches, schools, oak groves, and cottonfields, the League raised the level of political awareness of the freedmen and prepared them for a sustained struggle for power. In time, the League came to rival the black church as a center of power and community organization.

Union Leagues and party organizations also recruited and identified indigenous leaders and provided opportunities for

First municipal election in Richmond in
the postwar period attracted large numbers
of black voters. Observers said polls in
South were "thronged with eager crowds
of Negroes."

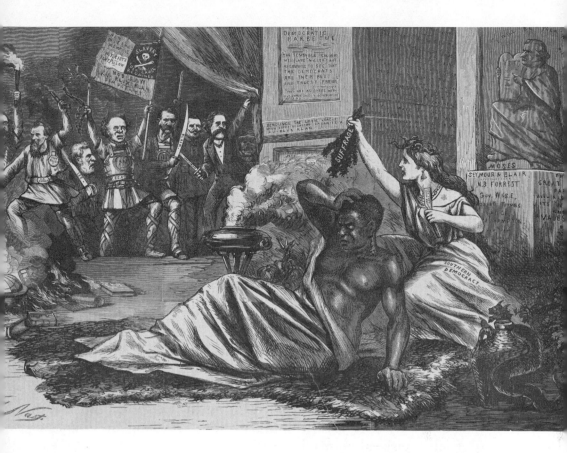

In a famous *Harper's Weekly* cartoon, Thomas Nast depicted "Modern Samson" awakening to power in the era following the Civil War.

them to learn parliamentary law. At league and party meetings, potential leaders also learned how to speak in public and how to identify interests and issues. The most talented of the indigenous leaders were encouraged to attend court sessions and political meetings as spectators in order to get the feel of power.

For the black masses, there were parades, barbecues, dances, mass meetings. The South, in this season, was a moving black mass of meeting, organizing, and electioneering. All over the South now, men and women were moving, hands and hearts uplifted, looking for a thing called freedom. Stopped here, rebuffed there, they moved again, believing always that it was around the next turning.

There was, in May and June and July of this summer, a series of huge outdoor political meetings of a frequency and intensity never since equalled in black America. Whole plantations moved en masse to meetings, walking all day, willing to sit and listen all night. "The blacks are kept in a state of camp meeting excitement," a reporter from the *Charleston Daily News* said. "Meetings are held everywhere, traveling disorganizers [sic]... visit all points...."

On Friday, May 3, five thousand black people gathered in Charleston to hear U.S. Senator Henry Wilson, the Radical Republican from Massachusetts. Thousands more gathered in groves and fields in Macon, Tallahassee, Montgomery, and New Orleans in June, July, and August. In Jackson, Mississippi, one to two thousand cheered the Rev. James D. Lynch, the magnetic orator who was known thereabouts as "the Henry Ward Beecher of the colored race." A local white Democrat stationed himself on the edge of the crowd. This is what he saw and heard: "Imagine one or two thousand Negroes standing en masse in a semi-circle facing the speaker, whose tones were as clear and resonant as a silver bell; and of a sudden, every throat would be open wide, and a spontaneous shout in perfect unison would arise, and swell, and subside as the voice of one man...."

Thus, in the summer and fall of 1867, the rivulets of hope and passion began to trickle down from their secret places high in the steep mountains of black despair.

Look closely at this scene as it stands now in 1867, and mark well the revolutionary mood of the black masses. In Alabama, black people were rushing into churches "without any changes having taken place, where the white people were sitting; not that they had no place to sit [i.e., the Negro pew] but simply to show their equality." Black people were also staging ride-ins and sit-ins in Charleston, Mobile, Richmond, and New Orleans. A *New York Times* correspondent caught with exceptional clarity an incident in Charleston:

On Tuesday afternoon, March 27, after the adjournment of the Freed-man's mass meeting in Charleston, S.C., an attempt was made by some of them to test their right to ride in the street car, which is denied them by the rules of the Company. One of them entered a car, and declined to leave it when requested to do so by the conductor, who at the same time informed him of the Company's rules. The conductor, however, insisted that he should at least leave the inside of the car, and finally his friends, who found he was liable to be forcibly ejected if the resistance were offered, persuaded him to yield. On its return trip the car was filled at the same place by a crowd of Negroes, who rushed into it, to the great discomfort of the white passengers, and although remonstrated with and appealed to by the conductor, declined to go out. The driver then attempted, by direction of the conductor, to throw his car from the track; and failing in this, unhitched his horses and left the car. The Negroes attempted to push the car forward, and threatened personal violence to the conductor, but the arrival of the police and detachment of soldiers caused the Negroes to disperse. Other cars were in the meantime entered in the same way, and the Negroes, finding the conductors would not permit them to ride, endeavored to interrupt the travel of the cars by placing stones on the tracks. . . ."

As the struggle continued in the streets and in places of public accommodation, military commanders began to lay down guidelines for the new order, appointing black and white registrars and public officials. In South Carolina, Beverly Nash was appointed magistrate by Major General Edward Canby.

General E. O. C. Ord appointed B. T. Montgomery, a wealthy Negro planter, justice of the peace at Davis Bend, Mississippi. In New Orleans, General P. H. Sheridan dismissed the board of aldermen and assistant aldermen and named new appointees, including several black men. In September, the New Orleans City Council appointed four assistant recorders, three of whom were Negroes, and two city physicians, both of whom were black. Two months later, Monroe Baker, a prominent black businessman and a free Negro, was appointed mayor of St. Martin, Louisiana.

By September, the South was ablaze with hope and fear. They were registering now in Natchez and Columbia and Waycross and Selma—in thousands of hamlets and cities in every state of Dixieland. Black people came from miles away, bringing with them bags and baskets, willing to wait all day if necessary. A hostile reporter saw a group in South Carolina and recorded that the freedmen's eyes "beaming with anxiety were constantly turned in the direction from whence the registrars came; . . . after their names were taken they went on their way rejoicing." By the end of November, 1,363,000 American citizens had registered in the old states of the Confederacy, and of that number 700,000 were black. Because of the disenfranchisement of some Confederate officials and the passive resistance of some whites, black voters constituted a majority in five states—Alabama, Florida, Louisiana, Mississippi, South Carolina—as can be seen in the table of population and registration figures.

How did Southern whites respond to all this?

Some Southern whites repudiated the Confederacy with what a disapproving historian called "unseemly haste"; others, notably Confederate General Pierre G. T. Beauregard, the hero of the Fort Sumter assault, sheathed their swords and joined the revolution; still others, fearful, fled to Mexico and South America. "I pray to God," General Sterling Price wrote from Mexico, "that my fears for the future of the South may

POPULATION AND REGISTRATION
IN THE RECONSTRUCTED STATES

State	Population 1860		Registration 1867	
	Negro	White	Negro	White
Alabama............	437,770	526,271	104,518	61,295
Arkansas............	111,259	324,143	17,109	49,722
Florida	62,677	77,746	16,089	11,914
Georgia.............	465,698	591,550	95,168	96,333
Louisiana	350,373	357,456	84,436	45,218
Mississippi	437,404	353,899	77,328	62,362
North Carolina	361,544	629,942	72,932	106,721
South Carolina	412,320	291,300	80,550	46,882
Texas	182,921	420,891	49,497	59,633
Virginia	548,000	1,000,000	105,832	120,101

never be realized, but when the right is given the Negro to bring suit, testify before the courts, and vote in elections, you all had better be in Mexico."

Some whites migrated, but most gritted their teeth and accommodated themselves to the realities of the hour. A considerable number of whites consoled themselves with the idea that the black man was destined to disappear "like the Indians." Said the editor of the *Natchez* [Miss.] *Democrat:* "The child is already born who will behold the last Negro in the state of Mississippi."

As this quote indicates, there was considerable confusion in white Southern ranks, and this confusion was manifested in the inability of Democrats to agree on a single strategy. One group adopted tactics of contemptuous abstention, boycotting the election and awaiting relief from Northern Democrats. Another group of planters supported the revolution, flattering themselves that they would be able to moderate and control it. This strategy was expressed with unusual bluntness by J. A. P. Campbell of Mississippi who "favored a prompt acquiescence on the part of our people, and to make the most of the situation and form an alliance with the Negroes politically by a full recognition of their rights to vote and hold office, acquire ascendancy over them, and become their teachers and controllers instead of allowing the Republicans to do so."

Pursuing this tactic, planters and New South commercialists wooed black voters at a series of interracial meetings and picnics. In Terry, Mississippi, for instance, an interracial meeting was held to prepare for a July 4th barbecue. A white man, a former Confederate, was elected president, and a black man, Alfred Johnson, was elected vice president. The committees named to arrange the interracial barbecue were conspicuously interracial, with three planters and three black men on each committee.

At these meetings, which were held in every Southern state, white men told the new black voters that Southern white men had always been their friends, that the North was responsible for slavery, and that it was to their best interest to vote with their old white friends instead of the "bad" Northerners.

Fraudulent in conception and fraudulent in execution, the planter campaign failed dismally. The black voters were illiterate—they were not dumb. They ate the planters' barbecue, drank their beer and went to the polls and voted solidly Republican. On election day, the polls were "thronged with eager crowds of Negroes." There was "wrangling, scrambling, fighting, almost suffocation in the eager rush to be first." In this, the first election of the new era, black people demonstrated a political sophistication that still frightens conservative historians. In South Carolina, for example, a larger percentage of the electorate (85 per cent) participated in the election than participates in elections in white America today. Sixty-nine thousand of the eighty-one thousand registered Negro voters went to the polls, and every one of these citizens voted for the constitution.

Now, after the electioneering and registering and voting, the Revolution moved to a climax. On Tuesday, November 5, the first constitutional convention opened in Montgomery, Alabama, with eighteen black men and ninety white men in attendance. Seventeen days later, forty-nine black men and forty-nine white men assembled at Mechanics Institute in New Orleans. In the first weeks of December there was action in Richmond and Atlanta. And, as the Revolution turned the corner of 1867, black men and white men began to gather in Little Rock and Raleigh.

It was in this climate that the historic Charleston convention convened.

And it was in this climate that a black man in a tattered frock coat mounted the rostrum in an old Baptist church and found the place in the Book. In a deep rolling tone he announced the text of that day and of that age:

> *He hath put down the Mighty*
> *From their seats*
> *And hath exalted them*
> *Of low degree!*

2

"The Glory Year"

A BLACK MAN is speaking.

He holds the floor in the amphitheatre-like assembly of the Greek revival capitol in Raleigh, North Carolina, where 15 black men and 133 white men have gathered to rewrite the organic law of the state. He has risen on a point of personal privilege to reply to disparaging remarks about the credentials of the new men of power who are sitting now in constitutional conventions across the South. The disparaging remarks came from Plato Durham, a white Southern irreconcilable who has just bemoaned the passage of power from privilege to poverty, saying that when he looked around him and saw Negroes filling the seats of Graham and Badger and Gaston, he felt ashamed.... He felt out of place.

Standing now in the well of the Commons Hall, one hand in the pocket of his frock coat, the other carving the air in graceful gestures, James J. Harris, a tall, forceful, black man from Wilmington, is saying, in reply, that he is not there to soothe the ruffled feelings of outraged aristocrats. Why, sir, "when such taunts are thrown as just heard," he always remembered "the 200,000 black men, who knew enough to fight for liberty and Union, and that great number who knew enough to vote against treason." Warming to the attack, focusing specifically on Durham, Harris, a free Negro, now thirty-five, says:"No doubt the delegate feels out of place. But if he leaves, the Convention will not send for him."

A ripple of laughter greets this riposte and Graham's face reddens as Harris continues, saying he is astonished to hear such uncharitable remarks from men of a race which had overridden his own and grown rich in their poverty — men, sir, "who had bathed their own country in blood." How dare such men come before the people speaking of education and political integrity! Why, sir, if black people had "only a tenth part of what they had earned, they would today have been educated." And why didn't they have the "tenth part"? Because white men had robbed black men "to provide themselves."

Somewhat prematurely, Harris predicts that that day is gone forever.

No longer, he says, will the rich and powerful and prejudiced be able "to arrogate to themselves the right to control the destiny of the State." No longer will they be able "to ignore the poor whites and Negroes." He and his colleagues were elected to create a new society, "to bury such old and tyrannical ideas, and form a Constitution that will shelter the. . . people of North Carolina."

Speaking thus of blood shed and debts not paid and "of the destiny of the State," speaking frankly and eloquently of poor whites and poor blacks and of the "tenth part" due, speaking of the right of *all* to participate and of the need for a new legal structure to shelter all, James J. Harris, a native of North Carolina, sketched in general outline the issues that agitated the South in what Henrietta Buckmaster has well called "the most revolutionary year in American history."

It was a year, this year of 1868, in which black people came onto the stage for the first time and spoke lines.

It was a year in which the pressure of the black presence stretched the fabric of the Commonwealth to the breaking point.

This was the year in which the secretary of war defied the President, barricaded himself in his office and had his successor arrested.

It was in this year and in this climate of turbulence and change that Congress came within one vote of dismissing the President of the United States.

In the North, in this year, there was wild talk of using troops to forcibly dissolve Congress and arrest its leaders; and in the South thousands on thousands of angry black people thronged the dusty roads, shouting defiance and demanding a division of the loaves and fishes.

This was the year of the Fourteenth Amendment; this was the year men made the Declaration of Independence walk in the streets; this was the year almost all things were made new.

It is against this background of worlds in collision that one must view the historic Reconstruction conventions which revolutionized the legal foundations of the South.

During the whole of this pivotal year, the South vibrated with the impassioned sounds of extraordinary assemblages of blacks, native whites, and Northern newcomers. As we have seen, this season of decision opened in November and December of 1867, with the convening of the Alabama, Louisiana, Virginia, and Georgia conventions. Alabama completed its work on December 6, but Louisiana, Virginia and Georgia reconvened after the Christmas holidays and were soon joined by five other conventions: Mississippi and Arkansas, January 7; North Carolina and South Carolina, January 14; Florida, January 20. As the Florida delegates gathered, Alabama was preparing to vote on its constitution. By the time Alabama completed its voting, Arkansas and other states were moving toward adjournment. Month after month, in leapfrog fashion, different states debated and voted until June when Texas, a late starter, opened its convention.

Never before—never since—had there been assemblies like these. Confederates, Unionists, poor men, rich men, black men, white men: all stood shoulder to shoulder in these conventions and grappled with questions that have not yet been answered in the Commonwealth.

What, precisely, is a government?

To whom does it belong?

Can the people participate?

Can the poor, the disadvantaged, the driven against the wall play a role?

Elected by a poor white and poor black constituency and composed of Northern-born whites, native white Southerners and Northern-born and Southern-born blacks, the Reconstruction conventions represented the first democratic assemblies in the South and, in some respects, the first democratic assemblies in America. Here was no asssemblage of middle-class lawyers and businessmen speaking for the people. Here, for the first and last time in America, was an assemblage of people, many of them poor, speaking for themselves. Here also was the first meaningful attempt, ninety-four years before the rise of Afro-Asia, of nonwhites to appropriate the symbols and images of white power.

Every real revolution demonstrates conclusively that more men have leadership potential than had been previously suspected. More than that: every real revolution proves that society pre-selects its failures and that a change in social structures changes and widens the creativity and social sensitivity of the excluded. The revolution of Reconstruction proved this on American soil by anticipating the experience of our own day that a basic change in the structural foundation of a society opens immense reservoirs of new talent which would otherwise have no opportunity for effective expression. In the wake of the Reconstruction revolution, thousands of impoverished men—black and white—scrambled onto the stage of power and repudiated by their presence the ideology and values in the name of which they had been excluded and stigmatized.

As Harold Laski has pointed out, the sense of wide horizons opening suddenly to a population confined for hundreds of years to narrow perspectives of opportunity evokes what is best in the spirit of that people. One could see this principle at work in the reconstructed South where there was hardly a plantation which did not produce in the context of its own peculiar needs a petit Martin Luther King Jr., capable of arousing it to efforts of which it had not previously known itself capable. This development was analysed with great subtlety and insight by Professor Vernon Wharton who was struck by the flowering of second-level leaders in Mississippi. There was "something amazing," he said, "about the suddeness with which, all over the state, [local leaders] emerged from the anonymity of slavery to become directors and counselors for their race. In general, it can be said that they were not Negroes who had held positions of leadership under the old regime; the characteristics which made a man a slave driver or foreman under the old regime were not those which would allow him to organize a Loyal League. Almost none of them came from the small group who had been free before the war. Such men, as barbers, artisans, or small farmers, had depended too long on the favor of the whites for the maintenance of their existence. Servility had become a part of them.... A large portion of the minor Negro leaders were preachers, lawyers, or teachers from the free states or from Canada. Their education and their independent attitude gained for them immediate favor and leadership. Of the natives who became their rivals, the majority had been urban slaves, blacksmiths, carpenters, clerks, or waiters in hotels and boarding houses; a few of them had been favored body-servants of affluent whites. Most of them were more intelligent than the mass of their fellows, and had picked up some smattering of education, at least to the point of being able to read and write. There was a general tendency for them to combine preaching with their politics; as Sir George Campbell has said, they were rather preachers because they were leaders than leaders because they were preachers."

It was believed by many men—North and South—that the new leaders would make fools of themselves in the official Anglo-Saxon world of whereases and wherefores. For how could a group of people without practical experience in business or government manage the affairs of the state? This question, which was asked repeatedly in the early days of Reconstruction, contained a veiled ideology in favor of the so-called natural leaders of the South. As a generalization on power, it was a tautological statement that only those who are permitted to govern can govern. As applied to the South of the Reconstruction period, it was palpably false. For experience in government in the South had been experience in exploitation and misgovernment. The new men of power had very little to learn from "the natural leaders" of the South, who, for more than a century, had kept their area in a state of underdevelopment and their people—black and white—in a state of misery and poverty.

Politics is not complicated.

People who say it is complicated say it to keep others from learning how very simple it really is. One learns to rule by ruling, and ruling is the same everywhere—the manipulation of emotions, myths, and pieces of foolscap.

It appears from the record that the black and white leaders of Reconstruction offended aristocrats and elitists most by exposing the myths of power. In the midst of a social convulsion unprecedented in American history, they proved how quickly men can learn all they need to know to make the wheels of government go around. Although experienced men, some of them lawyers and former legislators, moved to the fore in every state convention, there was, in every state convention, an articulate core of common people who spoke with uncommon authority, not because they had conferred with the people, but because they were the people. Not the least of these common men were the poor whites from the huts of the hill counties. For the first and last time in America, these men stood up in official assemblies and gave meaning to the phrase *government of the people.* (Some of the poor white politicians, incidentally, were illiterate. In the Florida legislature, only six men could not read or write — and four of them were white.)

Even more significant in terms of numbers and weight of previous exclusion were the former slaves, fifty-seven out of seventy-six in South Carolina, sixteen out of eighteen in Alabama. Many, perhaps most, of these men had been more than half convinced by an elitist ideology which was designed expressly to keep them out of the rooms of power. When the conventions opened, they were diffident and unsure of themselves. But as the days wore on they discovered how ridiculously easy it all was. By the end of the conventions, some of the former slaves were virtuosos of political in-fighting. As we shall see, the best men of the group were shrewd, cool, hard-headed types with a tight grasp of facts and keen insight into men and their motives.

Not only former slaves but self-educated free men, some of them wearing the simple and much-washed garments of the field, contributed to the thinking that changed the political architecture of the South. No one, for example, was more active in the South Carolina convention than Robert Carlos DeLarge, the self-educated tailor from Charleston. C. P. Leslie, a white delegate, said DeLarge, who was only twenty-five, was the best parliamentarian on the floor. No less active in the Louisiana convention was Pinckney Benton Stewart Pinchback, a rising young man whom we shall hear of again. Pinchback, who only had a common schools education, repeatedly outmaneuvered the white and black Creoles who sat in the Louisiana convention. He was aided considerably by shrewd, incorruptible former slaves like Oscar James Dunn, a forty-three-year-old plasterer with a fondness for violin airs.

As a group, the self-made delegates were handicapped by their lack of resources. Most were desperately poor, and many began their political careers with pressing debts. Daniel Richards, a white delegate to the Florida convention, noted that "probably three-fourths" of his black colleagues "had to borrow money to come with. . . ."

Some black delegates were fresh from the people, but some were very uncommon indeed. In fact, the best-educated and most cultured delegates in some conventions were black. This was certainly true in South Carolina where the black delegation was led by Francis Louis Cardozo, a graduate of the University of Glasgow, and Robert Brown Elliott, who had been educated at Eton. It was true also in Florida where Jonathan C. Gibbs, a graduate of Dartmouth and the Princeton Theological Seminary, easily outshone his white colleagues. A conservative white historian said that Gibbs was probably the most cultured member of the convention.

Foremost among the Black Bourgeoisie delegates were the representatives of the free black colonies of New Orleans, Charleston, and Richmond. Twenty-one of the seventy-six black delegates in the South Carolina convention came from this class. An even larger percentage of the Louisiana delegation came from the powerful free black colony of New Orleans which consisted of many professionals, some of whom were graduates of leading European universities.

There was, additionally, a creative core of lawyers and professionals, some of them migrants from the North. Some of the black Northern immigrants, however, were native Southerners who had returned to the South after extended periods of forced exile in the free states, Canada, and Europe. James J. Harris, for example, was a North Carolina native who fled his home state and sought refuge in Ohio. He returned to North Carolina in 1865. In that same year, Cardozo returned to South Carolina and James Thomas Rapier, the handsomely educated son of a white planter, returned to Alabama.

No portrait of the black delegates would be complete without mention of the black ministers: seven or eight out of seventeen in Mississippi, seven out of eighteen in Florida, and about thirteen out of seventy-six in South Carolina. Among the outstanding men in this group were T. W. Springer, AME, Mississippi; Henry P. Jacobs, Baptist, Mississippi; Francis Louis Cardozo, Presbyterian, South Carolina; Jonathan C. Gibbs, Presbyterian, Florida. Interestingly enough, three of the leading men in the state conventions were later elected bishops of their denominations: James Walker Hood, AME Zion, North Carolina; Henry McNeal Turner, AME, Georgia; and Richard Harvey Cain, AME, South Carolina. As we shall see, the African Methodist Episcopal Church and its ministers were integral parts of the new Southern power structure.

The black blocs in the conventions were by no means homogenous wholes. Some of the black men were so fair of skin that no one knows today and no one will ever know how many blacks were in attendance. Color apart, the black delegates differed considerably in their social attitudes. Although most were militant on racial issues, some were moderate, if not conservative, on economic and political issues. Not a few were separated from the black masses by chasms of interest and understanding. Some, like James T. Rapier of Alabama, were rich planters; others wanted to be rich planters. Many of the black professionals, moreover, were prisoners of unrealistic white middle-class ideals.

In general it can be said that many—though by no means all—black delegates were too anxious to prove that they could live up to the Anglo-Saxon ideal. These delegates were too anxious to prove they were "gentlemen" and that they, too, could protect the interests of the powerful. In the South Carolina convention, Francis Louis Cardozo, who gave excellent service in other respects, repeatedly lectured his colleagues on legalisms and the danger of "impairing the obligations of contracts." In the same convention, William J. Whipper, a gifted lawyer, indicated a desire to protect the interests of planters. The delegates, he said, were elected to serve all the people. The same general orientation was expressed in Georgia by Henry McNeal Turner, who was also an abrasively militant black nationalist.

What was true of South Carolina and Georgia was true of other states where delegates spent an inordinately large amount of time protecting the interests of men who would later become their executioners. Nothing illustrates this better than the attempts by some black delegates to restore the political rights of Confederate leaders, who were, at that very moment, organizing terrorist organizations and assassination squads.

What concerns us here is power — the acquisition, the organization and the use of power by black people at a plastic moment in American history. In the light of that concern we can see quite distinctly that long discussions on the morals and qualifications of black leaders are beside the point — which is power, or the lack of it. The worst thing that can be said about the black delegates to the convention is that some of them didn't understand that the only issue was power — that, and the obvious fact that some of them didn't know what time it was.

Reconstruction was a revolution, and a revolution imposes its own requirements in terms of strategy and tactics. First of all and most important of all, it is impossible to make a revolution in a short time without overwhelming force applied overwhelmingly. Nor can a revolution be made if the new men of power do not immediately uproot the tentacles of the old regime and mobilize the masses for a sustained and desperate struggle for the new. These were the tasks that confronted the black delegates to the conventions. Nothing in the literature of the time covered their situation. Not until the emergence of India and Ghana would there be a body of knowledge applicable to their situation. As I have said elsewhere, the great black leader of the Reconstruction period would have had the hardness of Kwame Nkrumah, the ascetic brilliance of Jawaharlal Nehru, the Machiavellian adroitness of Franklin Delano Roosevelt, and the love-thy-neighbor vocabulary of Martin Luther King Jr. He would have had a certain detachment from white values and white ideals and total faith in himself and his people. Above all else, he would have the vision to identify the interests of his people with the interests of society.

Few men approached this ideal—in the Reconstruction period or afterward—but some men moved in that general direction under the persistent pressure of an aroused black electorate and the exigencies of a situation which imposed its own requirements for political survival. Tentatively at first and then with increasing lucidity, black leaders projected a political posture which envisioned the destruction of the plantation system, the bulldozing of the color-caste system and a vastly expanded social welfare program which anticipated the New Deal.

One must see the black delegates, however, within the context of their times. To them, the Revolution was a developing event. They didn't know, as we know now, that they didn't have a great deal of time. And so, as the conventions approached, black delegates discussed their tasks in terms of developing stages. They believed apparently that it would be expedient to forego certain prerogatives and certain positions until America became accustomed to power in a black face. They certainly asked themselves difficult questions about timing and strategy.

How far, for example, should they go in moderating reform in order to placate the enemies of reform?

How far could they go without driving their anxious allies into the arms of the waiting planters?

Was the white man's opposition real or irrational? And if they confronted it honestly and frankly would it go away?

Seeking answers to these questions, the black delegates conferred among themselves and made discreet inquiries in Northern power centers. The South Carolina delegates, with supreme power in their own hands, sent a delegation to Washington to get the best thinking of congressional Radicals. They were told, Cardozo reported later, that it would be best to move with deliberate speed. Sumner and Stevens, Cardozo said, advised the delegates to seek the leadership of white Southerners. Significantly, neither of the great Radicals suggested a radical alliance between black people and poor whites under the leadership of blacks and poor whites.

The advice of congressional Radicals was accepted by many delegates, but there were significant dissents. The Pure Radicals of Louisiana and venturesome black men like William U. Saunders of Florida urged black people to take the reins of power in their own hands. The *New Orleans Tribune*, the organ of the Pure Radicals, demanded an effective share of the power of the convention, from "the President down to the doorkeeper, and from the clerk and the chief reporter down to the printer." The choices, the *Tribune* said, "should be made so as to convince the people of the State that the supremacy of a privileged class will be no longer fostered, and the time has come when the representatives of the colored race can find favor as well as white men. It is to be demonstrated that long services and unfaltering devotion to the cause of radicalism shall obtain the reward, irrespective of color or race, and to that effect it is important to choose officers from among both populations." The *Tribune* added:

But there is something more. It is important to show that the oppressed race will not be overlooked; that from this time forward the rights of the neglected race will be recognized to share in all departments of our state government. The Convention will have many things to do to break the spell under which we were laboring. The choice of officers will, therefore, have a political bearing, and cannot be dictated by fitness only.

The Convention will meet under very peculiar circumstances—circumstances of originality and grandeur. . . .As such this Convention has to take a position in immediate contradiction with the old assemblies of the *white man's government*. They will have to show that a new order will succeed the former order of things, and that the long-neglected race will, at last, effectually share in the government of the state.

In the general attempt to "break the spell" of the old regime, the black delegates labored under distinct disadvantages. South Carolina and Louisiana apart, black people were grossly underrepresented in these assemblies. The black delegations ranged from 9 out of 90 (10 per cent) in Texas to 18 out of 45 (40 per cent) in Florida, 49 out of 98 (50 per cent) in Louisiana, 76 out of 124 (61 per cent) in South Carolina. Although black voters had an absolute majority in Mississippi and held the balance of power in Georgia, Alabama, Virginia, and North Carolina, the black delegations from these states were relatively small: 17 out of 100 (17 per cent) in Mississippi, 33 out of 170 (19 per cent) in Georgia, 18 out of 108 (17 per cent) in Alabama. These figures are all the more remarkable since the black voters of Mississippi, for example, had overwhelming majorities in Black Belt counties which elected 70 of the 100 delegates.

How explain this?

The explanation is simple. At a time when the black population was largely illiterate and without political experience, the educated and organized minority was bound to exert a large influence. Moreover, as we have seen, some black people believed, in the first years of Reconstruction, that it was best to work through the white leadership. One must also remember that there had not been sufficient time to do the educational and organizational work necessary to mobilize a scattered population in an area characterized by limited communications facilities. In fact, as A. T. Morgan, an alert Northern newcomer, pointed out, several counties in Mississippi were without "active and capable" Republican leadership in 1868.

There were other reasons, including the varying material conditions of the states and the uneven development of the black population. Despite surface similarities, there were profound differences in the social and economic structures of the Southern states and these differences were reflected in the constitutional conventions. North Carolina, Georgia, and Virginia had a higher level of industrialization, a more diversified economy and a more developed middle class. In these states and in Alabama, which also had industrial potential, there was a more equal balance between the Black Belt and the poor white countries. In South

Carolina, Louisiana, and Mississippi, on the other hand, the Black Belt was a more decisive factor. At the same time there was a decisive difference between new states like Mississippi and well-established states like South Carolina and Louisiana with their crystallized social structure.

The delegations to the constitutional conventions naturally reflected the peculiar material and demographic factors of their state bases, varying according to the number of white Unionists in the population, the size and location of the Black Belt, the number of white Northern immigrants, and the posture of the Freedmen's Bureau and the commanding general. The extraordinary showings of the black people of South Carolina, Louisiana, and Florida can be explained, in part, by the large free black colonies (in Louisiana and South Carolina), the effective work of the Freedmen's Bureau and white missionaries (South Carolina), and the presence of inventive and imaginative black leadership (South Carolina, Louisiana, Florida).

Although the Reconstruction conventions were based largely on a black electorate and although black delegates played a large role in the thinking and legislating that gave them substance, none can accurately be called a black assembly. In point of fact, the delegates were broadly representative of the people as distinguished from the elites of their states. More: the conventions were supported by an astoundingly large number of white Southerners, some of them to the manner born. Perhaps as many as one out of every three white Southerners supported the Radical Reconstruction program in 1868. White support was particularly pronounced in the poor white sections of northern Alabama, western North Carolina, and northern and western Arkansas. Indeed, native whites had an absolute majority in North Carolina (100 out of 133), Georgia (128 out of 170), Arkansas (35 out of 66), and Alabama (59 out of 108).

Additional white support came from a number of Confeder-

ate generals, including P. G. T. Beauregard and James Longstreet, and former Governors Lewis E. Parsons, Joseph E.
Brown, J. M. Wells, James L. Orr, and E. M. Pease of Alabama,
Georgia, Louisiana, South Carolina, and Texas, respectively.
Indeed, there was something of a rush to get on the Republican
bandwagon. From Virginia, Samuel C. Armstrong, the founder
of Hampton Institute, noted: "Scores are getting down off the
fence and are rushing wildly to the Republican lines and
already begin to talk of what they have suffered for their
principles."

Whatever the size of the black and native-white delegations,
all conventions were dominated by an unstable coalition of
Northern-born whites, Southern Unionists and black men. One
would be well-advised to pause for a moment over this coalition
for one cannot understand what follows without a grasp of the
remarkable triple alliance between black men and Southern-
born and Northern-born white men. The white men have, of
course, been stigmatized as "carpetbaggers" (Northern-born
whites) and "scalawags"(Southern-born whites). These terms
have no descriptive value and should be discarded, for they
hinder rather than help understanding. The groups so stigmatized were composed of men with motives good and bad.
Some were ruthless opportunists who manipulated the tensions
of the time for selfish gain, but some, both Northern-born and
Southern-born, were men of large vision who embarked on
Albion Tourgee's celebrated "Fool's Errand" which he defined
as the attempt in any age to prove "that God teaches the
equality of rights of the several varieties of the human species."
As Tourgee also pointed out, the reconstructionists had to
work with the white human material available. And under
existing circumstances, the white human material had to come
from one of three classes: "martyrs, who were willing to endure
ostracism and obloquy for the sake of principle; self-seekers,
who were willing to do or be anything and everything for the
sake of power, place, and gain; and fools who hoped that in

some inscrutable way the law of human nature would be suspended, or that the state of affairs at first presenting itself would be temporary. The former class, it might have been known, would be naturally small. Martyrs do not constitute any large proportion of any form or state of society.... Self-seekers, on the contrary, those who can be swayed by motives of interest or ambition, regardless alike of principle and appro-bation of those by whom they are surrounded, are to be found in all ranks and classes; while fools who have stamina enough to swim for any great time against a strong popular current are not to be looked for in any great numbers in any ordinary community."

Fools, martyrs, self-seekers: white Republicans, Northern-born and Southern-born, came mainly from these three classes. For purposes of analysis, one can roughly divide the Northern newcomers into moderate commercialists who were primarily interested in a New South economic program and a New England political program, and a smaller number of idealists interested primarily in creating a new social structure.

As the advance tentacles of triumphant Northern industrial-ism, the Northern delegates constituted the middle core of the Republican coalition. With their training in politics and busi-ness and their detachment from the racial tensions of the Southern blacks on the left and the Southern whites on the right, Northerners were in an excellent position to control both by throwing their influence first to one side and then the other. This temptation was the undoing of many otherwise solid men who wavered chameleon-like throughout Reconstruction, chang-ing colors and purposes with the color of their environment. Historians have dismissed too lightly the overwhelming judgment of contemporary black politicians who attributed their ills to white politicians from the North.

To grasp the full dimension of the conventions, one must see the Northern newcomers as victims of their environment. As for the majority, however much their Unionism as well as their interests inclined them to satisfy their black allies, however ready they may have been to adopt radical measures to resolve the crisis, there is no evidence that they had reservations about white supremacy. Almost all of them had a sense of social distance which they wanted to maintain; almost all of them felt, as their letters and memoirs show, a racist-tinged repugnance to the black company they were forced to keep. But these feelings were not so deep-seated as to interfere with the realistic art of compromise and barter for immediate material ends.

What characterized the Northern whites as compared to the Southern whites was their freedom. They were not bound by the racial dogmas of the Southern past; nor were they encumbered by roots in the Southern social system. This freedom enabled them to play a role out of all proportion to their numbers in the conventions and the political maneuvering which followed.

This detachment was at once a strength and a weakness. For the danger of detachment is indifference. And it is not surprising that this was the precise weakness of newcomers who couldn't identify with the passions of either the former slave-owners or the former slaves. But to rule effectively one must identify with something or somebody. One must also identify the interests of one's group as the interests of the total community. Out of bad faith or naïvete, most newcomers attempted to avoid this dilemma by identifying with the state. But what was the state? To answer this question, the immigrants had to weigh the concrete demands of one group against the concrete demands of another group. The key to the conventions and to the Republican governments they foreshadowed is that the white newcomers, when pushed to the wall, invariably identified the interests of the state with the interests of affluent whites.

The situation was hardly better at the right end of the coalition which was contested by aristocratic Southern whites, who loathed poor whites, and poor whites, who envied and feared aristocratic whites. Both groups wanted to control the black voters for their own interests, which were, in most instances, antipathetical to the interests of the black voters. The aristocratic delegates were primarily old Whigs and merchant-businessmen who wanted to use the new voters and the new machinery to advance their own interests: low taxes, a cheap labor supply, government subsidies for levees, railroads, and industrial enterprises. With a greater sense of personal security than the poor whites, the aristocratic Whigs and the new commercialists were willing to accept the new black voters in the same resigned spirit as the white men of the North accepted the Irish voters of Boston and New York. They were prepared to accept them, in other words, so long as they stayed in their places, so long, in fact, as they didn't threaten social and economic arrangements.

Apart from slavery and the issue of which white man would rule, prosperous Southern whites shared the same basic values as the leading white newcomers. And in each state these groups soon banded together to form an informal but powerful "white wing" of the Republican party. By and large, members of the white wing believed that poor people—black and white—were incapable of governing and they reserved that right to their own race and their own class. In the conventions and afterwards, they championed conservative economic policies and maneuvered adroitly to dilute or distort the civil rights and social welfare demands of their poor white and poor black allies.

In these maneuvers, white wingers were aided considerably by the tensions between poor blacks and poor whites. The poor whites were basically agrarians who generally supported land reform and social welfare programs but opposed civil rights and subsidies to railroads and levees. A few poor whites transcended their background and articulated a vision of social and economic solidarity of poor whites and poor blacks; but most were hampered by the fact that although they knew what they hated they didn't know what they loved. In the beginning, poor whites were willing to cooperate with black men, but they never freed themselves of the conditioning which made them fear the rise of black people more than they feared poverty. Largely illiterate, lacking social and economic focus, they were the weakest link in the Reconstruction coalition, and they were the first to drop out when the price of freedom rose.

Whether Northern-born or Southern-born, whether educated or illiterate, the average white politician of the time regarded black voters and officeholders as necessary evils. Almost all of them thought black people should be content with voting for white men. Even the best of the Republicans, men like Albion Tourgee, believed in their hearts and said in their memoirs that black people were better voted than seen. Here and there a visionary like Hunnicutt of Virginia matched the black man stride for stride. But, in general, whites failed to rise to the challenge of the hour. "The essence of their failure lay," as Vernon Wharton noted, "in the fact that almost none of them could bring himself to deal with a Negro, however able or honest that Negro might be, as a political or social equal."

In all this, perhaps no one was to blame but events. The contradictions of role behavior which were reflected in the political acts of the disparate elements of the coalition were prefigured by contradictions in their situation. White men from the South struggled with white men from the North and both struggled with black men from the North and South because they occupied different positions in respect to the central force of the age—rampant industrialism. Their approaches differed because their situations or rather their interpretations of their situations differed. The inevitable result was that different elements in the coalition checked each other and served the interests of persons who were not on the scene (Northern businessmen) or not in the coalition (conservative white Southerners).

For the black man, the price of coalition was high. To

maintain the coalition, it was necessary to keep some issues in the background and to blur the edges of others. Even worse, black delegates had to divert needed energy to watching their allies who showed disturbing tendencies toward collaboration with white Democrats.

As the curtain rose on the Reconstruction drama, then, the black man's position was roughly this: He was entering a desperate and bloody struggle for political survival, flanked by two white allies, one Southern-born, the other Northern-born, neither of whom he could afford to turn his back on.

At this distance, in this safety, one must ask why black politicians submitted to these internal constraints.

Why didn't they turn their backs on their untrustworthy allies and strike out on their own?

They couldn't. Their situation was so structured that in order to keep their power they had to keep step with the coalition. For the North made it abundantly clear that although it was willing to sanction all-white government in the South it was not willing to sanction all-black governments in the South. To remain in power, then, the black man had to preserve the coalition. But to preserve the coalition, he had to make fatal concessions on radical reform.

Black politicians faced the even more excruciating dilemma of trying to organize radical state parties within the structure of a national party rapidly evolving into an instrument of the powerful and the privileged. In order to survive in the South, black politicians had to complete the Revolution by destroying the foundation of planter power — the large plantations — and by laying the foundation of a new power in a black and white yeomanry. But neither the North nor the freedmen's allies were prepared to go that far. National party leaders, Sumner and Stevens excepted, were prepared to see in the South, middle-class, white-dominated governments on the order, say, of Ohio and Massachusetts; they were not prepared to give their blessings to black-dominated governments with genuine labor interests. Since ultimate power lay in the hands of national party leaders, who could throw the black politicians to the planters any time they wanted to, black leaders had to operate within circumscribed limits. They could enact any law they wanted to, as long as the law didn't disturb the business climate. They could elect any officer they pleased, as long as the officer didn't try to do certain things congressional leaders were agreed he shouldn't do. Thus, the black politician as the constitutional conventions opened: He couldn't be revolutionary and remain in power but he couldn't remain in power if he weren't revolutionary. The question of questions, then, as the conventions opened, was simply this: Would black delegates scuttle their allies and take on society?

The economic stakes at the time were high, and men of power mobilized massive pressure to make sure this question was resolved in their favor. Northern newspapers fired volley after volley of editorial advice, and prominent editors like Horace Greely were busy behind the scenes, pulling wires. On at least one occasion, Greeley asked a military commander to remind the delegates that there were limits beyond which it was not prudent for them to go.

Congressional Radicals were even more persistent, dispatching wires and even emissaries to trouble spots. Particularly active in this regard was Senator Henry Wilson of Massachusetts who asked the military commander of Alabama to use his influence to moderate the radicalism of the convention delegates.

Pressure of another kind came from President Johnson, who did everything he possibly could to sow division and dissension in convention ranks. Wherever possible, he appointed conservative Democratic generals. And when these generals overstepped the bounds of conservatism by a vigorous enforcement of the Reconstruction acts, Johnson quickly transferred them. Johnson also had civilian representatives on the scene and in some cases was represented in the conventions by federal officeholders. Men close to Johnson, if not Johnson himself, also dispatched agents to the troubled capitals to bring pressure for conservative programs. Florida Radicals complained that E. M. Randall, brother of the postmaster general, was in Tallahassee "aiding the opposition with money and promises." In fact, the Radicals said, Johnson men were "like hungry wolves around a carcass." They were "congregating together there as with a common purpose, and that purpose [was] to defeat reconstruction on a Republican basis in that state. The caucuses of the organized lobby were held every night until nearly daylight, and money furnished by the Johnson officeholders, and every other influence was used to bring in delegates to join them."

The Johnson men were in open collusion with aristocratic Democrats who still controlled the white dailies of the South and who used these sheets to inflame public opinion, charging that the conventions were illegal assemblies of "baboons," "ragamuffins," and "thieves." The official state assemblies were referred to as the "Convention of Kangaroos" in Virginia, the "Black Crook" convention in Alabama, the "Congo Convention" in Louisiana and the "Bones and Banjo" convention in North Carolina. Even in Georgia and North Carolina, where native whites were in the driver's seat, Democratic newspapers denounced the "Africanization" of the South.

The old aristocrats also appealed to Northern public opinion on the basis of race and class. The South, so they said, was being run by poor men who paid no taxes. W. D. Porter of South Carolina said this was the first time in history that intelligence, education, and property had been subordinated to mere numbers. What Porter overlooked conveniently was that poor people paid proportionately more taxes than the owners of property. In fact, they were the ultimate source of all property and all taxes, as J. W. Hood pointed out in the North Carolina convention. "The poor people of North Carolina," he said, ". . . had paid all the taxes. As an illustration, suppose there was a landowner . . . who owned a piece of land. He puts a miserable apology for a house on it. For that house he charges a family $150 a year. In two years the whole value of that property would be paid for. The owner would . . . make . . . in one year, 50 per cent. Who, then, paid the State tax on this property? They said the people paid no tax. The idea was preposterous. . . ."

More dangerous than the outraged aristocrat without was the planter within. These planters, infinitely more resourceful than their irreconcilable colleagues, infiltrated the Republican organizations and sought their goals by subversion and bribery. In some cases, they distributed free railroad passes and opened the main hotels of the city to delegates who promised to thwart radical proposals. Harrison Reed, who was the power behind the scenes in the white wing of the Florida Republican party, was at that point and perhaps later a virtual double agent, working hand in cotton with David L. Yulee, the rich Democratic industrialist, and Charles E. Dyke, the resourceful and dangerous editor of the *Floridian.* Reed may have believed that he was sincerely serving the interests of conservative Democrats and Republicans. But the Democrats weren't interested in Reed or his theories. They were using him, as they would later use Henry Clay Warmoth and Daniel Henry Chamberlain, the white Republican governors of Louisiana and South Carolina, respectively.

Conservative pressures were transformed into gunpowder and the steel of bayonets in the conservative policies of the Union generals who held real power in the South in the transitional period. Strange as it may seem now, many Union generals used their influence to advance the interests of the former Confederate leaders.

General Alvin C. Gillem, who commanded the Mississippi and Arkansas military district, refused to implement the radical agrarian program of the Mississippi convention. In Louisiana,

Virginia, and Florida, hostile military commanders openly
sided with the big landowners and the conservative Republicans in generally successful efforts to blunt the thrust of the
radical delegates. In Alabama, Radical Republicans charged
that almost all of the Union Army officers were supporting the
opponents of Reconstruction. "Most of the soldiers," conservative white historian Walter F. Fleming wrote, "had no love for
the Negroes, carpet-baggers, and scalawags, and at a radical
meeting in Montgomery, the soldiers on duty at the capitol
gave three groans for Grant, and three cheers for McClellan
and Johnson."

There was strong counter-pressure from huge throngs of
black people who flocked to convention cities and camped on
the outskirts of town, confidently awaiting the distribution of
land. Many of these agrarian petitioners thronged the halls of
the conventions and unnerved delegates by hostile murmuring
in the galleries. The temper of these petitioners is reflected in
the comments of contemporary landowners. "Can you not stir
up the freedmen," a Kershaw, South Carolina, planter asked his
manager, "or are they waiting on the Convention." The mis-
tress of another South Carolina plantation observed at the time
that "the freed people are *universally dissatisfied*."

All these pressures beat against the walls of the buildings in
which 771 white men and 268 black men gathered in ten
separate conventions to rewrite the basic law of the South.
Most of the conventions were held in the Greek revival and
Italian Renaissance state capitols built, for the most part, by the
labor of black slaves. But the Georgia convention met in a
dingy room in the Atlanta City Hall.

It quickly became apparent that these assemblies were going
to be somewhat turbulent. In some states, reporters from the
venomously hostile white press were expelled from the floor for
writing insulting articles about the delegates. And in South

Carolina, the son of the convention president slugged a reporter who had written offensively about his father, who happened to be a native white South Carolinian with impeccable aristocratic connections.

Before the delegates could get down to business, they had to grapple with side issues unprecedented in the history of American assemblies. What, for example, were the black power brokers to be called? In North Carolina, James Walker Hood, "outraged and insulted," denied "that there was a Negro on the floor of the Convention, [and] insisted that the word *Negro* had no significance as to color, but could only be used in a reproachful or degrading sense, and he further declared that no man on that floor knew where the term originated, since it was not found in ancient history, inspired or profane." Hood's colleague, Abraham Galloway of Hanover County, was more nationalistic. He told the delegates that "the best blood of Brunswick County" flowed in his veins and, if he could do it, "in justice to the African race," he would lance himself and let it out. In Arkansas, a liberal white delegate interceded for his black colleagues, insisting that it was "disrespectful to style the gentlemen of the Convention Negroes." Speaking for himself, William Grey, soon to be Commisioner of Immigration, said he was not there to argue about names. He didn't object to the name Negro. How could he? For his "race was closely allied to the race which built the great pyramids of Egypt, where slept the remains of those whose learning had taught Solon and Lycurgus to frame the systems of their laws and to whom the present ages are indebted for the hints of art and knowledge."

The question of identity also troubled the South Carolina convention where T. J. Coghlan, a white delegate from Sumter County, offered a resolution which urged that steps be taken to "expunge forever from the vocabulary of South Carolina, the epithets, 'nigger,' 'negro,' and 'yankee' . . . and to punish this insult by fine and imprisonment."

Nothing was sacred in the new order of things, not even prayer. In Alabama, John Carraway, the assistant editor of the Mobile *Nationalist*, objected to the employment of chaplains with rebel connections. William P. Skinner of Franklin County said: "Let none offer prayer who are rebels and who have not fought under the stars and stripes." The matter was resolved by hiring a different loyal chaplain every day. Several black chaplains opened the proceedings, including one who asked God to rain down blessings on "Unioners and cusses on rebels."

Once over these hurdles, the delegates got down to the hard work of organizing. Black men were very active in this preliminary skirmishing. Charles H. Pearce, an AME minister, served as temporary president of the Florida convention and black men were elected to the positions of vice-president, doorkeeper, chaplain, clerk, and sergeant at arms in other states. They were also represented on important committees, serving, in several instances, as chairman. Francis L. Cardozo was chairman of the key education committee in the South Carolina convention and was a member of the powerful committee on review and consolidation of the whole convention. In Florida, the committee to recommend permanent officers was composed of three black men and two white men and was headed by a black man, William U. Saunders. In Louisiana, the committees on militia and the bill of rights were chaired by two black men; and the pivotal committee to draft the constitution was made up of four black men and five white men. This committee, incidentally, divided along racial lines, with the black members recommending a radical program of social welfare and the white delegates opposing laws regulating labor. In the end, a compromise was hammered out which contained proposals from the black and white committee reports.

In committee sessions and on the floor, black delegates were far from timid in pushing their major objectives. They were so vocal, in fact, that the white wings of the Republican parties allied with conservative Democrats to expel some black delegates who refused to play the game by the white ground rules. In Atlanta, conservative Republicans and Democrats turned on Aaron Alpeoria Bradley "who had made himself," a contemporary report says, "quite conspicuous in the convention by the advocacy of extreme measures, and a somewhat turbulent opposition to moderate counsels." The specific charge against Bradley was that his name had been stricken from the roll of attorneys in Massachusetts for contempt of court and that he had been convicted and sentenced to two years imprisonment in New York for seduction. Instead of making an abject apology, Bradley, like Adam Clayton Powell a hundred years later, said his white colleagues were guilty of the same thing. If eligibility were predicated on innocence of seduction, Bradley charged, the convention wouldn't be able to muster a quorum. Such a black man—defiant, daring, unchastened—was clearly a threat to the status quo, and Georgia Republicans and Democrats united to expel him. At about the same time, Louisiana Republicans were expelling six Pure Radicals from the Louisiana Republican party.

While Georgians and Louisianians were deradicalizing their ranks, Florida delegates were fighting in the streets of Tallahassee over a similar issue. The weather in Tallahassee was stormy, and the political climate was, if anything, stormier. Ice and frozen mud clogged the unpaved streets which were filled with speculators, soldiers and women—black and white —of indifferent morality. The air in the sleepy little village reeked with perfume, alcohol, and intrigue. In this setting a predominantly black faction and a white conservative group were struggling for control of the constitutional convention and people all over town were choosing sides. Hopelessly divided, the two factions were holding sessions in different buildings. The white wing was barricaded in the state capitol and the black wing was meeting in black churches. Open warfare seemed imminent, for black people, armed with pitchforks, guns and knives, were pouring into the city.

This struggle, the most dramatic of the convention season, grew out of a successful power play by a Black Power core which consisted of all but two or three of the eighteen black delegates and five radical white delegates, including two Floridians. This group was led by William U. Saunders, a charismatic black barber from Baltimore, and two white Northerners: Liberty Billings, a former colonel of a regiment of black Union troops, and Daniel Richards, a U.S. Treasury agent from Illinois. Of this trio, Saunders — Colonel Saunders to his colleagues — was easily the most outstanding. He was, according to contemporaries, a "bright, yellow mulatto, tall and handsome, active and strong," a striking figure "charged with eloquence and magnetic influence over a crowd." Saunders came to the state in 1867 as a political organizer and vaulted to power as the dominant influence in the Union League.

With Saunders, Richards, and Billings calling the shots, the Black Power faction seized control of the convention and relegated conservative white Republicans to a subsidiary role. Richards was elected permanent president, and Saunders, the power behind the scenes, was named chairman of the important committee on permanent organization. Stunned by the militancy and organizational cohesiveness of the black delegates, who acted and voted in a body, conservative Republicans counterattacked by forming a new coalition with conservative Democrats. The immediate aim of the new coalition was the expulsion of the leading Radical delegates and the fracturing of the united front of the black delegates. Supported by former Governor David S. Walker, industrialist David L. Yulee, and editor Charles E. Dyke, the prominent white Republicans launched a well-financed campaign of intimidation and subversion. The leading hotels of the city were thrown open to the poor black delegates who were wooed by champagne and oyster suppers and bullied by federal officeholders and army officers.

The black delegates refused to budge and white conservatives mounted a second offensive, trying to break up the convention by instigating disturbances and fights on the floor. But the conservatives were no match for Saunders who could hurl words and chairs with the best parliamentarians. Viewing the spectacle, a reporter for the *New York Tribune* said it "looks as though the white race was going backwards and the black race advancing in the scale of civilization."

Outmaneuvered in the caucuses and on the floor, eighteen white conservatives stalked from the convention on Tuesday, February 4, and organized a rump convention in the nearby city of Monticello. The remaining delegates—roughly twenty-two—completed the constitution and adjourned on Saturday, February 8. Two days later, the conservative bolters returned to Tallahassee at midnight, seized the capitol chambers and declared themselves the official convention. Lacking a quorum, they persuaded their Union Army supporters to arrest two black delegates, who were awakened in the middle of the night and dragged to the capitol. "The news," John Wallace, a conservative black Republican said, "went like wildfire through the adjoining counties. Large numbers [of black people] assembled in Tallahassee, ready, as they thought, for battle. Each one had his club, about two feet long with a string through the end of it, so as to be fastened to his wrist." Indignation meetings were held in black churches and in the capitol square, and speakers suggested a full-scale attack on the federal soldiers who were guarding the predominantly white assembly in the Italian Renaissance capitol on Adams and Monroe Streets.

To forestall this possibility, General George G. Meade, who was hostile to the Radicals, hurried to Tallahassee on Monday, February 17, and imposed a "compromise" which insured white conservative domination of the convention. On Wednesday, February 19, the reorganized convention expelled Saunders, Richards, Billings, and the AME minister Charles Pearce on the grounds that they were not citizens of the state. Saunders, who was nominated for lieutenant governor on the Radical ticket, continued the fight for several weeks but weakened in the face of the massive indifference of congressional Radicals. This strange, brilliant man made one last desperate attempt to push his white Radical allies aside and take the gubernatorial nomination. Failing in this effort, he threw in the towel and walked out of the pages of history.

But the struggle, of which he was the first great casualty, continued on the floors of the conventions, straining the Republican coalitions to the breaking point. However much black delegates were inclined to compromise to retain the support of white allies, they could not and would not compromise their humanity. In the South Carolina debate, Francis L. Cardozo, who represented Charleston, reminded white delegates that there were limits to compromise. "It was argued by some yesterday," he said, "with some considerable weight that we should do everything in our power to incorporate in the constitution all possible measures that will conciliate those opposed to us. No one would go further in conciliating others than I would. But we should be careful of what we do to conciliate.

"In the first place, there is an element that is opposed to us no matter what we do, which will never be conciliated. It is not that they are opposed so much to the constitution we may frame, but they are opposed to us sitting in the convention. Their objection is of such a radical and fundamental nature, that any attempt to frame a constitution to please them would be abortive.

"In the next place, there are those who are doubtful; and gentlemen here say if we frame a constitution to suit these parties, they will come over to our side. They are only waiting to see whether or not it will be successful.

"Then there is the third class who honestly question our capacity to frame a constitution. I respect that class, and believe if we do justice to them, laying our corner-stone on a sure foundation of republican government and liberal principles, the intelligence of that class will be conciliated, and they are worthy of conciliation. . . ."

   In South Carolina and elsewhere, most black delegates rejected a conciliation based on segregation; and their white allies, mindful of the power of the black electorate, beat a strategic retreat. In Alabama, for instance, Henry C. Semple, an aristocratic white Republican from Montgomery, proposed an ordinance banning intermarriage. John Carraway, the young newspaper editor from Mobile, countered with a demand for life imprisonment of white men living with black women. The convention backed away from the ticklish subject, defeating Semple's proposal by a vote of forty-eight to thirty. The potential power of the black delegations can be gauged by the fact that most conventions, even in states where the black delegation was relatively small, tabled or defeated Jim Crow provisions. A group of conservative Republicans in Alabama charged that the failure of the convention to ban intermarriage was an abject capitulation to the power of the black electorate. The dissidents said that "though the Judiciary Committee had *unanimously* reported a measure providing against amalgamation, yet the Convention tabled it; and *many members of the Committee, who had concurred in the report of the Committee,* receding from their position, voted to lay it on the table."
   On the issue of integrated schools, the debates became impassioned in all conventions, and latent discords were revealed. The discussions turned generally on whether the time was opportune for such a departure. Most of the black delegates warmly took the affirmative view, saying integrated schools were essential as a means of instructing the people in the principles of the new order. In rebutting that argument, B. O. Duncan, a white delegate from Newberry County, South Carolina, used words that are still current. First of all, he said, the provision would deprive white children of an education.

They would stay away from the schools and would "continue ignorant and degraded and prejudiced." If the convention attempted "to enforce mixed schools," it would "bring trouble, quarrelling and wrangling into every neighborhood." The question was too serious to the peace and welfare of the country for him "not to speak out plainly on the dangers before us." Black people were trying "to force upon South Carolina measures even in advance of Massachusetts. . . ."

Jonathan Jasper Wright, a lawyer, born free in Pennsylvania, now twenty-eight, answered Duncan, saying that to his mind it was "inconsistent that such an argument should come from a member of the Convention [for] the whole measure of Reconstruction is antagonistic to the wishes of the people of the State, and this section is a legitimate portion of that scheme." Wright added:

"The gentleman from Newberry said he was afraid we were taking a wrong course to remove these prejudices. The most natural method to effect this object would be to allow children, when five or six years of age, to mingle in schools together, and associate generally. Under such training, prejudice must eventually die out; but if we postpone it until they become men and women, prejudice will be so established that no mortal can obliterate it. This, I think, is a sufficient reply to the argument of the gentleman under this head."

Benjamin Franklin Randolph, a Northern-born Methodist minister soon to be assassinated by white Democrats, summed up the case for his black colleagues: "We are laying the foundation of a new structure here, and the time has come when we shall have to meet things squarely, and we must meet them now or never. The day is coming when we must decide whether the two races shall live together or not."

As the debates continued in Charleston and New Orleans and Montgomery, it became apparent that the main issue was not color but power, not race but money—and it was on the issues that blended color and class that the debates grew lively, taking a turn singularly menacing to the big landowners. Most conventions took immediate steps to relieve the needy by providing for moratoriums on the collection of debts. In Mississippi, white and black delegates approved a resolution levying a poll tax for the relief of needy freedmen. Mississippi delegates also passed a resolution which required the return of all property taken from freedmen by their former owners. General Gillem, who was in league with the large landowners, vetoed both resolutions.

More disturbing to the large landholders were attempts to regulate wages and employment. In South Carolina, James M. Allen, a native white delegate, offered an ordinance limiting landlords to one-half of the crop; and, in Alabama, Alfred Strother, Dallas County, demanded and the delegates actually passed a resolution empowering freedmen to collect pay from their former masters at a rate of ten dollars a month for services rendered from January 1, 1863, the date of the Emancipation Proclamation, to May 20, 1865.

This debate led naturally to the question of the hour—land. "We all know," C. P. Leslie, a white newcomer from Barnwell County, told the South Carolina convention, "that the colored people want land. Night and day they think and dream of it. It is their all in all."

Indisputably; and the question now was what were the delegates going to do about it. Franklin J. Moses Jr., the South Carolina native, wanted to meet the issue head-on. "You cannot make citizens out of these people unless you give ... land; give them houses. They deserve it from the people of South Carolina."

Francis L. Cardozo was in general agreement, but he opposed outright confiscation, suggesting a combination of federal action and state administrative action to break up "the infernal plantation system, one man owning his thousand, another his twenty, another fifty thousand acres of land." Cardozo added: "This is the only way by which we will break up that system, and I maintain that our freedom will be of no effect if we allow it to continue." Let the lands of the South be divided, then, he said, adding: "... We will never have true freedom until we abolish the system of agriculture which existed in the Southern states.... Give them an opportunity, breathing time, and they will reorganize the same old system that they had before the war. I say, then, ... now is the time to strike."

Another who saw things this way was Richard Harvey Cain of Charleston. It was a well-known fact, he said, that over three hundred thousand men, women and children were homeless and landless. How were they to live? "I know the philosopher of the *New York Tribune* says, 'root hog or die;' ... My proposition is simply to give the hog some place to root.... I want these lands purchased by the Government, and the people afforded an opportunity to buy from the Government.... I propose to let the poor people buy these lands, the government to be paid back in five years time."

These were fine words, but fine words alone would not provide forty acres and a mule for a single freedman. What would the delegates do? What could they do? It soon became evident that they would not and could not do much. Under strong pressure from Union generals and conservative Republican politicians in the North, the delegates in South Carolina and other Southern states backed away from demands for outright confiscation. On request from General Robert K. Scott, who feared a sharecropper uprising, the South Carolina convention finally passed a resolution "to disabuse the minds of all persons whatsoever throughout the State who may be expecting a distribution of land by the Government of the United States." The resolution went on to say that it was the conviction of the convention that there would be no distribution of land and "that the only manner in which any land can be obtained by the landless will be by purchase."

Thus, in Charleston and New Orleans and Montgomery and

In the power vacuum of the postwar period, the
U.S. Army stood between contending groups of
planters and freedmen. The Army was the real
source of power until the inauguration of
Reconstruction governments.

"Victory," a *Harper's Weekly* cartoon of 1868,
symbolized the triumph of Radical
Republican forces in a year marked by
meetings of historic Reconstruction
conventions.

other Southern capitals, in the spring of 1868, the Revolution came to the Rubicon and halted on dry ground. It is true, of course, that the delegates were limited by internal and external constraints. It is true also that the Radicals in the state conventions, like the Radical Stevens and Sumner in Congress, capitulated when it became clear that America would never sanction wholesale confiscation and redistribution of land. All this—and more—is true. But it is certainly true also that History does not forgive men who, having put their hands to the plow and having a clear majority, look back.

The delegates looked back. But all was not lost—not yet. The billowing pressure in black communities, as well as the delegates' uneasy awareness that political survival depended on the destruction of the plantation system, led to a flanking movement by which the Reconstruction governments sought to accomplish this basic objective by taxation. It was a generally unstated but widely held objective of these governments to tax land, especially uncultivated land, so high that the planters would be forced to sell large units. South Carolina's tax policy was expressed with militant bluntness by Niles G. Parker, who was soon to become treasurer of the state. He said:

> Taxes, always (at least in hard times) a burden, will be assessed yearly upon all lands, and they must be paid. The expenses of the State (constantly increasing, will be a continual drag upon those who attempt to carry on large landed estates with a small amount of money), will alone force sufficient lands upon the market at all times to meet the wants of the landless. This Convention will cost the State quite a large sum of money. A legislature will soon assemble, and that will cost money. Education, once limited, is to be general, and that will be expensive; and, to keep up with the age, it is fair to presume that the State tax will be greater next year than this, and increase yearly; this will be felt, and will be the stimulus to many for owning less land, and cause them to see the necessity for disposing of their surplus.

The flanking movement began in the conventions and continued throughout the Reconstruction period. Beverly Nash of

South Carolina and black and white delegates in other assemblies proposed provisions that would have taxed uncultivated land at a higher rate. Unsuccessful efforts were also made to pass measures providing that land sold by court order should be divided into tracts not to exceed 150 or 160 acres. When these maneuvers failed, militant members of the South Carolina convention passed a resolution, sponsored by Alonzo J. Ransier, which asked Congress to lend the state one million dollars to buy land for poor whites and blacks. Congress rebuffed this overture and the South Carolina convention created a land commission which was charged with the responsibility of buying land and reselling it at reasonable prices to poor South Carolinians.

Militant black and white delegates also succeeded in turning back attempts to limit the suffrage by literacy and poll tax requirements. Robert Brown Elliot of South Carolina opposed these attempts, saying the convention couldn't limit the suffrage of the electorate which gave it being. His colleague, Franklin J. Moses Jr., focused on the power requirements of the hour. "You strike at the freedom of South Carolina," he said, "You will allow power to go again in the hands of the aristocratic element." Alonzo J. Ransier, the suave free Negro who would soon be lieutenant governor of South Carolina, told the convention that the right to vote "belongs alike to the wise and ignorant, to the virtuous and vicious." He hoped "that the music of the nineteenth century will inspire every man upon this floor to view it in the light of progress and reason, and strike out every word that puts a limitation upon the manhood of the citizen, so far as regards the right to vote." So fervent were black delegates in supporting one-man, one-vote provisions that many of them opposed—unwisely as it turned out—the anti-Confederate provisions angry poor whites and shrewd Northerners inserted in the constitutions of Arkansas, Alabama, Mississippi, Louisiana, and Virginia. These provisions generally disfranchised and barred from office leading

Confederates and Confederate supporters. A handful of black
delegates supported these provisions, saying it was bad public
policy to give weapons to irreconcilable enemies of the state.
They also pointed out that "God had never converted an adult
generation."

Ballots, Bread, Land, Money, Education, Power: such were
the preoccupations of the black and white delegates as they
struggled amid the Greek revival ruins to give birth to a new
society.

Let us go back in time and see if we can see what these men
saw. In Montgomery, at this hour, eighteen black men and
ninety white men, fifty-nine of them Southern whites, are
debating the issue of equal public accommodations. Henry C.
Semple has just reported an ordinance requiring separation in
public places and on public conveyances, and the assembly is in
an uproar. A. Griffin, a Northern immigrant, upbraids Semple
for daring to propose such "an iniquitous measure." James K.
Green, a carriage driver from Hale county, takes the floor and
observes that it is the custom to put Negroes in the second-
class section "with drunk and low white folks." He objects to
the practice. "We want never to be subject to such disgrace."
James T. Rapier of Lauderdale County rises to say that he is
appalled by the manner in which black ladies and gentlemen
are treated in America. He has dined with lords and doesn't
feel flattered by sitting beside white men. Ovid Gregory, a
barber from Mobile, takes the floor to object to the strategy of
the native white Republicans, pointing out that Semple and
other white Republicans were elected by black people but don't
want to ride in the same car with them. How can the delegates
go back home to their constituents, nineteen-twentieths of
whom are black, after denying them rights enjoyed by white
men. Does Semple feel polluted by sitting beside his black

colleague, Peyton Finley? Semple replies that he doesn't feel polluted. Well, then, continues Gregory, why does he object to sitting in the same car with him? Gregory says he is tired of such foolishness. He is, he says, "as good a man as Napoleon on his throne" and he can't be honored by sitting by a white man, but "in the old world the colored folks ride with the whites," and so it will be here.

On now to Richmond where Thomas Jefferson's temple-like capitol resounds with the angry cries of men Thomas Jefferson and the Declaration of Independence had excluded. James W. D. Bland from Prince Edward County is proposing that the words "all men" in the bill of rights be replaced by the words, "mankind, irrespective of race or color." He thinks that the delegates should state distinctly what they mean by mankind and what they mean by the words *all men.* "When I recollect that the word 'men,' as written in this first section, has been construed to mean white men only in Virginia, and as mankind takes in all the men, women and children on earth, I propose the words 'mankind, irrespective of race or color' as an amendment, as men upon this earth are of different races and colors...." Another black delegate, Dr. Thomas Bayne, a dentist from Norfolk rises to say that it is imperative for the assembly to pass a measure to prevent planters from discharging black laborers because of their political opinions. "I claim," Bayne says, "to be an ignorant man, one not wholly acquainted with this kind of work.... I give this convention notice that unless they settle this question mentioned at this time and in the commencement of the sessions, we ignorant men will settle it ourselves and to satisfy ourselves...." John L. Marye, a white delegate, objects. "Why is it that the cry is coming up from the colored men, actually now taking the form of a petition to Congress, that they cannot get employment because the white people hustle them out of it?" Bayne is on his feet. "Will the gentleman allow me to answer his question? The colored people will not work because the employers do not pay them.

Six dollars a month will not pay a man and feed and clothe his wife and children."

The same issues and the same archetypal figures — militant blacks, conservative whites — dominate the Louisiana convention, which is drawing to a close. The Pure Radicals, a predominantly black group led by the *New Orleans Tribune*, are disenchanted with "the white adventurers" of the convention. The Pure Radicals are specifically displeased by the failure of the convention to provide for land reform and by the failure of party leaders to divide offices equally between black and white men. "The Republican party," the *Tribune* charges in an editorial which is being discussed now in the bars and grog shops, "is headed by men who, for the most part, are devoid of honesty and decency, and we think it right that the country should know it. The active portion of the party in Louisiana is composed largely of white adventurers, who strive to be elected by black votes.... Some of them intend, if elected, to give a share of offices to colored men. We admit that, but they will choose only docile tools, not citizens who have manhood." With the issue out in the open, the Pure Radicals of the convention demand and get a strong public accommodations section and an explicit sanction of integrated schools. Finally, on Monday, March 9, the convention closes with an extraordinary prayer by the Rev. Josiah Fisk. "Bless the President of these United States. Enable him to pause in his career of vice and folly. May he cease from doing evil, and learn to do right."

The final words are also being said in the creamy white capitol on the banks of the Arkansas River in Little Rock. James P. Johnson, a black delegate, has the floor. "I believe, he says, "this constitution to be the best one that Arkansas ever had. The gentleman from Ashley has undertaken to show that the class of men of whom he is a representative are our best friends. My God! I hope he will put his hand over his mouth and never speak that word again. We are very much inclined to believe the men who are trying to secure equal rights of voting according to the true Republican doctrine of the equal rights of all men; you do not want us to have any rights, but just let us stay in slavery as we were before the war."

James T. White, the delegate from Phillips County who will serve later as a commissioner of public works and internal improvement, asks leave to explain his vote in favor of the constitution. "Another reason why I shall vote, and why if I had 10,000 votes I would give them all for the constitution, is that I see in it a principle that is intended to elevate our families—the principle of schools—of education. That is the only way that these Southern people can be elevated. Were they properly educated they would not be led from any prejudice to oppress other men. Were they educated they would not hate us because we have been slaves; but like these gentlemen, if they should puzzle their brains and risk their lives upon the battlefield for the Union, they would stand up for our rights. Away with Union men who will not give all men their rights! Talk about friendship! The devil has such friends locked up, and hell is full of them!"

"Great God!" Anthony Hinkle replies. "Great God! is there no help for the widow's son!"

So it went everywhere as the historic Reconstruction conventions drew to a close. The Arkansas delegates adjourned in February after a short session of 31 days. The next month, delegates in North Carolina (55 days), South Carolina (53 days), Louisiana (81 days) and Georgia (67 days) packed their bags and went home. Mississippi (115 days) ended protracted deliberations in June. Alabama had the distinction of finishing its constitution in the record time of 23 days. Texas, on the other hand, opened its convention on June 1, and debated on and off until December.

The conventions ended, as they began, in a cloud of controversy. Fourteen Mississippi delegates refused to sign the constitution as a protest against the article on suffrage. Sixteen whites refused to sign in Alabama because the constitution didn't require separate schools. Fifteen whites refused to sign in Arkansas, and nine Radicals, most of them black men, signed under protest in Florida.

Although there were vigorous protests from both the black left and the white right, most delegates gave thunderous approval to the constitutions. In North Carolina, black and white delegates ended their session with a harmony session that was doubtless fueled by copious quantities of beverages. The delegates sang "The Star Spangled Banner", "John Brown," "Hang Jeff. Davis" and "Negro melodies." In South Carolina, A. G. Mackey, convention president, delivered a valedictory in which he praised the delegates for democratizing the foundations of the state. For the first time, he said, manhood suffrage had been written into the law of the state. Serfdom, he said, had been uprooted and provisions had been made for the first time for universal education. He was pleased that "that most pernicious heresy of state sovereignty" had been destroyed. "We do not claim," he said, "a preeminence of wisdom or virtue, but we do claim that we have followed in the progressive advancement of the age; that we have been bold and honest enough and wise enough to trample obsolete and unworthy prejudice under foot." In honor of the occasion, one South Carolina delegate proposed that 1868 be designated "The Glory Year."

The constitutions which emerged from these cockpits of conflicting world-views were, on the whole, excellent documents. They were so good, in fact, that most Southern states were content to live under them for decades after Reconstruction. It can be said of these documents generally what Francis B. Simkins said of the South Carolina document specifically: "The learning of the leaders bore fruit in a constitution written in excellent English and embodying some of the best legal principles of the age. In letter it was as good as any other constitution the state has ever had, or as most American states had at that time. This assertion is supported by the practical endorsement which a subsequent generation of South Carolinians gave it; the Conservative whites were content to live under it for eighteen years after they recovered control of the state government, and when in 1895 they met to make a new constitution, the document they produced had many of the features of the constitution of 1868."

Here, as elsewhere, however, the reconstructionists erred, not because they fell below the level of Anglo-Saxon jurisprudence but because they didn't rise above it. In the context of the needs of the population to which the constitutions were addressed it was probably a mistake to stick too closely to forms and patterns which were invented to check the development which the delegates represented. It was to the interests of the poor black and poor white delegates to simplify the administration of the state as much as possible by reducing the number of officials and by encouraging local communities to create organs of their own. Above all, it was necessary to involve the new citizens at every level of the government. Some of the old forms retained frustrated these purposes. A unicameral legislature, for example, would have been far more practical than the bicameral forms retained. Instead of retaining the outlandishly archaic legal forms of the North, it would have been far better to draft legal codes which didn't make members of a priestly legal caste necessary intermediaries between the people and power. As it was, a black population with few lawyers tied themselves, through the shortsightedness of their representatives, to a form of government that forced them to depend on white lawyers of doubtful sincerity and oftentimes doubtful integrity.

Such as they were, however, the new constitutions were grand pages of public law which would revolutionize the South if adopted there today. Most of the constitutions began, J. R. Ficklen, a conservative white historian noted, by reciting "portions of the Declaration of Independence, with slight modifica-

tions of language suitable to the existing circumstances and
with a practical application of principles which would have
shocked the author of that immortal document." The key
words here are *practical application of principles*. These constitutions were, in essence, practical attempts to concretize the
phrase: All men are created equal. The black delegates to the
conventions had had their fill of vague phrases and they tried,
as B. F. Randolph said of the South Carolina constitution, "to
settle the question [of human rights] forever by making the
meaning so plain that a wayfaring man, though a fool, cannot
misunderstand it." Thus it was that the South Carolina bill of
rights stated: "Distinction on account of race or color, in any
case whatever, shall be prohibited, and all classes of citizens
shall enjoy equally all common, public, legal and political
privileges." The Louisiana constitution was equally forthright,
declaring that all places of business or public entertainment, as
well as all businesses which required a license, were public
places, open to the accommodation and patronage of all persons, without regard to race or color. Mississippi delegates
played the politics of loopholes but did manage to state that
"the right of all citizens to travel upon public conveyances shall
not be infringed upon, nor in any manner abridged in this
state."

The slippery word *all* meant not only all black people but all
white people. If a democracy is based on the consent and
participation of at least a majority of the people, the South had
never been a democracy, not even for white people. What
Roger W. Shugg said of Louisiana was true of the whole South.
"Suffrage or representation, and sometimes both, were arranged
to exclude a majority of the people, white or black, from
effective control of their government." The Reconstruction
constitution reversed this process, giving poor whites and
white women privileges the aristocrats had denied them. In one
fell blow, the old feudal system of duelling, imprisonment for
debt, and whippings for punishments was swept away. The
homestead laws, which protected small holdings from legal

expropriation, were designed primarily to protect poor whites, for most black people did not have holdings of any kind at the time. The constitutions also began the emancipation of white women—rich and poor. The South Carolina constitution gave the state its first divorce law and declared that the property of a married women couldn't be sold for the debt of her husband.

Although the documents differed in detail, they generally extended the force and function of government, making the state a creative force in the everyday activities of the people. Of even greater importance were articles which widened the circle of men who could participate directly in decisions affecting their lives. The Florida constitution was a notable and interesting exception to this general rule. After capturing the Florida convention, white conservatives wrote an anti-Negro constitution which was frankly designed to nullify the power of the eight heavily populated Black Belt counties. The constitution limited each county, no matter how large, to four representatives in the General Assembly. "By the apportionment provided for in said constitution," the Radicals charged, "less than one-fourth of the registered voters will elect a majority of the State Senate, and less than one-third will elect a majority of the Assembly; 6,700 voters in [white] counties elect as many senators (twelve and one Indian) as 20,282 voters elect in [black] counties. Seven senators are elected by 3,027 voters in [white] counties, and only *one* senator is elected by 3,181 in a Union country (Leon), and *twenty-three* voters elect *one* senator in a [white] district." More ominous was a provision which permitted the governor to appoint practically all of the state officers, effectively nullifying black power in the election of sheriffs, assessors and other county officials. These provisions were designed, according to Harrison Reed, the state's leading white Republican, "so as to secure the sparsely settled white counties against the domination of the populous black belt," and "to save the State from a threatened war of races...."

Florida and Arkansas apart, the new constitutions generally gave more people more power over local and state offices.

Property-holding qualifications were abolished. Local government was reformed, and a larger number of offices were made elective. In addition, the constitutions provided for direct government participation in the founding and managing of asylums, deaf and dumb schools, and other institutions of social welfare.

The most revolutionary provisions of the constitutions related to universal education and universal suffrage. Some Confederates were temporarily deprived of political privileges in five states, but the new constitutions opened the political arena for the first time to the mass of poor blacks and poor whites.

Closely allied to this provision were articles requiring the state to create and sustain a public school system for all children. Although scattered and unsuccessful attempts had been made to create a school system for poor whites, the Reconstruction constitutions were the first in the South to provide for tax-supported statewide systems for all. It should be noted also that the public school sections were adopted largely at the insistence of black delegates and the black masses. Du Bois was right: "Public education for all at public expense, was, in the South, a Negro idea."

Although some constitutions sought consensus through silence, some provided that public education for all would be in schools attended by all. The Louisiana constitution said: "All children of this state between the years of six and twenty-one shall be admitted to the public schools or other institutions of learning sustained or established by the State in common, without distinction of race, color, or previous condition. There shall be no separate schools or institutions of learning established exclusively for any race by the State of Louisiana...." There was a similar provision in the South Carolina constitution.

The constitutions were words on pieces of paper; it remained now to give the words force by organizing political instruments and taking over the state. In most states political brokers met in the final days of the conventions, nominated state officers, and prepared for the referendum on the constitutions. Although black voters formed the base of every state Republican organization, few black politicians were nominated for state offices in 1868. The Republican party faced a national Presidential election that year, and Republican leaders told black politicians once again that it would be inexpedient for them to assert themselves at that stage of the game. This advice was accepted in North Carolina where James J. Harris refused a unanimous nomination for Congress and in South Carolina where Francis L. Cardozo declined the nomination for lieutenant governor. Cardozo said that "to have yielded to [the office] would simply have been a surrender to the enemy by going beyond the limits of true victory." He was finally persuaded to accept the post of secretary of state.

If Cardozo didn't know the difference between true victory and true defeat, Louisiana black men did. They not only demanded a fair share of cabinet officers but they also organized a strong campaign for governor. At the Louisiana convention, two black men, P. B. S. Pinchback and F. E. Dumas, and four white men were nominated for governor. Pinchback withdrew, believing apparently that there was plenty of time to seek the prize he coveted. Dumas, unlike Pinchback, stood his ground. He was a wealthy free Negro who had recruited, outfitted, and captained a company in the Union Army. As a war hero and a member of the free Negro colony of New Orleans, he enjoyed huge support among the Pure Radical faction. On the first ballot, however, neither Dumas nor his white opponents received the forty-five votes necessary for nomination. Dumas received forty-one votes, Warmoth thirty-seven, G. M. Wickliffe four, and J. G. Taliaferro three. This ballot indicated that the main contest was between Dumas and Henry Clay Warmoth, a twenty-six-year-old Northerner. In the spirited contest for the nomination, Warmoth was served by his audacity, his color, and his opponent's background.

The first black man elected to the
House of Representatives, John W. Menard
of Louisiana, was denied a seat. He
became the first black man to speak
in Congress.

A federal official arbitrates an economic
dispute between a freedman and a
planter in Freedmen's Bureau office in
Memphis, Tennessee.

Dumas, though a Negro, was a former slaveholder, and although the freedmen were willing to forgive converted white slaveholders, it was hard for them to forgive a former Negro slaveholder. In the frantic period of horse-trading before the second ballot, Warmoth and his men made good use of the fact that Dumas had once owned slaves. Even so, he failed to make an appreciable dent in Dumas' support. On the second ballot, Warmoth squeaked by, forty-five to forty-three, with seven additional votes coming mainly from supporters of white conservative candidates. As a consolation, Oscar J. Dunn, a former slave, was nominated for lieutenant governor, and a free Negro, Antoine Dubuclet, for state treasurer. Another Negro, John Willis Menard, thirty, was also nominated and elected to Congress by a vote of 5,107 to 2,833. Congress refused to seat Menard, although he became the first Negro to deliver a speech on the floor of the House. Congressman James A. Garfield of the committee on elections stated frankly "that it was too early to admit a Negro to the U.S. Congress. . . ."

In all states, there was action in this season on the local level where county conventions nominated black candidates for sheriff, county commissioner, and other posts. A South Carolina reporter covered a local convention in Georgetown. "The freedmen from their respective plantations," he wrote, "assembled en masse to participate in the selection of their representatives in the General Assembly. Prior to the meeting, groups were to be seen in every direction on Bay Street, holding their caucuses and discussing the merits and demerits of the respective candidates for nomination. The shrill shriek of the fife, however, soon summoned them to their rendezvous where a hot contest ensued between the friends and supporters of the several candidates."

The Republicans weren't the only organizers in this seminal season. Outraged Democrats, saying and apparently believing that civilization was about to come to an end, bestirred themselves, organizing economic and political boycotts. Democrats generally adopted a tactic of nonsupport, refusing to recognize the legitimacy of the conventions and urging their supporters to refrain from voting in the hope that this would insure defeat under a congressional law which said that state constitutions had to be affirmed by a majority of the *registered* voters.

Democratic conservatives also relied heavily on terrorist organizations like the Ku Klux Klan, a white supremacist organization founded in 1865 by Confederate war veterans. Dedicated to the preservation of white supremacy and the destruction of the Reconstruction governments, the terrorist organization spread across the South and reached a peak of effectiveness in 1868. More than one thousand black voters were killed that year in massacres and riots, and scores of black and white politicians were assassinated by masked gunmen.

In the face of this challenge, black Republicans and their white allies girded themselves for an all-out war. Eighty-eight Republicans of the North Carolina convention put white Democrats on notice:

Did it ever occur to you, ye gentlemen of property, education, and character—to you, ye men, and especially ye women, who never received anything from these colored people but services, kindness, and protection—did it never occur to you that these same people who are so very bad, will not be willing to sleep in the cold when your houses are denied them, merely because they will not vote as you do; that they may not be willing to starve, while they are willing to work for bread? Did it never occur to you that revenge which is sweet to you, may be sweet to them? Hear us, if nothing else you will hear, did it never occur to you that if you kill their children with hunger they will kill your children with fear? Did it never occur to you that if you good people maliciously determine that they shall have no shelter, they may determine that you shall have no shelter?

The same spirit of bitter determination informed a rousing speech given by Alfred Gray, a Black Belt grass-roots politician, on the eve of the Alabama election. Standing in the town square in Tallapoosa, Alabama, Gray said:

"The Constitution, I came here to talk for it—If I get killed I will talk for it. I am not afraid to fight for it, and I will fight for it until hell freezes over. I afraid to fight the white men for my rights? No! I may go to hell, my home is hell, but the white man shall go there with me."

Gray leaned in close to the crowd and continued: "Gentlemen, I am no nigger, I am neither white nor black. Will some one be smart enough to tell me what race I belong to?"

"Mr. Gray," one onlooker said, "you is a white man's son by a black 'oman."

"Yes," another man shouted, "and if your mother had been as honest as mine, you'd been as black as I is!"

"Yes," Alfred Gray said—"Yes, that's my stock; and my father, god damn his soul to hell, had 300 niggers, and his son sold me for $1,000. Was this right? No! I feel the damned spirit of damnation in me and will fight for our rights until every rascal who chased niggers with hounds is in hell."

"Gentleman," Gray said, changing the subject, "you hear a good deal about social equality, and black and white children going to school together. Well, ain't that right? We pay our $1.50, and make them pay tax on the land that you cleared and which you have the best right to. Then send all to school together. Didn't you clear the white folks' land?"

"Yes," the crowd screamed, "and we have a right to it!"

Gray told them they could get the land if they would only stand up and fight for their rights.

"Boys," he said, "now I want you to hear. Remember the 4th of February. And every one come in and bring your guns and stand up for your rights! Let them talk of social equality, mixed schools and a war of races. We'll fight until we die, and go to hell together, or we'll carry this constitution."

They carried it—almost everywhere. An overwhelming majority, including many whites, endorsed the Alabama constitution, although conservatives temporarily blocked implementation by a boycott of the polls. This tactic backfired when Congress passed a new law requiring only a majority of the votes cast. Only in Mississippi did the conservative campaign of intimidation and fraud succeed. In the same elections, Republican slates—predominantly white—were swept into office in seven states of the old Confederacy.

By July, South Carolina, Alabama, Florida, Georgia, Louisiana, North Carolina and Arkansas had been readmitted to the American Union on condition "that the constitutions of neither of said states shall ever be amended or changed as to deprive any citizen or class of citizens of the United States of the right to vote in said states who are entitled to vote by the constitutions thereof herein recognized." Tennessee, which did not undergo formal Reconstruction, had already been admitted; Texas was still debating its constitution; Mississippi had rejected its constitution; and a hostile commanding general had refused to authorize a referendum in Virginia. These states were admitted in 1870.

Now began the pageants of power. On Tuesday, April 2, America's first integrated legislature (eight black men and ninety-six white men) opened in Little Rock, Arkansas. More important, however, were the festivities on Monday, June 29, in New Orleans, where the Louisiana legislature held its first session, with Oscar J. Dunn, a former slave, presiding over the senate and R. H. Isabelle serving as acting speaker of the house. Of the thirty-six men in the Louisiana senate, seven were black. About half of the 101 representatives were black.

The political temperature rose perceptibly in July. On July 2, Clayton Powell, a former Union general, was inaugurated in Little Rock and rows of chairs were placed under the oaks in front of the capitol to accommodate the throng of blacks and whites. Two days later, on Saturday, July 4, the governors of North Carolina and Florida were inaugurated before huge crowds of blacks and whites. The capitol square in Tallahassee was packed with thousands of Republicans of all ages, classes, and colors. "Probably the largest crowd was here, than ever before at any time," the *Floridian* said. Black people took over the city streets and there was "much marching and counter marching, beating of drums and shouting."

The highlight of the month, however, came on Monday, July 6, in Columbia, South Carolina, where the first legislature in America with a black majority (84 blacks and 72 whites) held its first session in temporary quarters at Janney's Hall. Three days later, on July 9, the state officers were inaugurated and Francis L. Cardozo, the secretary of state, became the first Negro state cabinet officer in America. Cardozo was joined almost immediately by Antoine Dubuclet, the Louisiana treasurer, and Oscar J. Dunn, the Louisiana lieutenant governor, who were inaugurated in New Orleans on Monday, July 13.

Meanwhile, on the national scene, the architect of all this hope and passion lay dying. Thaddeus Stevens, who had said he intended to "die hurrahing," couldn't have arranged a better scenario for his departure. Three weeks after ratification of the Fourteenth Amendment and a little over a month after the meeting of the first American legislature with a black majority, the Great Commoner breathed his last in the company of a predominantly black band of mourners. The South was jubilant — "Hell," one newspaper said exultantly, "will now be reconstructed" — but black Americans went into national mourning for the great liberator who was buried, by his own request, in a Negro cemetery in Lancaster, Pennsylvania. The stone above his remains carried the words he wrote:

> I repose in this quiet and secluded spot
> not from any natural preference for solitude
>   but finding other cemeteries
>   limited by charter rules as to race,
> I have chosen this that I might illustrate in my death
>   the principles which I advocated through a long life
>   Equality of Man before his Creator.

With Stevens' death, idealism as a political force passed from the Republican scene. There were, to be sure, idealists still around—men like Charles Sumner, George W. Julian, Frederick Douglass, and Wendell Phillips. But these men didn't control the levers of power. The power Stevens had wielded as boss of the House passed now to coarser organizational men. The new symbol of the party was General U. S. Grant, a war hero who had the usual weakness of generals in politics: unlimited faith in the virtue of businessmen.

Grant, stolid, unimaginative, dour, came on the scene at a crucial moment. The new states were struggling for survival in an increasingly hostile atmosphere, and Democrats hoped to doom them at birth by winning the Presidential campaign of 1868. The Democrats nominated Horatio Seymour, a conservative Copperhead from New York, and denounced "military despotism" and "black supremacy" in the South. The Radical Reconstruction program was called "unconstitutional, revolutionary, void."

At the Chicago convention which nominated Grant for the Presidency, Republicans defended the Reconstruction program and charged that the Democrats intended to repudiate the national debt. This convention marked the debut of the African-American as a political force. P. B. S. Pinchback of Louisiana and James J. Harris of North Carolina were delegates to the convention and Harris served on the committee which waited on Grant to inform him of his nomination. African-Americans also served for the first time as Presidential electors. Robert Meacham was a presidential elector in Florida and the South Carolina electoral ticket included three black men, B. F. Randolph, Stephen Swails, and Alonzo J. Ransier.

Of even greater significance was the fact that African-Americans supplied the crucial votes that sent Grant to the White House and insured the continuation of the Radical Reconstruction program. Although Grant won by a majority of 309,000 votes, he polled a minority of the white vote. The nearly half-million votes cast by African-Americans insured his election. John Roy Lynch, the rising young black politician of Mississippi, noted: "The Republicans were successful, but not by such a decisive majority as in the Congressional election of 1866. In fact, if all the Southern States that took part in that election had gone Democratic, the hero of Appomattox would have been defeated. It was the Southern States giving Republican majorities through the votes of their colored men that saved that important national election to the Republican party."

Recognizing the national importance of the black vote and the fragile legal prop which supported that vote, black and white leaders immediately mounted a national campaign to cement Negro suffrage into the basic law of the land. The grand outcome was the Fifteenth Amendment which was passed on February 26, 1869. With passage and ratification of this crucial amendment, the Reconstruction legal scaffolding was almost complete. In the wake of that triumph, a mood of political euphoria moved across the face of black America. "I seem to myself," Frederick Douglass said, "to be living in a new world. The sun does not shine as it used to.... not only the slave emancipated, but a personal liberty bill, a civil rights bill, admitted to give testimony in courts of justice, given the right to vote, eligible not only to Congress, but the Presidential chair — and all for a class stigmatized but a little while go as worthless goods and chattels...." Even Wendell Phillips was overwhelmed. "Slavery," he said, "is dead." "We have not only abolished slavery, but we have abolished the Negro. We have actually washed color out of the Constitution."

Let us go now from state to state, beginning with South Carolina, and sample the mood and doings of a people who believed, almost one hundred years ago, that all things had been made new.

3

South Carolina:

Post Bellum Paradise for Negroes

IT WAS BEGINNING.

She knew it was beginning.

Even in the dim room with the windows shut tight against the red July sun and the hot black hopes of the men she and her husband had once owned — even in that secluded place, she knew that a new thing, terrible (to her) in its implications, was beginning and that the old world she had loved was ending. She could visualize it — black men and white men sitting on the same platform, the white men fawning over the black men, promising them things, flattering them, ruining them. She could see it in her mind's eye, the old white woman; she could feel it — and her blood boiled at the thought of it. Soon, they would shoot the big guns and there would be cheering and it would all be over: a whole way of life, a whole civilization, cotton, crinoline, blooded horses — and black people in their place.

In the hot old house near the university in Columbia, South Carolina, Louisa McCord, widow of a leader of the old regime, put down words that reflected these thoughts in a letter she wrote to her daughter while waiting, bodefully, for the guns to

announce the inauguration of the first Radical Republican
government in the state of South Carolina. Rigid with rage,
almost hysterically angry, the aristocratic white woman struggled furiously to find words sufficiently corrosive to express her
horror of the "crow congress," the "menagerie," and the "Yan-
kee-nigger government program."

As she wrote, angrily stabbing the paper with her pen, the
scene she saw in her mind's eye unfolded in living color at
Janney's Hall where officials of the new South Carolina government were taking the oath of office that would release to them
the keys of power. From this place, or near this place, John
Calhoun had risen to fame and power. From here, or near here,
would come "Cotton Ed" Smith, James Byrnes, Strom Thur-
mond, and a Clarendon County school segregation suit that
would, one hundred years later, turn the clock of history back
to this day when white men and black men swore before white
men and black men and God that they would govern South
Carolina in the name of all the people. First, on that faraway
day, came Robert Kingston Scott, a heavily-mustachioed former Union general who had sought yellow gold in California
and Mexico and had found black gold, unexpectedly, in the
political mines of South Carolina. After Scott came the new
lieutenant governor, Lemuel Boozer, a native South Carolina
white man; and the new attorney general, Daniel H. Chamberlain, another Union veteran, cold of mien, elegantly turned out,
a brilliant, complex man who had graduated near the top of his
class at Harvard and Yale Law School. No less brilliant and no
less elegant was the black man who followed, Francis L.
Cardozo, the tall, portly secretary of state. There were others:
Justus K. Jillson, the perceptive Northern-born superintendent
of education; and John L. Neagle, the Confederate Army
veteran who held the portfolio of comptroller-general.

When, at length, the procession of newly elected state officials
ended, the big guns boomed, noisily announcing to friend
and foe alike the inauguration of a new order of things:

an integrated government, elected by black men, answerable to a predominantly black legislature, charged with the responsibility of governing 415,000 black people, 289,000 whites, 114 Indians and one Chinese living in a thirty-thousand-square-mile area between the Atlantic and the mountains. This area, which was shaped roughly like a triangle, was sharply divided into the predominantly black lowcountry and the largely white upcountry. Both lowcountry and upcountry were rural. When the Radical Republicans came to power, there were only three towns in the state with a population over four thousand: Charleston, Columbia, and Greenville.

On inauguration day—Thursday, July 9, 1868—all over this area, from the Atlantic to the mountains in the north and west and the Georgia boundary to the south, power began to change habits and colors. Nowhere yet was it all-black, but nowhere was it still all-white. The black population just then had a clear voting majority of thirty thousand in the state and overwhelming majorities in the lowcountry Black Belt; and this ballot power was reflected in the skin tones and political tints of the men who were moving now into the seats of power, replacing aristocrats long accustomed to exclusive control of the state apparatus. To the dismay of aristocrats, a bumper crop of black sheriffs, county commissioners, clerks and other functionaries bloomed in small hamlets and rural counties. Toward the center of power in Columbia, the capital, and Charleston, the commercial center, there were black aldermen, magistrates, and federal officials. From both the center and circumference came representatives and senators who gave black people a majority in the state house of representatives and the balance of power in the state senate. "Here," Edward King wrote from South Carolina, "the revolution penetrates to the quick."

On both the state and local level and in both the legislative and the executive departments, there were exceptionally able black politicians who would leave a permanent mark on the proud Palmetto state. Of the characteristics and qualifications of the major black leaders, we shall have much to say later. For the moment, let us say merely that they were like politicians everywhere: some, in other words, were good, some were bad, and some were indifferent. In the following pages, we shall meet time and time again the adroit, scrupulously honest but somewhat moderate Cardozo; the handsome black lawyer, Robert Brown Elliott, who was without doubt the ablest and most powerful black politician in the state; Beverly Nash, another brilliant black man, who weaved webs of power from his commanding position in the state senate; Richard H. Cain and Robert C. De Large, the powerful leaders of the Charleston area; Joseph H. Rainey, the first black congressman and the dominant political force in the Georgetown area; and Alonzo J. Ransier, the first black lieutenant governor and a major influence as chairman of the state Republican executive committee. There were others, particularly the charismatic Robert Smalls, the bold Stephen A. Swails, the flamboyant William J. Whipper and the dedicated supreme court justice Jonathan Jasper Wright.

Of the men named here, at least nine should be spotlighted for the record, for in their intertwined careers they summed up the spirit of the new regime and the old regime it contradicted.

The name of Francis Louis Cardozo, for example, recurs repeatedly in this narrative and in records of the day. Who was this urbane and conspicuously able black man? How did he come to his position of eminence in the South Carolina state house? Cardozo came by a circuitous route. He was born free in Charleston on January 1, 1837, to a Jewish economist and a free black woman; and he soon fled the totalitarian air of ante bellum South Carolina, seeking refuge in Europe where he was graduated with honors from the University of Glasgow after winning prizes in Latin and Greek. After two years of graduate study at the London School of Theology, he returned to America in 1864 and pastored the Temple Street Congregational Church in New Haven, Connecticut. The next year the

American Missionary Association sent him to Charleston where he became principal of Avery Institute, the largest black school in the area. He went from this post to the state convention where he conducted himself with such distinction that his colleagues persuaded him to run for higher office. Cardozo, who was an expert accountant and a brilliant administrator, became the black anchor in the predominantly white state administration, serving successively as secretary of state (1868-72) and treasurer (1872-77).

By temperament, Cardozo was cautious and conciliatory. Unlike Elliott, he seems to have lacked an instinct for power. A hard-working and unspectacular figure, he seems to have preferred the bureaucratic background which separated him from the perspectives of popular concern, and militated against the creation of a popular base. For these reasons and perhaps others, he tended to take on the coloration of the white administrative leaders with whom he associated. But, for all that, Cardozo made a large contribution. Punctiliously honest, with a superb administrative sensibility, he saved the state millions of dollars by blowing the whistle on white colleagues who were trying to defraud the government. On several occasions, he refused to affix the state seal to fraudulent bonds.

In the summer of his accession to power, Cardozo was only thirty-one years old. He was a handsome figure — tall, elegantly tailored, with a square face and side whiskers. His presence in the gray granite capitol in Columbia spoke volumes about the possibilities of the new regime and the deficiences of the old.

No less persuasive was the presence in the state senate of Joseph Hayne Rainey of Georgetown (13,000 Negroes, 2,000 whites) and Alonzo Jacob Ransier of Charleston County (60,000 Negroes, 28,000 whites). Ransier and Rainey were South Carolina natives who went from the bottom rungs of the old regime to the top perches of the new. Rainey, who was thirty-six in this summer, represented Georgetown where he had been born in slavery on June 21, 1832. His father, who was

Alonzo Jacob Ransier is sworn in as lieutenant governor of South Carolina at his inauguration in Columbia in 1870.

In the predominantly black South Carolina legislature, a black representative takes the floor in support of a civil rights measure.

Joseph H. Rainey became the first black
member of the House of Representatives
on December 12, 1870.

a barber, purchased the family's freedom and young Rainey grew up in freedom. A barber like his father, Rainey trimmed the hair of planters for many years at the Mills House in Charleston. He went from his barber chair to the corridors of power, representing Georgetown in the convention, the state senate, and the U.S. Congress, where he was the first black representative.

Though self-educated, Rainey was polished and fluent. In appearance, he was a fair, stout man with an oblong face covered partially by side whiskers. He had a look, a contemporary said, "of great courage and sagacity." Though something of an introvert, he was militantly effective in pushing the interests of his constituents.

Also self-educated and enormously able was Alonzo Jacob Ransier, a thirty-six-year-old free Negro. Ransier represented Charleston, where he had worked before the war as a shipping clerk. He had little formal training but he was extremely effective as a parliamentarian and political tactician. He was to serve as chairman of the state Republican executive committee and lieutenant governor before going to Congress in 1873.

No one, as these examples indicate, has ever devised an IQ for power. No one has ever been able to determine, on the basis of educational qualifications and prior experience, precisely which men in a newly assembled political formation will rise to the top. Some men, with brilliant ideas and impeccable qualifications, fall by the wayside for want of staying power. Others, less brilliant perhaps but quietly tenacious, burrow in like unromantic chiggers and it is impossible to dislodge them until they have made their point and their mark. Robert Smalls, Robert Carlos De Large and William Beverly Nash were in the latter category. As the race for power began in Columbia, it would have been difficult, if not impossible, to predict their future eminence on the basis of their records. Robert Carlos De Large, for instance, was a self-taught tailor who had made himself a professional parliamentarian by organizing and chairing the post-Emancipation meetings of freedmen in the Charleston area. Like many other black leaders, he began his rise to power as an agent of the Freedmen's Bureau. Shrewd and practical, he was very influential in the house, where he served as chairman of the ways and means committee. De Large, who was only twenty-six when the legislature opened and thirty-two when he died suddenly in 1874, was to serve as commissioner of the sinking fund, land commissioner, and U.S. congressman.

Slightly older than De Large and other leading members of the black directorate was Beverly Nash, the middle-aged former slave who had more native ability, a hostile white reporter said, "than half the white men in the senate." As a slave, he blacked boots in a Columbia hotel and painfully taught himself the ABC's. Now, with the turn of the wheel, he was the most powerful politician in Richland County (Columbia) where he had once waited tables in a hotel. Six feet tall, "black as charcoal, handsome of face and commanding of figure," Nash was an imposing politician in the senate, where he headed the ways and means committee. Despite, or perhaps because of, his limited education, Nash was a formidable foe on the floor and in committee sessions. "He handles them all," a black colleague said. "The lawyers and the white chivalry, as they call themselves, have learned to let him alone. They know more of law and some things than he does; but he studies them all up, and then comes down on them with a good story or an anecdote, and you better believe he carries the audience right along with him. All the laugh and all the ridicule is on his side. And when he undertakes a thing, he generally puts it through, I tell you. No, sir, there is now nobody who cares to attack Beverly Nash. They let him alone right smart."

Across the hall, in the lower chamber, was Robert Smalls, a man of similar force and background. The son of a Jew and a black woman, Smalls was a big-framed brown man with a thick neck and a Van Dyke beard. Born a slave in Beaufort in 1839, he mastered the nautical arts and was employed on ships operating in the Charleston harbor. While working there during the war, he stunned the South and gave new heart to the North by sailing the steamer "Planter" out of the heavily fortified harbor and presenting it to surprised Union naval officers. During the latter part of the war, he served as noncommissioned captain of the "Planter".

Like Nash, Smalls excelled at political in-fighting and was particularly effective on the stump. He was idolized in the Beaufort area (29,000 Negroes, 5,000 whites) which sent him to the convention, the state house, state senate and the U.S. House of Representatives. A white Northerner heard a young cynic rebuke one of Smalls' elderly Beaufort admirers. "Smalls ain't God!" the young man declared. "That's true, that's true," the old man replied, "but Smalls' young yet."

Smalls' Beaufort colleague, Jonathan Jasper Wright, was a typical example of the brilliant band of black professionals from the North. A native of Pennsylvania, Wright was reportedly the first African-American admitted to the bar of that state. He came to South Carolina in 1865 as an agent of the American Missionary Association and served as legal advisor to the Freedmen's Bureau in the Beaufort area. Nearly six feet tall, black, with "a finely chiseled face and a handsomely developed head," Wright was twenty-eight when he entered the state senate and thirty when he was elected, on February 1, 1870, to the South Carolina Supreme Court. Although he lisped, Wright was a forceful speaker and an excellent jurist.

Another black migrant who played a large role in the new senate and in the South Carolina Republican party was the charismatic minister-politician, Richard Harvey Cain. Cain was a man of dramatic presence and power—tall, black, with a broad nose, large expressive eyes, and luxuriant side whiskers. He was very influential in the Charleston area where he pastored the huge Emanuel African Methodist Episcopal Church. Eloquent, witty, and militant, Cain excelled in organization and propaganda. "Church by church," a contemporary wrote, "sprang into existence as if by magic under his charge." But Cain felt, as he put it, that "his people had need of him in other fields." The fields were many and various. He edited the *Missionary Record*, the most influential black-oriented newspaper in South Carolina, and speculated heavily in real estate and business enterprises. As a politician, he led a black reform bloc which consistently denounced the machinations of Northern-born white politicians.

Cain was born free on April 12, 1825, in Greenbriar County, Virginia. Carried to Gallipolis, Ohio, as a child, he enrolled in Wilberforce University and later entered the ministry. During the war, he pastored an AME Church in Brooklyn. Like Cardozo, like Wright, he hurried to the South in 1865 and settled in Charleston, where he developed a political base which carried him to the state senate and the U.S. Congress.

To the names listed here must be added lastly the name of Robert Brown Elliott, who was one of the most remarkable politicians of the Reconstruction era. Born free in Boston on August 11, 1840, Elliott, who was of West Indian descent, was educated in England, where he attended High Holborn Academy and Eton. Returning to the states, he completed his education by studying law for two years in Boston. He came to South Carolina as editor of the *Leader*, a Charleston newspaper, and was soon deep in the political whirlpools of the state.

Elliott was a handsome man of imposing physical presence. Broad-shouldered, full-lipped, with an oval face and a heavy mustache, he was, a white contemporary wrote, a "pure African" with "all the traits of his race . . . and the soul looking through lightens the shadows that cover them like a flash of sunlight."

Elliott, who spoke French, German, Spanish, and Latin and had the largest private library in the state of South Carolina, was no ordinary politician. On his feet, speaking, he surpassed all his associates, black and white. Frederick Douglass thought him one of the greatest black orators of all time. And Carter G. Woodson considered him the most brilliant of all Reconstruction politicians. Like most black politicians of this era, Elliott was consistently maligned by the white Democratic press. But there is no hard evidence to substantiate the charge that he was involved in the financial manipulations of the time.

Unlike some of his contemporaries, Elliott preferred the substance to the pomp of power. In an age when Washington was the height of the average politician's ambition, Elliott resigned from Congress twice in order to return to South Carolina where there was black power to be organized and used.

Elliott was power-oriented. He intended to make himself governor and political master of the state of South Carolina. Time and a violent counter revolution thwarted that ambition, but he was always a force to be reckoned with and white politicians, who scorned some of their black associates, were always deferential in his presence. An awed white reporter said Elliott's motto seemed to be: "I am what I am and I believe in my nobility."

In addition to major black politicians like Elliott, there were, on both the state and local levels, many white officials, Northern-born and Southern-born, who began, in July of 1868, to think black, either out of conviction or opportunism. A number of poor whites like James M. Allen of Greenville, Solomon Dill of Kershaw, and Joseph Crews of Laurons got in on the ground floor of the Revolution and were elected to the first legislature. An even larger number of old citizens of the state manned the judiciary. The supreme court consisted of two native whites and one Northern white. Of the eight circuit court judges elected by the first legislature, six were native white South Carolinians.

More significantly, the state cabinet was composed of four Northern newcomers, three native whites and one black man. Among the dominant whites in the new power structure were

Daniel H. Chamberlain, the clever and equivocal attorney general; Niles Gardiner Parker, the unscrupulous Northern-born treasurer; John L. Neagle, the Rock Hill storekeeper who was not overly careful as comptroller-general; Franklin J. Moses Jr., a hundred per cent integrationist with grave defects of character; and Robert K. Scott, the genial but pliable chief executive.

One ought to linger awhile with Robert Kingston Scott, for there were Scotts in power in every Southern state and the limitations of Reconstruction were largely the limitations of men made in Scott's mold. Born in Pennsylvania in 1826, Scott was an adventurous spirit who had wandered across the face of the world, mining for gold in California and Mexico, practicing medicine and selling real estate and merchandise in Ohio. Scott threw himself into the Civil War with the passion that characterized his whole life, organizing and leading a regiment of Ohio volunteers.

He remained in Charleston after the war and was breveted major general and named director of the South Carolina Freedmen's Bureau, a post he held until his nomination. Scott's nomination on the Republican ticket came as a surprise to some men, for he had never been accused of undue sympathy for the freedmen. His record as director of the South Carolina branch of the Bureau was marked by the same painful ambivalence that characterized his two terms as governor.

Drive, daring, a penchant for long shots and adventure: these qualities informed Scott's formative years, and they were not absent as he completed a remarkable power play by moving from the Freedmen's Bureau to the governor's office in Columbia. He was in his early forties then—a handsome, self-possessed man with a full mustache and vague gray eyes. Men who saw him then said he was not without a certain charm. But they also said he had the usual weaknesses of the adventurer. On one occasion, it is said, the manipulators of the white bond ring plied him with whiskey in a New York hotel room and left him in the hands of a famous actress who reportedly agreed to seduce him for a percentage of the fraudulent bonds she persuaded him to sign.

Even so, Scott was not without redeeming qualities which would have made him an outstandingly ordinary chief executive in the ordinary tradition of American state executives. He tried hard, according to his lights, to impose discipline on his wrangling subordinates. But he failed ultimately because of contradictions in his role and character. The qualities that served Scott in the gold mines of California and the volatile speculator circles of South America were not the only qualities he needed as chief executive of the most improbable social revolution in American history. In the former, he needed nerve, courage, tenacity; in the latter, he needed nerve, courage, tenacity, social passion, and a clearly defined social base. When Scott assumed direction of the South Carolina political machine, he not only lacked a social base but he also lacked a clearly defined group purpose. Lacking purpose himself, he naturally could not instill a sense of purpose in others.

It would be irrelevant to charge Scott with unfaithfulness to his black allies, for the interests of his black allies had never been uppermost in his mind. The revolution of Reconstruction opened a door; he walked through that door, telling his black allies that the demands of the hour required their absence and their patience.

Robert Scott may not have been acting as a conscious agent of conservative white interests, as Harrison Reed and Henry Clay Warmoth were doing at that very moment in Florida and Louisiana, respectively. But it is certain that he entered on his task with a state of mind that can only be called collaborative. His inaugural address, which was remarkably similar in tone and emphasis to the inaugural addresses of Warmoth and Reed, artfully subordinated the interests of the black men who elected him to the interests of the prewar rulers. It was necessary, he said, to respect the rights and the feelings of the former Confederates. He therefore recommended segregation in public schools and urged the Assembly to petition Congress for a removal of the political disabilities of leading Confederates. The *Charleston Daily News* found Scott's address "reassuringly moderate in sentiment," an indication that Scott was "anxious to gain the good will of the respectability and intelligence" of the state. In all this, Scott merely foreshadowed the dominant thrust of the white newcomers whom he represented. It is an interesting fact, worthy of long thought, that in the final showdown, Scott and the first Republican governors of Florida, Louisiana, Mississippi, and Virginia would align themselves with the Klan-oriented counterrevolutionaries.

In South Carolina, as elsewhere, black voters were unusually unlucky in their choice of allies. They were so unlucky, in fact, that the explanation must be sought in the situation, not in personalities. In South Carolina, as elsewhere, black voters had to work with what they had. And what they had, in the main, were business-oriented types with little real sympathy for the basic aspirations of the black electorate. Worse, many of the white Republicans were ruthless opportunists on the make. The one thing that was certain of the main body of white officials in South Carolina (and elsewhere) was their hostility to basic, revolutionary reform. There were exceptions to this rule, laudable exceptions like Justus K. Jillson, but it can be said that the average white politician of that day, whether Northern-born or Southern-born, asked not what he could do for black voters but what black voters could do for him. The sincere leaders—black and white—of the South Carolina Republican party never really came to grips with a problem which all revolutionary regimes face. Every real revolution forces its leaders to make a basic distinction between administrators who are experienced but hostile and administrators who are inexperienced but faithful. And every revolution that survives instinctively casts its lot with the faithful. South Carolina Republicans doomed themselves by ignoring this elementary rule. Seeking hastily to improvise an administrative apparatus which would satisfy their sworn enemies, they made the enormous, but understandable, mistake of entrusting its administration, especially in law, to white men of the old regime who were, at worst, hostile, and, at best, cool and suspicious. The consequences of all this were disastrous. By 1870, when black politicians turned on the white administrators, the Revolution had been betrayed, almost beyond redemption. But this was not, by any means, entirely the fault of the white administrative elite. Nor was it the fault entirely of black voters, who had little freedom of choice, situated as they were in a no-man's land with uncertain friends on one side and certain enemies on the other. To grasp the weight and meaning of the story that follows, we must accustom ourselves to viewing all the participants in the drama, black voters as well as black and white leaders, as human beings caught in a cataclysmic social upheaval that deviated and distorted most needs. Like most men, the leaders of Reconstruction were both accomplices and victims. Like all politicians, South Carolina's leaders — black and white — were limited by the human material at their disposal and the web of relations history had spun.

To understand the full tragedy of this story, to understand how black people came into their time of daylight, how they fought with and against white allies and how the sun finally ceased to shine, it is necessary, first of all, to understand that leaders and led faced tasks that were well-nigh insuperable in the parallelogram of forces existing at the time. To formulate and carry through a revolutionary program in the interests of Negroes and poor whites in a power situation dominated economically by old planters and new businessmen looking for a quick dollar and a big deal; to communicate this program to a rural, illiterate population, most of whom, black and white, lacked a viable political tradition; to galvanize into life and draw into movement this huge mass, impotent because split and scattered; to insure breathing space for the Revolution by

creating a mobile defense force which would counter any effort
on the part of hostile aristocrats to take advantage of the new
government's weakness; to be wise as serpents and harmless as
doves, crushing ruthlessly Ku Klux Klan terror, yet holding out
the right hand of fellowship to repentant racists; to be, in a
name, both a Martin Luther King and a Malcolm X, the better
to weld into effective unity black and white people burdened
by the inertia of a powerful tradition deliberately fashioned to
keep them apart; not only to be but to do; to fashion basic
reform that would retain the loyalty of the black masses and
yet not alienate Northern financial and political circles on whom
the life of the regime ultimately depended; to go beyond this by
initiating economic and educational programs that would persuade poor whites that the interests of the Revolution were
something they, too, must defend; to break down especially the
ingrained economic and sexual fears that made poor whites
their own worst enemies; rapidly to break up the plantation
system, developing on the one hand a black and white yeomanry and on the other a business and manufacturing middle
class; constantly to innovate and experiment upon a scale
where financial and human limitations left the narrowest margin of safety; all the time to thread one's way amid the
complexities of Northern political forces; to buy time, therefore,
by building a creative administrative structure that would
inspire confidence; to evoke and train, quickly, black and white
talent proportionate to the scale of the enterprise; to build
quickly new roads, new social agencies, new schools; to persuade Wall Street and conservative bond buyers to finance this
revolutionary program; to do all this in a climate of terror and
violence amidst a people impoverished and embittered by a
hard and bloody war; these were the tasks, Gargantuan on any
showing, which faced the black and white politicians as they
assembled in the temporary statehouse in Columbia on the
morning after the night of celebrations of the accession to
power. It cannot be said that these tasks were met, even in large

outline; yet no one can read the record of Reconstruction with an open heart without something approaching awe at how close the new men of power came against such great odds.

Taking over a discredited state government with ten million dollars in debts and only forty-five dollars in the till, South Carolina's new leaders moved with dispatch to re-establish the substance of government. The center of initiative at this point lay in the hands of the eighty-four black legislators and seventy-two white legislators who held a special session in July in their temporary quarters at Janney's Hall. With black leaders conspicuously prominent, local government structures were revamped and strengthened to the permanent benefit of a state which had been backward in adopting democratic procedures. The legislature also appointed a three-man committee, including the black lawyer William J. Whipper, which revised the state's legal code. This was a step of permanent benefit to the state. "The adoption of the code gave well-nigh universal dissatisfaction to the lawyers," John S. Reynolds, the conservative, anti-Negro chronicler of Reconstruction in South Carolina, commented. "But after thirty-five years' use, with immaterial changes suggested by experience, it has come to be regarded an admirable system—the product of legal minds of extraordinary power, worthy of close study by every man aspiring to be an educated lawyer, and of great merit as a specimen of terse, technical and yet scholarly English."

The interests of black people and poor whites were not neglected. The first legislature gave clear notice of its political posture by passing a homestead law to aid poor farmers, and a civil rights bill to protect the public rights of citizens of color. In pressing the claims of black people and poor whites, the legislature deliberately used the public credit for social purposes. More significant were measures which pointed to an equally deliberate use of taxation to accomplish changes considered socially desirable. The old planters had created a regressive tax system which spared the rich and soaked the poor. The new legislature reversed this policy by shifting the burden of taxation from mercantile to landed property. Under the new tax system, all property was taxed at full value.

This policy was designed, at least in part, to encourage productive development of the land which had never been fully utilized in the ante bellum South. Another motive, openly avowed by some Republicans, was the destruction of the plantation system.

If the tax policy was indeed designed to break up the large plantations, it was partially successful. For thousands of acres—five hundred thousand in 1874 alone—were forfeited to the state because of the inability of owners to pay taxes. Big landowners charged that the new tax program amounted to virtual confiscation. The Republicans replied with truth that the South Carolina tax rate—an average of nine mills for the first four years of Reconstruction and an average of eleven mills for the second four years—was less than the tax rate in most Northern states.

While awaiting collection of the first taxes, the new regime had to borrow money on state securities in order to survive. The legislature therefore created a financial board—Governor Scott, Attorney-General Chamberlain, Treasurer Parker and Comptroller-General Neagle—and empowered it to market $2,600,000 in state bonds in order to pay interest on the state debt and to relieve the pressing wants of the treasury. The financial board employed as its financial agent, H. H. Kimpton, a young and dubious New York businessman who had attended college with Attorney-General Chamberlain, and waded into the murky waters of high finance. Both Kimpton and Scott received frosty receptions in Wall Street, where financiers expressed intense concern over the bad credit rating of the prewar regime and the unsettled racial conditions in the new. After long and delicate negotiations, the new governor succeeded in borrowing money at the rate of four dollars in bonds for three dollars in cash. The loan was consummated, however, at the near-usurious rate of interest of 18 per cent a year—"a rate," Scott noted, "only demanded on the most doubtful paper." Subsequent bond issues were floated at a higher valuation, but at rates of interest varying from 15 to 20 per cent. In all, Scott said later, South Carolina only realized three million dollars in hard cash for over nine million dollars in bonds. As a short-term expedient, the financial scheme was perhaps necessary; but as a long-term solution, the bond plan carried grave risks, particularly in the hands of the state's Wall Street financial agent and the all-white financial board. The state financial agent and some members of the financial board were either corrupt or inept or both. By an incredible over-sight, the young financial agent, who had few assets, was not required to post a bond. Nor did the members of the board exercise the foresight and discretion the situation required. The board, for example, issued almost three million dollars in bonds to meet debts incurred prior to Reconstruction. Most of this debt was contracted during the war and "was clearly for-bidden to be paid," a congressional committee noted, "by the terms of the Fourteenth Amendment...." The committee added: "Had the credit of the State been unsullied up to 1868, it might have been expedient to make light loans on almost any conditions to preserve her good name, or a great emergency might have justified such terms temporarily for limited amounts; but for a State to go upon the 'street' as a mendicant borrower, and remain there buffeted from broker to broker for three years, raising money to pay old and dishonored debts at a cost of three dollars in new obligations for every dollar paid, seems to us indefensible."

So it seemed also to black leaders when they investigated the financial affairs of the state in 1871. But the details of the bond scheme were not known to the legislators in the summer and fall of 1868, when the new government faced the cruel necessity of realizing money at any price or surrendering the govern-

ment. In addition to the day-to-day needs of provision and
defense, the new government faced the necessity of raising
huge sums to meet the additional expenses of dealing with four
hundred thousand new citizens, who had not used the courts
and other political facilities as slaves. By floating bond issues
and by a uniform rate of taxation on land and property at full
value, the new leaders succeeded in raising enough money to
get the ambitious reform programs off the ground. Before the
first year ended, they had improvised an administrative apparatus and had embarked on an ambitious social welfare program,
breaking new ground in education, social welfare, legal administration, and race relations. By 1870, the insane asylum and the
new penitentiary were operating under mixed boards, and a
deaf and dumb school had been established at Cedar Springs.
By that time, the new school system was taking shape. A
temporary scaffold for the new system was thrown up by the
first legislature, which indicated its full support of the new
superintendent of education, J. K. Jillson, who said: "The
education of *all* classes and castes is indispensable to the
highest and best welfare of the community." Acting on this
premise, the legislature completed the legal foundations of
South Carolina's first universal education system by passing
laws in 1870 and again in 1871 which provided for the free,
integrated education of all children. The legislature established
another precedent by providing free textbooks for poor children.
A. D. Mayo, an educational authority, said the new school
law "was sufficient to realize the ideal of the most radical
schoolmen of the state. It, indeed, proposed a scheme in some
particulars in advance of the large majority of the Northern
states at this period." As for higher education, the legislature
reorganized the state university under an integrated board of
regents and established a normal school for the education of
teachers. Another law provided for scholarships for students
from each county.

In the sensitive sphere of economics, the new state adminis-

tration alarmed planters and businessmen by making a real
effort to protect sharecroppers and laborers, oftentimes shifting
the emphasis of lien, credit, and bankruptcy laws to the
advantage of debtors instead of creditors. In 1873, the legislature passed a law which gave laborers first claim on the crops
they produced, and protected sharecroppers by limiting the
amount a landlord could attach to one-third of the harvest. The
legislature also created a Bureau of Agricultural Statistics
which was a thinly disguised state-level Freedmen's Bureau
charged with the responsibility of protecting the economic
interests of poor farmers and sharecroppers.

Outraged businessmen were mollified by a series of laws
which opened the state to intensive capitalistic development.
The legislature extended liberal tax subsidies and business
incentives to manufacturers and industrialists. Cotton manufacturers, for example, were exempted from taxation for four
years. These benefits were later extended to other industrialists
who opened factories in the state. The new government also
gave indirect subsidies to big landlords and businessmen by
channelling public money into social overhead facilities
(roads, levees, railroads). It was at the urgent request of South
Carolina conservatives, led by the prestigious Charleston Board
of Trade, that the new legislature entered the thorny field of
railroad financing, guaranteeing more than six million dollars in
bonds for the Blue Ridge, Greenville and Columbia, and South
Carolina railroads. Since railroad bonds constituted the largest
item in the public "debt" of almost every Southern state, it is
important for us to recognize precisely what was at stake.
Under the railroad financing plans, which had been used
extensively by white Democrats before the war, the state lent
its name and credit to private railroad operators who floated
bonds which were guaranteed by the state. The amount guaranteed became a contingent debt of the state which agreed, in
the event of failure, to pay the interest and principal.

These plans reflected a railroad fever which seized every

Southern state. Convinced that transportation was the key to opening the potentialities of the state and maintaining or improving the state's economic position vis-à-vis its rivals, every Southern state embarked on a mania of railroad building which engulfed all classes and colors. The possibilities of fraud and manipulation in this situation were enormous, and hard-eyed speculators were soon hard at work exploiting the techniques they had perfected in Washington, D. C., and the capitals of Northern states. It was these men and their patrons on Wall Street and in the major financial centers of London and Amsterdam who were primarily responsible for the frauds and corruption of this period. On the local scene they were aided considerably by prominent aristocrats like Confederate General J. W. Harrison of the Blue Ridge Railroad. Protected by their connections and the institutional rituals that stand between big business bribers and their deeds, few of these men were caught. It was their agents or their victims, those men unpracticed in business deceit and inept enough to be caught exchanging a vote for money, who were stigmatized in the public eye. Such men — big business bribers and their political tools — were an unavoidable evil in the social upheavals of the period. With time, they could have been exposed and weeded out. But time was the very element that South Carolina and other states lacked.

Of fraud and corruption, we shall have much to say in a later chapter. For the moment, let us say frankly that, yes, there was corruption in South Carolina between 1867 and 1877, as there was corruption in this same period in the lily-white governments of New York and Washington and as there is corruption today in New York and Washington and Chicago. What I am concerned to emphasize here is that corruption is a constant variable in American politics — a constant that varies with socioecononomic conditions and the nature of political structures rather than with the color of men's skin. Some black leaders were peripherally involved in corruption in South

Carolina as receivers of bribes and improper pay certificates; but the major operators, by all accounts, were white Republicans and Democrats, some of them highly placed Confederates with impeccable connections in the Charleston Board of Trade and the Columbia Chamber of Commerce.

These things happened offstage. Onstage, the legislature pushed ahead, authorizing approximately $700,000 for the purchase of improved and unimproved land to be divided into plots of not less than twenty-five and not more than one hundred acres, to be sold to actual settlers on easy terms. To carry out these provisions, the legislature created the office of land commissioner. The commissioner was to be supervised by an advisory board consisting of the governor, comptroller-general, treasurer, attorney general, and secretary of state. The legislature also made rapid strides in the field of race relations. Despite the pleas of Governor Scott and other whites who advised a go-slow policy, the legislature quickly passed a strong civil rights bill which forbade segregation on public conveyances and places of public business and amusement. The new law was probably the strongest public accommodations act ever passed in America. Not only the owners of public places but also their employees and public officials who failed to enforce the act were made subject to stringent penalties, including fines and imprisonment. An interesting feature of the South Carolina public accommodations act was that the burden of proof of innocence lay on the alleged violators. Here are some excerpts:

Whereas, in this State the government is a democracy, the people ruling, and the government is also a republican one, in which all things pertaining to the government are in common among all the people; and whereas, it follows that no person is entitled to special privileges, or to be preferred before any other person in public matters, but all persons are equal before the law; and whereas, these propositions lie at the very foundation of our policy, and the American people have embodied the same, in the most emphatic manner possible, in their organic and statute laws, and the same do by their sovereign will and pleasure sustain; and whereas, notwithstanding all these great and glorious facts, there are found some brutal, ill-disposed and lawless persons in the State who persist in denying and trampling upon sacred rights of certain of the people; therefore

Section 1. It shall not be lawful for any common carrier... to discriminate between persons on account of race, color or previous condition....

.   .   .   .

Section 3. Whoever, conducting or managing any theater, or other place of amusement or recreation... shall wilfully make any discrimination against any person lawfully applying for accommodation in, or admission to, any such theater or place, on account of the race, color, or previous condition of the applicant... shall... on conviction, be punished by a fine of one thousand dollars, and also imprisonment at hard labor in the penitentiary for three years.

.   .   .   .

Section 7. In every trial for violating any provisions of this act... the burden shall be on the defendant party, or parties, so having refused or denied such admission or accommodation, to show that the same was not done in violation of this act.

In passing this law, militant black legislators had to meet substantially the same argument advanced one hundred years later against another public accommodations law. It was said, for example, that the law invaded a private arena and that it attempted to legislate social equality. Speaking on the floor of the house of representatives, William J. Whipper rebutted this argument. "Our race do not demand social equality," he said. Turning to a native white Republican who had defended segregation, Whipper continued with devasting sarcasm. "No law can compel me to put myself on an equality with some white men I know, but talk about equality and the member imagines he must take you into his arms—as he probably would your sister, if she was good looking."

Whipper and his colleagues repelled the conservative attack. Not only was the law passed; it was vigorously prosecuted, oftentimes by black officials who staged personal sit-ins and arrested offending businessmen on the spot. The effect of all this was immediate. A Northern teacher, who returned to South Carolina in 1868 after a trip to the North, reported: "We took a small steamer from Charleston for Beaufort. Here we found a decided change since we went North. Then no colored person was allowed on the upper deck, now there were no restrictions,—there could be none, for a law had been passed in favor of the Negroes. They were everywhere, choosing the best staterooms and best seats at the table. Two prominent colored members of the State Legislature were on board with their families. There were also several well-known Southerners, still uncompromising rebels. It was a curious scene and full of significance. An interesting study to watch the exultant faces of the Negroes, and the scowling faces of the rebels...."

An interesting field of inquiry opens up just here. Given the long history of Negro protest since Reconstruction, the question naturally arises: How did whites protest when black people had power? Since power operates the same way everywhere and since men—black, white, brown and yellow—respond to power in the same way, we should not be surprised to learn that the white man out of power acted in much the same way as the black man out of power. So long as black power was organized and sustained by the intractable will of a federal government determined to maintain a republican form of government in South Carolina, *so long as people thought that it would never end,* white people accommodated themselves to the situation, grumbling, some of them, but obeying, almost all of them. In fact, as James S. Pike and other visitors observed, there was "an air of mastery among the colored people" and the whites were "wholly reserved and reticent, and apparently fearful." Pike was shocked at "how reticent the whites are in their dealings with the blacks, & how entirely self-contained and self-assertive, the blacks appear to be."

What of the aristocrats? What were they doing all this time?

"Many of the old families," Pike reported, "remain in Columbia, but they are no longer rich, and keep themselves secluded from the general current of affairs. Their places, which used to be tidy and bright, are growing shabby and dilapidated, and the occupants live on the departed glories and what they have been able to save from the wreck of their estates. They are like the old St. Germain aristocracy during the latter empire who used to say of Louis Napoleon and the promiscuous crowd who occupied the Tuileries in his reign: 'We know none of these people.'"

They spoke often in these days, the old aristocrats, of the French Revolution. Eliza T. Holmes, a proper Charlestonian, said in a letter: "We are being made, however, day by day, to realize the equalities of all things, and brings to my mind the scenes I have read of during the Revolution in France of the hundred days, when the Nobility were so terribly treated. Surely our humiliation has been great when a Black Postmaster is established here at Headquarters and our *Gentlemen's Sons* to work under his biddings."

In this period, the average white accommodated himself to the power realities of the hour; so did the average white leader who, according to visitor Pike, felt "that the iron hand of Destiny [was] upon him." Pike, who was vehemently anti-Negro, went on to observe: "The gray heads of this generation openly profess that they look for no relief. They see no way of escape. The recovery of influence, of position, of control in the State, is felt by them to be impossible. They accept their position with a stoicism that promises no reward here or hereafter. They are the types of a conquered race. They staked all and lost all." Perhaps the best indication of the state of mind of white leadership was that many placed their hopes in the unrealistic idea of dividing the state, giving one portion to Georgia and another to North Carolina in order to get rid of the black majority.

By all this, we must understand that in the first stage of the game white Democrats were demoralized, confused and totally ineffective. In 1868, the Democrats demanded "a white man's government" and sent an all-white committee, headed by John P. Thomas and Wade Hampton, to Washington to present a petition on behalf of "the proud Caucasian race, whose sovereignty on earth God has ordained." When the white South Carolinians told Congress that South Carolina was being ruled by its black majority, Thaddeus Stevens replied that "what the protest claimed as grievances were regarded as virtues."

Thwarted in Washington, the Democrats returned to South Carolina and appealed to black voters on the basis of the "close ties" of the past. They organized "Coloured Auxiliary Democratic" clubs and held separate-but-equal political meetings where they urged black people to trust "old friends" who had treated them "humanely and justly." When a committee of black voters proved from the record that the Hamptons and Thomases had never been their friends, the white Democrats turned mean, rattling sabers. "We shall not give up our country," the white Democrats warned Negroes, "and time will soon restore our control of it. But we earnestly caution you and beg you in the meanwhile to beware of the use you make of your temporary power. Remember that your race has nothing to gain and everything to lose if you invoke that prejudice of race which since the world has ever driven the weaker tribe to the wall. Forsake, then, the wicked and stupid men who would involve you in this folly, and make to yourselves friends and not enemies of the white citizens of South Carolina."

But the Democrats were whistling — literally — in the dark. At that point, they didn't even speak for all the planters and businessmen. Nor, it seems, did they speak for "the white citizens of South Carolina" whose apathy and general indifference to Democratic appeals appalled the Democratic irreconcilables. In the face of widespread indifference, the Democrats of Sumter issued the following appeal: "Fellow citizens of

Sumter District arouse from your lethargy. Think of your wives and children. Let the love of them stimulate you to action." These appeals fell on deaf ears, largely because of the difficulties inherent in the mobilization of people for certain defeat. It was apparent to the rank and file, if not to the leadership, that white Democrats could not outvote black Republicans in South Carolina. Faced with even a token Republican party, the Democrats could only have attained serious relevance to the situation by making large concessions to the legitimate demands of the black majority. The white Democrats scorned this course, refusing even to admit the essential humanity of the black population. This strategy condemned the white Democratic leaders to impotence within the democratic framework.

Under the impact of this situation, the Democratic party fissured, with one faction trying to outflank the Republicans by devious campaigns under the Conservative banner and another faction going underground and pursuing a campaign of sedition and subversion. Led by big landowners and big business men, the seditionists openly conspired to destroy the credit of the state in order to undermine the government. The Charleston papers, which were controlled by prominent Democrats, railed against "the bayonet bonds" issued by "the so-called Governor of the State, with the sanction of the pretended Legislature, to carry on an illegal government." The *Charleston Daily News* told the financiers of Boston and New York that the white men of South Carolina would never recognize the legitimacy of the government elected by a majority of South Carolina voters. At the same time, South Carolina irreconcilables used their levers of power to push an organized tax boycott which deprived the state of millions of dollars of operating revenue and added two or three millions dollars to the bonded debt.

Even more disquieting was the tendency of white Democrats to adopt terrorism as a normal method of political struggle. As early as 1868, the Ku Klux Klan entered the state and pushed down deep roots, particularly in the poor white hill counties. Strategically organized on a military basis and led by former Confederate colonels and brigadiers, the Klan became a potent political force in South Carolina, assassinating black leaders like B. F. Randolph and white radicals like Solomon Dill and James Martin.

Alarmed by the inroads of the masked terrorist group, the Radical Republicans counterattacked by passing an anti-insurrection law and organizing a state militia of some ninety thousand men. Here again, however, black people were cheated by history. For Scott, who feared a general racial holocaust, never adequately used the predominantly black National Guard. By this time, however, Klan terror had become a national issue and Congress seized the initiative, passing a series of laws which made conspiracy to deprive citizens of their civil rights a federal offense. Proceeding under these statutes, President Grant declared a state of rebellion in nine South Carolina counties and dispatched additional troops who arrested more than one thousand whites, including many prominent professionals, businessmen, and educators. Some of these persons pleaded guilty and received fines and sentences; others fled the state, going to Canada and England; still others were tried before mixed juries, convicted, and sentenced.

Meanwhile, the South Carolina Revolution was stumbling from crisis to crisis, hampered by the opposition and indifference of white administrators. There were potentially unreliable elements at every level of the state administration, and the reform programs were bogged down in a swamp of treachery and corruption. The federal government had saved South Carolina Republicans from their enemies. Who was going to save them from their friends?

Black Republicans came to grips with that question in the winter of 1870 by organizing an informal black caucus which was charged with the responsibility of monitoring the machinations of the white administrators. This caucus was composed of leading legislators — Rainey, Whipper, Elliott, Ransier, Nash — and Cardozo, who was of invaluable assistance because of his position in the statehouse. According to Thomas E. Miller, who later served in the U.S. Congress, the black caucus held a meeting and decided, in so many words, that black people had to learn finance fast or die.

Cardozo pointed the way by resigning from the advisory board of the Land Commision to protest the unorthodox and questionable transactions of Charles P. Leslie, the aging, unprincipled white newcomer who served as land commissioner. Cardozo was seconded by a powerful group of black legislators who began to ask embarrassing questions about the operation of the land commissioner's office. When the black legislators determined to their satisfaction that large tracts of worthless land had been bought at artificially inflated prices and that Leslie and the financial agent had diverted or stolen tens of thousands of dollars, they banded together and refused to appropriate additional money for the Land Commission. Since the leading whites involved desperately needed additional money to cover unauthorized expenditures, the maneuver succeeded and Robert C. De Large replaced Leslie. The duties of the land commissioner were subsequently transferred to the secretary of state's office where Cardozo and, later, Henry E. Hayne, a free Negro and a Union army veteran, did excellent work in retrieving a badly bungled venture. As a result of the work of Hayne and Cardozo, a substantial number of citizens were provided with homes and land. The legislature later charged the remaining members of the advisory board — Scott, Neagle, Parker, Chamberlain — with "neglect of duty and unwarrantable violation of law."

Stung by the mounting evidence of the unfaithfulness of their allies, who were not above blaming the ignorant assembly" and the illiterate black electorate for their own misdeeds,

black politicians began in 1870 to see the necessity of direct
control. The immediate result was a demand for a larger share
of offices for black politicians. In the spring of 1870, Senator
Cain brought the issue into the open with a demand for an
equal division of all offices. Martin R. Delaney, the old abolitionist who was practicing medicine in Charleston, also joined
the movement, saying "black men must have black leaders." He
called for "a colored lieutenant governor, and two colored men
in the House of Representatives and one in the Senate, and our
quota of state and county offices."

In support of these demands and others, black politicians
mobilized mass pressure, holding meetings in Charleston
churches and on outlying plantations. Robert Elliott, for example, was the leading figure in an integrated state labor convention which demanded a purification of the administrative
apparatus and radicalization of the Republican program. The
convention said agricultural laborers should get one-half of
the share of the crop or a minimum daily wage of 70 cents.
They also demanded that (1) the claims of agricultural laborers
for wages due shall operate as a preferred lien on the land;
(2) that the governor appoint in each county a commissioner of contracts to examine and attest all contracts for labor;
(3) that suits of all classes of laborers and employers for wages
due them shall have precedence on the calendar of courts; (4)
that the governor appoint in each county an officer to supervise
jury lists "in order that the laboring classes may have a fair
representation on the juries."; (5) that land, sold by the sheriff,
should be divided into tracts not exceeding fifty acres; (6) that
the legislature pass an act establishing a nine-hour day.

Meanwhile, DeLarge, Smalls and other black leaders were
mobilizing forces for a third party. "If the white men in the
party think that the Republican party was made for them," De
Large said, "they are badly mistaken." Black people, he said,
would no longer submit to white leadership. "When a colored
man is capable of filling an office, I say give it to him; and I

shall fight this over the entire state." DeLarge added ominously: "I hold that my race has always been Republican from necessity."

White men in Columbia and Washington, D. C., got the message and moved quickly to meet the spiralling aspirations of black leaders. In a compromise settlement, Scott was renominated for governor in 1870, but a black man, Alonzo J. Ransier, was slated for the No. 2 spot of lieutenant governor. Cardozo was again nominated for secretary of state, and Ransier became chairman of the powerful Republican state executive committee. In a parallel development, two whites withdrew from the congressional races in favor of black politicians.

Foreseeing certain defeat under the Democratic banner, conservatives joined bolting Republicans and fielded a Union Reform ticket headed by Richard B. Carpenter, an apostate Republican judge, and M. C. Butler, an anti-Negro Democrat. This ticket was a product of the flanking fusion movement organized by conservative white Democrats who saw no other way to overcome the thirty to forty thousand black majority. The fusionists in the Union Reform party promised to respect the rights of black voters, but this was sheer campaign oratory. The fusion idea, as its architect, Francis W. Dawson of the *Charleston Courier*, frankly explained, was designed to "overthrow our Negro government and re-establish white supremacy." Dawson and other fusionists said this privately as white Democrats. But as members of the Union Reform party they composed an ingenious platform which denounced "the incompetent, extravagant, prejudiced, and corrupt administration" and deplored the hostility between labor and capital and "the absolute and sharp antagonism between the races."

Campaigning on a program of reform and "good government," the Union Reform party made a desperate effort to win black votes, but failed, chiefly because of the anti-black company it kept. In a cynical maneuver, the party stressed the "close ties" that existed between Negroes and planters "who had grown up together and played together." The gist of the black response can be gauged from a huge campaign poster which hung across the streets of Charleston:

WE HAVE PLAYED TOGETHER, YOU SAY;
BUT WERE WE EVER WHIPPED TOGETHER?

Black people were not fooled; nor, it seems, was anyone else. Several prominent native whites announced publicly for the Republican party. James L. Orr, a former speaker of the House of Representatives and a former South Carolina governor, said he would vote for the Scott-Ransier ticket because the Republican party "had done much to ameliorate the condition of the white people—adoption of homestead exemption, prohibition of collection of debts incurred for purchase of slaves, in abolition of imprisonment for debt, in raising the price of state bonds from 26 in January, 1868, to 90 at the present time." John Winnsmith, a Spartanburg doctor, and Robert F. Graham, the Confederate hero of the Battle of Fort Wagner, also declared for the Republican ticket.

Outmaneuvered on the political field, the Democrats resorted to terrorism. The terrorists were hampered, however, by the possibility of retaliation in Black Belt counties. In a speech at Yorkville, John L. Neagle, the Confederate veteran and state comptroller general, told his listeners to stand firm. "Matches," he said, "are cheap."

Backed by a solid black vote and the support of a large number of whites, the Republicans scored a smashing victory, winning by a 34,000 plurality. Joseph Rainey was elected to fill an unexpired congressional term and became, on December 12, 1870, the first black congressman. Also elected to Congress were DeLarge (he was later unseated on contest) and Elliott. More important perhaps was the fact that the black majority in the General Assembly increased to 85 out of 154. With ten members of the senate and seventy-five of the 124 in the house, black men now had a majority of sixteen in the General Assembly.

Despite campaign promises, Scott failed in his second term to alter the climate of South Carolina politics. Financial affairs became even more tangled, and fraud continued. Scott was no sooner inaugurated than the state and Wall Street were rocked by revelations which indicated that there had been a large and unauthorized issue of bonds by the financial agent and the financial board. To make matters worse, black legislators couldn't get precise information about the exact amount of the state debt. The whole matter was extremely complex and experts are by no means agreed on the details, even today. Suffice it to say that there had undoubtedly been, either through accident or design, an overissue of bonds of at least six million dollars.

Had the Revolution been betrayed?

Could it be saved?

An aroused legislature, with black politicians in the front ranks, named a joint special financial investigating committee "to make a complete and thorough examination of all the accounts of the State Treasurer, Comptroller-General, and Financial Agent...." This committee concluded that the governor and financial board had been guilty of dereliction of duty and perhaps fraud by making unwise appointments, giving bad advice, and sanctioning extravagant expenditures. An attempt was made to impeach Governor Scott and Treasurer Parker for "high crimes and misdemeanors," but both men survived with an ingenious defense in which they blamed the financial plight of the state on a white tax boycott, Ku Klux Klan violence and the threat of prominent whites to repudiate obligations made by the Republican administration.

What we have to deal with here is not corruption but a Revolution trying to realize itself, balked here, stymied there, turning this way and that, stumbling in the dark, betrayed by friends, black and white. We must also understand that some

men, black and white, were trying desperately to get the
Revolution back on the track, bogged down all the while in red
tape, ritual, finances, and petty personal controversies.

Rightly or wrongly, black leaders placed the blame for this
state of affairs on the white financial agent and the white
members of the financial board — Scott, Neagle, Parker, Chamberlain. And they resolved in the early seventies to clean house
with a black broom. Cain, who was a leader of the black reform
bloc, rained invectives on the Northern-born whites. "These
long, lank, sharp-nosed gentlemen," he said, "may prepare for
defeat.... The colored people have been sold often
enough.... We venture to say that not one of these pretending
scamps will ever go to misrepresent them again." Samuel J.
Lee, the self-educated sawmill worker who had made himself
one of the most feared criminal lawyers in the state, sounded
the same theme. "We, as a people," he said, "are blameless of
misgovernment. It is owing to bad men, adventurers, persons
who, after having reaped millions almost from our party, turn
traitors and stab us in the dark. Ingratitude is the worst of
crimes, and yet the men we have fostered, the men we have
elevated and made rich, now speak of our corruption and
venality, and charge us with every conceivable crime."

Disappointed by their Northern-born friends, black politicians made the profound, but intelligible, mistake of shifting in
1872 from Scott, the Northern-born white, to Franklin J.
Moses Jr., the charming Southern-born white who was liked by
everybody and trusted by nobody. Moses, who had evolved
from a racist into a self-proclaimed social revolutionary, was
worth anybody's study. The son of a well-to-do lawyer, he had
married the daughter of another well-to-do lawyer and had
served the old aristocracy in various posts. It was Moses who
pulled down the U.S. flag at Fort Sumter, and it was Moses
who championed a more sophisticated form of white
supremacy as the postwar editor of the *Sumter News*. While
serving in this post, Moses went through a remarkable conver-

sion and began to champion the cause of the freedmen. Fired by his outraged superiors, he nimbly leaped to the side of the Republicans and was elected to the constitutional convention and the house where he served as the first speaker.

In his life and in his career, Moses embodied the deterioration of an aristocratic elite which had been doomed by history. Lacking moorings in the present and hope for the future, members and hangers-on of this class drank deep of the draughts of nihilism, turning away from reality and seeking solace in the medieval horse tournaments which were popular in the postwar period. The old aristocrats and their professional retainers refused to face reality, because reality had made them obsolete. Eschewing a real partnership with the black and white masses, they saw only a forced choice between what they considered two different kinds of humiliation — domination by black people or domination by Northern whites. Most of Frank Moses' old friends refused to choose and pretended that they were King Arthur and his knights. Moses, who was more sensitive than his contemporaries and probably more despairing, made his choice immediately, plunging into the heart of a revolution he didn't feel, abandoning his white wife and pretending that he was a Negro. Declassé, deracinated, anchorless, Moses came out for instant integration and gave himself completely to the image of the black women which had long dominated the fantasy life of the old aristocrats. Moses' transformation, however, was not complete. Like his old friends, he was evading reality, not confronting it. And it is no surprise to learn that he later became a dope addict, drifting across the North in a self-destructive flight from reality.

But all this was far in the future when Moses, charming and extremely able, was nominated for governor of his native state by men who were impressed by the fact that he at least lived the transformation of color that almost all of their white colleagues merely mouthed. Richard H. Gleaves, a suave black businessman from Pennsylvania, became Moses' running mate;

and Cardozo was slated for the crucially important post of treasurer. Henry E. Hayne, a former sergeant in the famous First South Regiment, was named to succeed Cardozo as secretary of state and Robert E. Purvis, the well-to-do son of a famous abolitionist, was nominated for adjutant general.

A large group of Republicans, including Cain, Whipper, Smalls and DeLarge, withdrew from the convention and nominated an Independent Republican slate headed by Reuben Tomlinson, a Quaker from Pennsylvania, and James W. Hayne, a talented black legislator from Barnwell County. Tomlinson, colorless and dour, was no match for the magnetic Moses and the formidable Republican machine, which won by more than thirty-three thousand votes.

This election was an excellent barometer of the mood of black voters who clung to the regular Republican machine throughout Reconstruction despite well-financed efforts to confuse and mystify them.

With rare sophistication, black voters perceived that the conservatives were more interested in white supremacy than in reform. Though disheartened and discouraged by fraud and corruption, they refused, as Cardozo told a *New York Times* reporter, to vote for "concord and harmony, if concord and harmony meant the sacrifice of political and civil rights."

Throughout this period, black voters were faced with situations in which all their options were bad. Since Democrats refused to enter into a serious dialogue and since Independent Republicans showed a disturbing tendency to collaborate with Democrats, there was no real alternative to the regular Republican candidates. Ransier bore down hard on this point in an 1870 campaign speech, asking his audience: "Would you not prefer [Republican] legislation to the old state of things, though not perfect?" "Yes! Yes!" the black voters replied, indicating by their enthusiasm that they recognized that there was no way out of the Republican party that didn't lead into the arms of the waiting Democrats. In South Carolina, at least,

Frederick Douglass' celebrated dictum was true: The Republican party was the ship—all else was the sea.

In 1872, and in every other election year in South Carolina, black voters were almost unanimous in their support of the regular Republican party. Their cohesiveness in the 1872 election advanced Black Power to record heights in South Carolina and the South. Black men won four of the eight state cabinet offices, four of the five congressional seats and 106 of the 157 General Assembly seats. When the assembly met, Stephen A. Swails, a Union war hero and the political boss of the Williamsburg area, was elected president pro tem of the senate, and Samuel J. Lee of Aiken County became the first black speaker of the house.

Although Moses pushed integration to new heights in South Carolina, it cannot be said that he governed either wisely or well. Instead of raising the tone of government, he lowered it. Instead of focusing the energies of the government, he diffused them. Moses not only appropriated public funds for his private use; he also presented a broad and inviting target for conservatives seeking ammunition to discredit the Republicans.

It was during Moses' administration, however, that the Republicans initiated the first of several sweeping reforms which returned the Revolution to its course. In 1873, the legislature passed an act which provided for the scaling of the state debt at 50 cents on the dollar. Under this act, more than six million dollars in fraudulent bonds were repudiated and the total debt was adjusted to a reasonable seven million dollars. The legislature also decreased the number of officeholders and provided for periodic public reports by officials charged with the responsibility of handling money. During this same period, the legislature passed and sent to the people a constitutional amendment which placed a ceiling on the state debt.

Frank Moses may have been dissolute; he was certainly corrupt—but nobody could say that he was dull. A lean, long-legged man with a bushy, gray-brown mustache and a flair for histrionics, he paid forty thousand dollars for the old Wade Hampton mansion, the finest house in Columbia, and gave a dazzlingly lavish series of interracial receptions and balls which horrified his old friends. One of these balls was described by a hostile white witness who said: "The colored band was playing 'Rally Round the Flag'. . . . There was a mixture of white and black, male and female. Supper was announced, and you ought to have seen the scrambling for the table. Social equality was at its highest pitch. . . . "

Moses also scandalized aristocrats by doing in public what they had been doing in private. The native-born white governor of South Carolina drove around the capital city, aristocrats charged, in his "handsome landau drawn by a spanking pair of Kentucky horses" in the company of four black belles "arrayed in low-neck and short sleeves, their black bosoms and arms covered with real jewels."

The cost of all this ran high. When, a few years later, Moses filed a bankruptcy petition, he revealed that his debts totalled $225,000 and that his assets amounted to only $67,000.

The cost to Radical Republicans was higher. For while Moses danced, the financial situation got worse, and wily Democrats moved in to capitalize on the situation. A convention of white taxpayers met in Columbia and arraigned the Republican regime for extravagance, corruption and inefficiency. The taxpayers sent a committee of fifteen to Washington to present a memorial to President Grant against "the monstrous oppression" and the "the unprecedented spectacle of a State in which the government is arrayed against property." The white taxpayers were disturbed by the fact that "the department of the State Government which exercises the taxing power is administered by those who own a mere fraction of the property of the State." Having described their theory of government, which rested on the premise that the owners of property should rule, the taxpayers went on to charge that the public debt had been raised in six years from five to ten million dollars and that annual appropriations had advanced from four hundred thousand dollars a year to more than two million dollars a year.

The central committee of the Union Republican party of South Carolina immediately issued a counter-memorial which said that these figures were "wholly inaccurate and untrue." In fact, said the Republicans, they were spending less on government than the prewar Democrats. Since this reply contains an excellent summary of the main issues of Reconstruction, it would be well to consider it at some length.

The Republicans began by comparing the expenditures of the Republican administration (1872-73) and the annual expenses of the last Democratic administration (1859-60) before the war. Here are the salient points:

	1859–60	1872–73
Salaries	$81,000	$94,989
Contingents	73,000	47,600
Free schools	75,000	300,000
State normal school	8,704	25,000
Deaf, dumb and blind	8,000	15,000
Military academies	30,000	–
Military contingencies	100,000	20,000
Roper hospital	3,000	–
State lunatic asylum	–	77,500
State normal and high school	5,000	–
Jurors and constables	50,000	–
State orphan house (colored)	–	20,000
State penitentiary	–	40,000
Sundries	184,427	444,787
	$618,231	$1,184,876

Remember that the appropriation of 1859-60 represents gold value.

By the census of 1860 there were in South Carolina at that time 301,214 free population and 402,406 slaves. By the census of 1870 there were 705,606 free population. Now, "remember," in the eloquent language of another, "that in 1860, 402,406 souls, now a part of our body politic, voters amenable to our laws, the cost of governing whom is now chargeable to the Government of our State, were in 1860 chattels, merchandise, with not one civil or natural right which white men were bound to respect. In 1860 the slave was no charge on the State Government, save when he was hung for some petty misdemeanor, and the State compelled to pay his loss."

It would be, therefore, but just and fair to divide the amount appropriated in 1859-60, viz. $618,231, by the then free population, 301,214, and it will be found that the cost of governing each citizen was $2.05; and then divide the amount appropriated in 1872-73 by the free population now, viz.: 705,606, and it will be found that the cost of governing each citizen is $2.05 in 1859-60, during the boasted Democratic period, and $1.67 in 1872-73, under the so-called corrupt radical rule—a difference of 38 cents per capita in favor of the latter. So that if the Democrats had the same number of free citizens to govern in 1859-60 that the Republicans had in 1872-73, it would have cost them $261,616.30 more than it cost us.

The State having been organized upon a free basis necessarily creates a larger number of offices, and, therefore, a larger amount of salaries. We are not ashamed of the fact that our appropriation for schools in 1872-73 is four times greater than in 1859-60. Ignorance was the cornerstone of slavery and essential to its perpetuity, but knowledge prevents the existence of that "sum of all villainies." Now in every hamlet and village of our State "the schoolmaster is abroad." In 1857 the number of scholars attending the free schools was only 19,356, while in 1873 the number of scholars attending the schools was 85,753 (of which 37,218 were white, 46,535 colored).

It will also be observed that there were no appropriations for the State lunatic asylum and penitentiary in 1859-60. The lunatic asylum was then supported by the friends of its wealthy inmates and the counties. But in 1872-73 this was found to impair the efficiency of the institution, and the State assumed its support and made liberal appropriations for its unfortunate patients.

The erection of the penitentiary was not begun until after the war, and there was, therefore, no appropriation for it in 1859-60.

The appropriation in 1872-73 for military purposes was but $20,000. We had no occasion to appropriate $130,000 for military academies and contingencies, in order to furnish nurseries to train the young to strike at the nation's life, and to purchase material for the War of Secession.

There was no appropriation in 1859-60 for a colored State orphan house. The colored orphans that were then uncared for were free, but their parents, when living, were heavily taxed to support white orphans, while their own children, after their death, were neglected.

As for the state debt, the Republicans said that of the $10,000,000 valid debt, five million dollars were issued by Democratic administrations and five million dollars by Republican administrations. The committee added: "But of the amount issued by the Republicans, they are only really responsible for $1,700,000, issued for the 'relief of the treasury' and the 'Land Commision.' The remaining $3,300,000 were issued to pay the past due interest on the debt that had accrued previous to [the Republicans'] ascension to power. . . ." The Republicans concluded by admitting "the existence of evil amongst them." They acknowledged "mistakes and errors in the past, which they deeply regret." But "those mistakes and errors were being corrected daily." There were "enough able and good men among them," they said, "to right every existing wrong."

At the 1874 Republican convention, reformers righted one wrong by dumping Moses for the colorless, ambivalent and yet able Daniel Henry Chamberlain. Chamberlain, whom we have met before, was a native of Massachusetts and a former lieutenant in the Fifth Massachusetts Colored Volunteers. A product of America's leading schools—Phillips Academy, Amherst, Harvard, Yale—he settled in Berkeley County after the war and served in the constitutional convention. As attorney general and as a member of the financial board and the advisory board of the Land Commission, he was partially responsible for the irregularities of the Scott administration. On one occasion, he recommended a questionable, to say the least, railroad bond plan to his old friend, the corrupt state financial agent, with the following comment: "There is a mint of money in this or I am a fool." Chamberlain later admitted that he was caught up in the get-rich fever of the white immigrant colony. "That I hoped," he said, "to make money—dreamed of thousands—there is no doubt."

After leaving the government in 1872 and entering private law practice with a conservative white Republican, Chamberlain tended to blame "Negroism" and "the ignorant assembly" for the blunders and/or crimes he and his white colleagues perpetrated. Always ambivalent on the race question, Chamberlain deeply desired the company and approbation of the "white gentlemen" of South Carolina. He was particularly pained by the walls which confined him and his pretty wife to the company of white and black people he considered his social and racial inferiors.

This was the man who presented himself to the Republican convention of 1874 as a champion of reform and the black man. Naturally, there were cries of disbelief. Robert Brown Elliott, then one of the most powerful men in the state, denounced Chamberlain as a racist and opportunist; and Whipper, Cain, and Rainey ventilated his record as "a reformer." In an impassioned speech, Chamberlain explained away his anti-Negro statements and disclaimed any connection with the irregularities of the Scott administration.

After a heated session, a compromise was reached which made Chamberlain the gubernatorial nominee and Elliott the chairman of the state Republican central committee. The slate also included Cardozo, treasurer; Gleaves, lieutenant governor; and Hayne, secretary of state.

Republican dissidents again bolted and nominated Judge T. Green, a white South Carolinian, for governor and Martin R. DeLaney for lieutenant governor. Although the Independent Republicans received the enthusiastic support of white Democrats, they were soundly defeated, but by a reduced margin—80,403 for Chamberlain and 68,818 for Green. More ominous was the sharp drop in the black representation in the General Assembly. For the first time, whites outnumbered blacks in the house, eighty to seventy-seven. Despite this fact, Elliot was elected speaker of the house, and Swails was again elected president pro tem of the senate.

Under the Chamberlain administration, the movement for reform reached new heights of fulfillment. By 1875, the abuses of the Scott and Moses administrations had been largely corrected, the debt had been scaled at a relatively modest figure, and social welfare programs had been established on a sound basis. All this, however, was accomplished at a tremendously high price; for, focusing on retrenchment, many men forgot the Revolution. More disquieting was Chamberlain's tendency to collaborate with anti-Negro forces.

Even so, the accomplishments of the Revolution were real and were rightly regarded as such by the black electorate. In education, especially, the achievements of the Republicans were of permanent value. When Radical Reconstruction began, there were thirty thousand students attending four hundred schools conducted by five hundred teachers. By 1876, there were 123,035 students attending 2,776 schools taught by 3,068 teachers, one-third of them black.

Some of these children attended integrated schools. Although the Republicans indicated a willingness to let blacks and whites feel themselves into the new order, the law was clear and specific, and some students took advantage of it, particularly in higher institutions of learning. Early in the new administration, the aristocratic University of South Carolina was reorganized under a law which opened the school to all races and provided a system of liberal scholarships. The legislature emphasized its intent by electing two black politicians to the new board of trustees. Within a short time, black men had a majority on the board. The able black lawyer, Samuel Lee, was later elected president of the board of trustees.

Perceiving the drift of things, whites urged Negroes to bypass the sacrosanct (to them) university. They even offered to barter Citadel Academy in Charleston in return for a lily-white University of South Carolina. But black people, insisting on "equal and exact justice," spurned the offer. On Tuesday, October 7, 1873, Henry E. Hayne, the black secretary of state, enrolled in the university, precipitating the resignation of three white professors. In accepting the resignations, the predominantly black board of trustees said, in effect, good riddance:

Resolved, That this board accepts the resignations of M. La Borde, M.D., A. N. Talley, M.D., and R. W. Gibbes, M.D., in the University of South Carolina; and in accepting the same this board deem it due to the public to place upon record their conviction that the resignations of these gentlemen were caused by the admission, as a student of the medical department of the University, of the Hon. Henry E. Hayne, a gentleman of irreproachable character, against whom said professors can suggest no objection except, in their opinion, his race; and recognizing this as the cause of these resignations this board cannot regret that a spirit so hostile to the welfare of our State, as well as to the dictates of justice and the claims of our common humanity, will no longer be represented in the University, which is the common property of all our citizens without distinction of race."

This was clear enough and, to racists, bad enough. Samuel Lee, the black president of the board, later dotted the i's, reporting: "In the chapel, recitation rooms, on the ball ground and in the study the lessons of equality and mutual self-respect have been inculcated."

Not long after that, several other black men, including C. M. Wilder, Joseph D. Boston, Lawrence Cain, Paris Simkins, N. T. Spencer, and Francis L. Cardozo, entered the university. A new plateau was reached in 1874 when Richard T. Greener, a graduate of Harvard, became professor of mental science.

In this same year, Republicans pressed the issue of integration at the deaf and blind school at Cedar Springs. Learning, in 1873, that the directors of the school were equipping a separate building for black students, Jillson laid down the law in a sharp letter: "The following points relative to the admission of colored pupils into this institution will be strictly and rigidly insisted upon: 1. Colored pupils must not only be admitted into the institution on application, but an earnest and faithful effort must be made to induce such pupils to apply for admission. 2. Such pupils when admitted must be domiciled in the same building, must eat at the same table, must be taught in the same classrooms and by the same teachers, and must receive the same attention, care and consideration as white pupils."

In protest, the director and faculty members resigned, thereby forcing the closing of the institution. In his annual message to the legislature, Governor Moses took note of the widening controvesy, expressing satisfaction that "the narrow spirit of bigotry and prejudice has been banished from its [the university's] portals." He was especially pleased by the hiring of a black professor, for, said he, this was an "onward stride in the march of civilization" and "the harbinger of the happy day which is coming when all class distinctions shall be forever laid in the dust of the past." As for the resignations at the deaf and blind school, Moses said: "It was hoped that even political malice would have felt some touch of pity in contemplating the victims of the most awful bereavement that Providence has visited upon humanity, and that no discrimination would have been made as to those whom God himself had reduced to the same common level of helpless calamity. . . . You will see by the action above referred to of the board of directors of the asylum for the deaf and dumb and the blind, as well as by the action of the board of trustees of the State University, that at least in South Carolina 'the chaff is being rapidly winnowed from the wheat' and that we are fast getting rid of influences prejudicial in our State institutions."

The chaff was separated from the wheat in other fields, to the benefit of black voters. By 1875, Negro land ownership was up. There had also been real advances in the material position of the Negro masses. Although most Negroes still worked from dawn to dusk only to end up at "settlin' time" owing "the man," the tide was changing. Black people were still down, but they were rising and they knew it—and white people knew it.

Above all else, black people were political persons. No public place was barred to them; no public position was beyond their reach.

Black men in blue were directing traffic and arresting criminals who were tried, more often than not, before predominantly black juries and black magistrates. There were black mayors, black directors of railroads, and black presidents of oil companies.

Did one want a birth certificate? It was necessary to see a black man. Was there trouble in the schools? It was necessary to see the predominantly black school commission. Perhaps the problem was a death certificate. The man to see was black. Did one have business with the post office? The clerks were often black and so, oftentimes, were the men in charge like postmaster C. M. Wilder of Columbia and Postmaster Benjamin A. Boseman of Charleston.

It could not be escaped in those days—the power of blackness.

It certainly could not be escaped in Columbia, the political nerve center of what some visitors called the Black Commonwealth. It was hard for visitors to this small town (population: 12,000) of broad open streets and fine shady residences to miss the new beat and color of history. Most of the voters in Columbia were black and their representatives were the dominant force in the life of the community. The policemen and market men were black. So were most of the officials at city hall and the Richland County courthouse. An 1873 visitor was told that "everybody in office was a darky."

How was Columbia faring under the blacks?

The blackened ruins of war were still conspicuous, but the city hummed with new life and purpose. By 1873, Main Street, the commercial center, had been rebuilt to a considerable extent, and new buildings—warehouses and an opera house— were going up on surrounding streets.

Farther to the east, there was unusual ferment at three institutions which linked Columbia to the dominant forces of the age. There was, first of all, the U.S. barracks on the outskirts of town. Though garrisoned by a token force, the U.S. camp was a concrete contradiction of the old regime and all Columbians looked to it, some with fear, some with contempt, some with hope. At sunset, the broad, tree-shaded avenues of Columbia were thronged with carriages whose owners were driving to the parade ground of the barracks to watch the troops drill. On these occasions, there was indiscriminate mixing, and the military band often saluted South Carolina with "John Brown's Body."

Near the parade grounds were the buildings of the state university which accommodated black and white students from all over the state. And two blocks away was the Italian Renaissance capitol which stood on an eminence, dominating the whole scene. This three-story building, with its porticoes supported by fluted Corinthian columns, had been built laboriously over a period of years by black slaves, and it was virtually controlled in this period by the descendants of its makers. On official days, black people thronged the capitol grounds and the entrance ways. On the first floor were the offices of the governor, treasurer, secretary of state, and superintendent of schools; and these offices, visitor Edward King noted, were "usually filled with colored people discussing the issues of the hour."

On the second floor were the chambers of the supreme court (which consisted of the classic trio, a Southern-born white, a Northern-born white, and a Negro), and the spacious and commodious chambers of the state senate and house of representatives. A broad entrance hall, "resounding with echoes at every footfall," separated the senate, which had a small white majority, from the house, which was overwhelmingly black in 1873.

No trip to South Carolina was complete without a visit to the General Assembly. The density and weight of blackness in this assembly overwhelmed both friendly and hostile critics. Viewing the assembly in 1870, Robert Somers said it was "a Proletariat Parliament the like of which could not be produced under the widest suffrage in any part of the world save in some of these Southern states."

What one could see from the galleries of the house was so unusual that some conservatives fled the building in hysterical fits of anger. On the dais, presiding, was a black man (Samuel J. Lee in 1873) whose color contrasted strongly with the crimson plush gothic chairs. Before Speaker Lee, at banks of desks, were ninety black men and thirty-four white men. Many of the black men, a witness said, bore testimony "in their color to the natural possibility of miscegenation." Some of the representatives were dressed in fine black broadcloth; others, poorer, wore frock coats "of infirm gentility, glossy and threadbare."

Black and white, Democrat and Republican, "were sandwiched in a way," one visitor said, "that would disturb the dead bones of many of Caroline's proud sons." Black pages ran to and fro, distributing letters and documents, knocking away specks of dust and attending to the wants of the honored gentlemen. Clerks and attachés — black and white — hovered in the background, waiting the representatives' pleasure.

Crossing the broad entrance hall to the senate, one would have found a similar scene. At the president's desk sat Stephen A. Swails, a black man from Williamsburg County. He was attended by clerks and attachés. For the rest, the floor was occupied by whites and blacks, more of the former than the latter, some native South Carolinians of both races and some of both races from other states. From time to time honored guests were admitted to the floor. One visitor reported that "a fine looking quadroon, or possibly octoroon woman, and the ebony gentleman escorting her, were admitted to the floor of the Senate, and sat for some time listening to the debates." Visiting the same scene in March, 1869, Martha Schofield, a Northern schoolmarm, was seized "with strong feelings" as she sat "in that body where all men were equal before the law, where those whose race had been oppressed for two centuries, were now making laws for the oppressors." The black senators, she noted, "appear as much at ease and at home as the others."

Many observers were struck by the seriousness of purpose and the social passion of the black senators and representatives. James S. Pike, who was enraged by the spectacle of black power, was strangely impressed by what he called the Black Parliament. "It is not all sham," he wrote, "nor all burlesque. They [the black representatives] have a genuine interest and a genuine earnestness in the business of the assembly which we are bound to recognize and respect, unless we would be accounted shallow critics. They have an earnest purpose, born of a conviction that their position and condition are not fully assured, which lends a sort of dignity to their proceedings."

As the focal point of policy and politics, the General Assembly gave coherence and direction and continuity to the state. The legislators had immense power vis-à-vis the governor and they were not loath to use it. They elected judges and had a veto power over most appointments. They also had the power of inquiry and appropriation. In addition, the budget of each county had to be approved by the legislature.

Through their command of a network of strategic points in the legislature, black politicians exerted a major influence on public policy. James Pike's celebrated complaint, though exaggerated for polemical purposes, reflected the power realities at the time of his 1873 visit. "The speaker is black," he wrote, "the clerk is black, the door-keepers are black, the little pages are black, the chairman of the Ways and Means is black, and the chaplain is coal-black."

Most of the black power brokers surprised their contemporaries by the speed with which they assimilated the mechanics of parliamentary play. David R. Duncan, a conservative white senator, and other contemporaries admitted that black legislators learned rules and procedures "like a flash" and had "a wonderful aptness at legislative proceedings." By 1873, black legislators were familiar with the uses of the caucus and had learned the advantage of combination and concentration of forces. Edward King, who visited the state about this time, was impressed by the level of culture of the black delegates. "The President of the Senate," he wrote, "and the speaker of the House, both colored, were elegant and accomplished men, highly educated, who would have creditably presided over any Commonwealth's Assembly."

In the face of massive evidence to the contrary, white conservatives continued to believe that the government would fall because of the inability of black men to work the government machinery. They also told themselves that the only thing that prevented the fall of the government was the white blood in the veins of the black leaders. James Pike told South Carolinians they were living in a dream world. He urged them to wake up and prepare for a full-scale revolution. "There is a strong disposition," he wrote, "among the old whites of the State, to say and believe that it is the white blood in the Negro race which is managing affairs in the new *régime*. The pure blacks have been set so low in the scale, that it would show great want of penetration or great misrepresentation on the part of the old masters for them to admit the capacity of the black to conduct civic affairs, even as well as they are conducted here. Hence, all credit is apt to be denied them, and given to the element of white blood that courses in the veins of their lighter colored brethren. Let us look about the legislature and see how this is. The man who uniformly discharges his duties in the most unassuming manner and in the best taste is the chaplain of the House. He is coal-black. In the dignities and proprieties of his office, in what he says, and, still better, in what he omits to say, he might be profitably studied as a model by the white political parsons who so often officiate in Congress. Take the chairman of the House Committee of Ways and Means. He is another full-black man. By his position, he has charge of the most important business of the House. He was selected for his solid qualities, and he seems always to conduct himself with discretion. Two of the best speakers in the House are quite black. Their abilities are about equal. Their moral qualities differ. One appears to be honest, and the other to be a rascal. They are both leaders rather than led. Go into the Senate. It is not too much to say that the leading man of the Republican party in that body is Beverly Nash, a man wholly black. He is apparently consulted more and appealed to more, in the business of the body, than any man in it.... There is the senator from Georgetown. He boasts of being a Negro, and of having no fear of the white man in any respect. He evidently has no love for him. He is truculent and audacious, and has as much force and ability as any of the lighter-colored members of his race about him...."

Throughout the Reconstruction period, black legislators, to quote Simkins and Woody, "outnumbered, and, in many cases, outshone their carpetbag and scalawag contemporaries." One can gauge the tone and temper of their political posture from the reply of a black politician in a debate on a bill to exempt manufacturers from taxation. Addressing himself to white conservatives, he said he had "heard, or overheard, a good deal from the class of people whom this legislation was designed to benefit; that it was intended to overslaugh and crowd out the blacks by foreign immigrants, to be introduced into the State by wholesale." Now, he wanted everybody to understand that "the blacks did not intend to be crowded out," but that "they proposed to stand their ground and fight this thing out to the bitter end."

Faced with militancy backed by votes, white conservatives tended to withdraw. At the time of Pike's visit, the white conservatives were huddled together in a corner for warmth and protection. "There they sit," he wrote, "grim and silent. They feel themselves to be but loose stones, thrown in to partially obstruct a current they are powerless to resist. They say little and do little as the days go by. They simply watch the

Franklin J. Moses Jr., a
native of South Carolina,
served as governor from
1872 to 1874.

Richard H. Cain served
in the South Carolina
legislature and
U.S. Congress.

Robert K. Scott, a Union
general, was the first
Republican governor of
South Carolina.

Francis L. Cardozo, a
native of Charleston, served
as secretary of state and
treasurer.

Robert B. Elliott was
probably the most powerful
black politician in
South Carolina.

Jonathan Jasper Wright
was elected to the state
supreme court in
February, 1870.

rising tide, and mark the progressive steps of the inundation. They hold their places reluctantly. They feel themselves to be in some sort martyrs, bound stoically to suffer in behalf of that still great element in the State whose prostrate fortunes are becoming the sport of an unpitying Fate."

The leading legislators participated fully in the social life of the state. They were leading lights of the brilliant official society of Columbia where black and white men of power rode in fine carriages and attended elaborate balls and receptions in the governor's mansion. Governor Scott, one witness reported, "made no distinction among members of the legislature.... All alike crowd around his luxuriant refreshment tables, where, as his accomplished lady told me, no invidious distinctions are made."

From Columbia radiated concentric circles of black expressiveness that was reflected at every level of South Carolina society. On the county level, black men dominated Black Belt boards of supervisors. In cities like Charleston and Columbia, they exerted equal weight on the aldermanic boards and the police force. Black men also served as magistrate, probate judge, justice of the peace, constable and sheriff. On the state level, there were black majorities and black chairmen on the governing boards of the university, the lunatic asylum, and the orphan asylum. Robert Smalls and Prince R. Rivers were major generals in the National Guard. Among the leading black officeholders were:

Alonzo J. Ransier	Lieutenant Governor, 1870–72
	U.S. Congress, 1873–75
Richard H. Gleaves	Lieutenant Governor, 1872–77
Francis L. Cardozo	Secretary of State, 1868–72
	Treasurer, 1872–77
Robert B. Elliott	U.S. Congress, 1871–74
	Speaker, General Assembly, 1874–76
	Attorney General, 1876–77
J. J. Wright	Associate Justice,
	S. C. Supreme Court, 1870–77

H. E. Hayne	Secretary of State, 1872–77
Robert Purvis	Adjutant General, 1872–76
Joseph H. Rainey	U.S. Congress, 1870–79
R. H. Cain	U.S. Congress, 1873–75, 1877–79
Robert C. DeLarge	U.S. Congress, 1871–73
Robert Smalls	U.S. Congress, 1875–79
Samuel J. Lee	Speaker, S. C. Assembly, 1872–74
Stephen Swails	President Pro Tem, S. C. senate, 1872–77

If, as some people contended, South Carolina was the black man's paradise, it was not, by any stretch of the imagination, a white man's hell. Sir George Campbell, a member of the British Parliament, visited the South at the end of this period and commented: "Before I went South I certainly expected to find that the Southern States had been for a time a sort of pandemonium in which a white man could hardly live. Yet it certainly was not so.... When I went to South Carolina I thought there at least I must find great social disturbances; and in South Carolina I went to the county of Beaufort, the blackest part of the State in point of population, and that in which black rule has been most complete and has lasted longest. It has the reputation of being a sort of black paradise, and *per contra*, I rather expected a sort of white hell.... To my great surprise I found exactly the contrary.... White girls go about freely and pleasantly as if no black man had ever been in power...."

Instead of crumbling under black power, the state as a whole prospered. In fact, South Carolina produced a larger proportion of America's cotton during Reconstruction than before the war. During the Republican regime, there was a sharp rise in the production of wheat and corn and a firm foundation was laid for the important textile industry. The *Charleston Daily News*, no defender of the black man, said that despite "the rapacity and tyranny [of the Republican government], South Carolina was better off than before the war."

Thus, in whole and in part, stood the Palmetto State in the sixth year of the black man's accession to power.

Black men were marrying white women and white men were marrying black women, and black and white youths were reading books in the same classrooms. They were riding in that year on the same streetcars and drinking in the same bars. God was in Heaven, the black man was in power and, despite that fact or perhaps because of it, South Carolina was thriving.

4

Democracy Comes to Mississippi

I F IT COULD HAPPEN ONCE in Mississippi, it could happen again anywhere.

If a black man could move into the governor's office and rule Mississippi as acting governor, and if two black men could go from *that* place to the U.S. Senate; if black sheriffs could dominate rich Delta counties, and if a black politician could sit in the mayor's chair in Natchez; if one Benjamin Montgomery could preempt Jefferson Davis' baronial mansion and plant cotton and entertain in *Gone With The Wind* style, and if a white state senator from Yazoo County could make social news by marrying a beautiful black teacher from Hinds; if black chancery clerks and county supervisors and superintendents of education could function in the place where Schwerner and Goodman and Chaney died, and if almost one-third of the white electorate, including some of the wealthiest white planters, could support them with their voices and votes: if all these things could happen almost one hundred years ago in the ill-starred state of Mississippi, if they could be done *there*, then, without doubt, they can be done again everywhere.

Strange as it may seem now, these things—all of them—happened in the state of Mississippi in the six-year period from 1870 to 1875. Alexander K. Davis, the black lieutenant governor, did run the state during the month-long summer vacations of Governor Adelbert Ames; Hiram Revels and Blanche Bruce did go to the U.S. Senate; Robert H. Wood did serve as mayor of Natchez; and Albert Morgan did marry Carolyn Highgate and take her home to Yazoo. These things happened in Mississippi and the world did not end and cotton did not cease to grow. It is of record that they happened. It is of record that the worst state was once close to being the best state and that twenty to thirty thousand white Mississippi voters actively supported a political program that most white voters would not support in New York City and Chicago today.

How explain all this?

The explanation is simple: *Power.*

Power simplifies many things.

It was so, as we have seen, in South Carolina; it was so also in Mississippi where, during the period under discussion, black people constituted 53 per cent of the population (444,000 Negroes, 382,000 whites) and had a statewide voting majority of from twenty to thirty thousand. Black voters had large majorities in thirty-three of the sixty-one counties. They constituted 91.7 per cent of the population in Tunica, 86.2 per cent in Washington, 82.2 per cent in Coahoma, 78.8 per cent in Adams, and 77.6 per cent in Sharkey.

Power simplifies, but it also individualizes, imposing its own requirements according to the network of relations in which it is exercised. By this we must understand that there are majorities and then there are *majorities*, and that it is necessary to know how to do more than count in order to make power real. We can see this distinctly in Mississippi where black people encountered formidable problems in translating their numerical strength into the manna of politics: bread, land, clothes, housing, money, and space for the heart.

Unlike South Carolina, which was relatively civilized (for white people) when black people came to power, Mississippi was a barbarous, sparsely settled frontier state which presented immense problems in communications and political organization. There were no cities in the state then and only a half-dozen towns of any size. Jackson, the capital, was "a good-sized village of five or six thousand," and Vicksburg, the largest town in the state, was a violent trading center of about fifteen thousand. Travel was uncertain, and social relations were primitive. Then, as now, Mississippi was a violent place where knifings, beatings, and shootings occurred daily, and women appeared on the streets at the risk of insult or worse.

Then, as now, the black population was concentrated in the large towns and the Black Belt counties in the Delta, a fan-shaped region of fertile soil which covered the western edge of the state from Memphis in the north to New Orleans in the south. The black people of Mississippi had several characteristics that, in some respects, set them apart from their countrymen in other states. Slavery was harsh everywhere, but in Mississippi it was a man-made inferno. In the huge concentration camp-like Delta plantations, black people were seared from sole to soul and, of course, they carried the scars of slavery — illiteracy, poverty, social vagueness — into the tense Reconstruction struggle.

Unlike South Carolina, Mississippi had few (less than a thousand) free Negroes. This meant, of course, that there were fewer trained black leaders in Mississippi at the beginning of Reconstruction. Still another element that made an immense difference in the development of Reconstruction in Mississippi was land. The freedmen of Mississippi, unlike the freedmen of South Carolina, were effectively denied access to land. Realizing that land was the major issue, the old planters moved swiftly, after Appomattox, entering into agreements to keep black people from buying land. They even attempted to write into law a provision making it illegal for freedmen to buy or rent land outside incorporated areas. If life was hard for the freedmen, it was little better for the poor whites who lived in the Tennessee Hills in the northeast and the piney woods of the southeast.

The old planters of Mississippi were wise in their generation. Playing a double game, appealing on the one hand to black people and subtly inflaming the fears of poor whites on the other, the planters succeeded for a spell in controlling both. As soon as Congress enfranchised the freedmen, the planters moved to the offensive, making a verbal commitment to the Fourteenth and Fifteenth Amendments and proposing a coalition between black people and "old citizens, *gentlemen* whom they had known all their lives." To a very great extent, this was open fraud. Most of the planters had no intention of supporting a political program that would ease the plight of black people and poor whites. Their strategy was to bow to the inevitable, join the Revolution, and control it. As former governor Albert G. Brown put it: "We cannot afford to be illiberal."

In addition to the Democrats in Republican clothes, there were many white radicals who sincerely supported the Republican economic program and a not inconsiderable number who accepted, with some reservations, the Republican racial program. What distinguished Reconstruction in Mississippi, above all, is the fact that a large number of wealthy native whites entered the Republican ranks. Among the white defenders of the new order were James L. Alcorn, a prewar slaveholder and former Confederate general who owned twelve thousand acres in Coahoma County; Reuben W. Millsaps, wealthy merchant and financier whose name graces one of Mississippi's finest colleges; and R. W. Flournoy, a fiery radical and fervent integrationist who had been one of the largest planters and slaveholders in northeast Mississippi. In all, some twenty thousand Mississippi whites actively supported the Republican program. At least one-third of the Republican congressmen, two of the three supreme court justices, one of the two governors, thirteen of the fifteen circuit court judges and one-third or more of the members of the General Assembly were old residents of the state.

One final element in the unique Mississippi equation requires emphasis. In Mississippi, many federal military officers openly backed the planters. During the crucial formative phase, the Mississippi area was under the command of General Alvin C. Gillem, a Democrat and Southerner who gave black people little protection and sanctioned brutal suppression of black demonstrations for "forty acres and a mule." Even worse, some Gillem subordinates organized and supported anti-Negro Democratic organizations and, in one instance, helped Ku Klux Klan terrorists to escape.

If all this seems confusing to the reader, consider the plight of Mississippi voters who beheld, as the curtain rose on Reconstruction, a bewildering panorama of old slaveholders damning Jefferson Davis and preaching integration and Union soldiers damning Ulysses S. Grant and calling for black subordination.

Because of the hostility of Gillem and Union soldiers (who offered only minimum protection) and the skill of the planters (who adroitly combined the use of terror, gentle persuasion, and intimidation) and the ineptness of Republicans (who failed to organize Negroes), Reconstruction was delayed in Mississippi for two years. In 1868, when most Southern states re-entered the Union, Mississippi opted for continued military occupation by decisively defeating the new constitution in a canvass punctuated by widespread violence and fraud. The white strategy at this point was to accept military occupation under the popular and pliable General Gillem and wait for the election of a Democratic President in the fall of 1868. The election of Republican U. S. Grant dashed that hope. Worse, Grant immediately replaced Gillem with Adelbert Ames, a crusading Union general who began to turn white supremacists out of office and enforce the letter and spirit of the Reconstruction acts.

Nerve center of Radical Reconstruction regime in
Mississippi was the slave-built Capitol in Jackson.
So-called Black and Tan Reconstruction convention met
in the building in 1868.

OLD CAPITOL

Begun in 1833. Here Henry
Clay, Andrew Jackson, and
Jefferson Davis spoke. Was
scene of 1861 Secession
Convention. Black and Tan
Convention of 1868, & 1890
Constitutional Convention.

James L. Alcorn, a wealthy
planter, was the first
Republican governor of
Mississippi.

Hiram R. Revels became
the first black U.S. senator
in 1870.

John R. Lynch, speaker of
the Mississippi house and
a U.S. congressman.

Within a short time, the diehard rebels were routed and
Congress sanctioned the resubmission of the constitution to the
electorate but authorized a separate vote on a controversial
section which barred Confederates and Confederate sympa-
thizers from office. Faced with a determined Congress and a
determined occupation force, Mississippi's monolithic white
front cracked. Diehard irreconcilables urged continued resistance, but the bulk of the new power structure—old planters,
the major newspaper editors, the major commercialists—
counselled submission. Joining in a policy of opportunism,
these disparate groups abandoned the name Democrat, organized the National Constitutional Union Republican party, and
nominated Lewis A. Dent, a brother-in-law of General Grant,
for governor. Dent was an absentee operator of a Delta plantation, but his connection with the state was tenuous (he was then
living in the White House). This didn't faze the frenetic
Democrat-Republicans, who also nominated a black man,
Thomas Sinclair, for secretary of state. It is a point of immense
and ironic significance that the first black man nominated for
state office in Mississippi was nominated by never-say-die white
supremacists. There was method in this seeming madness. By
nominating a black man, the Democrat-Republicans hoped to
fragment the black vote. By nominating Dent, a Northern non-
resident, the white power structure hoped to win the support
of President Grant and split the white Republican vote. Both
strategies failed. President Grant quickly repudiated the
Democrat-Republican party, and black people expressed open
contempt for Sinclair, a servile and obscure black man who was
a puppet on the string of the planters.

To counter the Democrat-Republican thrust, Republicans
nominated James L. Alcorn for governor and slated a black
man, James D. Lynch, for secretary of state. Republicans completed their ticket by dividing the remaining state officers
between white newcomers and old residents and by nominating
a substantial number of black men for the legislature.

"The spectacle presented by the two tickets," John S. McNeily, a conservative white historian, said, "was a peculiar one. In a supreme struggle against a party composed of Negro voters and led by Northern adventurers, the white people had for the head of their ticket, a Northerner who was not even a bona fide resident of the state. With an undying repugnance to the recognition of the Negro as a voter they were pledged to vote a Negro into a high state office. The inconsistency of such a ticket was matched by having at the head of the one which had for its cardinal principle, Negro political equality, a large and typical slaveholder—one of the haughtiest of the class."

The Republican ticket was not, as McNeily said, led by Northern adventurers. Balanced with old residents, white newcomers, former Confederates, former Union soldiers, free Negroes and former slaves, the Republican ticket had an obvious and broad appeal. The candidate for attorney general was Joshua S. Morris, a Roman Catholic and a Confederate veteran from Port Gibson. Another old slaveowner, William H. Vasser, was the candidate for treasurer. James Lynch, the nominee for secretary of state, was a brilliant example of the emerging black directorate. Lynch had been born free in Baltimore in 1839 and had graduated from Kimball University in Hanover, New Hampshire. An indefatigable traveler and organizer, bold, able and aggressive, he came to Mississippi in 1868 after helping to found Republican organizations in South Carolina and Georgia. As a Methodist Episcopal missionary and as an aggressive champion of a radical Reconstruction program, Lynch helped Mississippi Republicans overcome the backwashes of the 1868 debacle. By 1870, he was the most popular black man in the state and the best Republican stump speaker, black or white. Even Democrats respected this slender, fiery politician with the massive head and the direct, no-nonsense approach. A Democratic paper said he was "the most popular carpet-bagger in the State—the best educated man, and the best speaker, and the most effective orator, of that party, in Mississippi; and, withal, as much a gentleman as he can be with his present white associations."

Equally formidable was gubernatorial nominee James Lusk Alcorn. In some respects, Alcorn was the most imaginative white Southerner of his class. Thick-necked, barrel-chested, pugnacious, looking for all the world like the eagle for whom his Eagle's Nest plantation had been named, Alcorn, then fifty-four, had grave limitations as a man (arrogance, pettiness) and politician (inflexibility, impulsiveness) but he saw vividly that security was no longer available to the planters on their own terms. "The terrible necessities of our position," he told his old friends, "demand blunt speaking.... The old master, gentlemen, has passed from fact to poetry!"

Unquestionably; but who was to take the old master's place? That was the question, and Alcorn couldn't or wouldn't face it. His plan, in essence, was a very sophisticated (for the time and place) form of graduated tokenism. Since there was no escape, he proposed "to vote with the Negro, discuss politics with him, sit, if need be, in council with him, and form a platform acceptable to both...." The key words here are "if need be." Alcorn didn't suffer integrationists gladly, but he was prepared to suffer them, if need be, in order to control the Republican party of Mississippi for conservative policies.

What made this all the more remarkable was Alcorn's background. A lawyer and businessman with a baronial plantation at Friar's Point on the Mississippi, Alcorn was an old resident of the state. He had been born in 1816 in Illinois, but he had spent most of his life in Kentucky, where he was reared, and Mississippi, where he made his fortune. When the war came, he opposed secession but grudgingly went along with his state, serving as a brigadier general in the Confederate Army. After a bitter dispute with his old enemy, Jefferson Davis, he left the Confederate Army and spent the last years of the war tending his cotton. He was not an original reconstructionist. His friend and political associate, Joshua Morris, said: "He wanted that cup to pass from us. And so did I until the measure was adopted by Congress." With the passage of the Reconstruction acts, Alcorn bowed to the inevitable, but he bowed, as Morris indicated, in the spirit of the game cock in Daniel Defoe's fable. "When he was among the horses in the stable and there was no way for him to get out," Morris explained, "he looked up and said to the horses, 'Gentlemen, let us not step on each other's toes.'"

It might, in the end, be said of Alcorn that he was, in some respects, the Booker T. Washington of the planters. Alcorn, like Washington, accepted what he couldn't change; unlike Washington, however, he accepted in order to dominate and control. He accepted the *principle* of equality in order to moderate the *practice* of equality. In fine, Alcorn was riding two horses, a difficult feat at best, impossible when the horses are going in different directions.

Remarkably, the balancing act worked for a time. With Alcorn out front, dazzling Democrats and Republicans with his foot-in-both camps posture, the Republicans organized an exceedingly effective campaign. We catch a glimpse of this campaign and of the electioneering of the whole Reconstruction era in a contemporary description by Albert T. Morgan, a young white newcomer who was running for the state senate on the Alcorn ticket in the predominantly black county of Yazoo. Morgan was nominated at an integrated county convention which also selected an integrated slate of officers, half of whom were native white Mississippians.

Yazoo County Democrats very wisely abandoned the name Democrat and nominated a Conservative National Republican ticket headed by Major W. D. Gibbs, a scion of one of the state's most aristocratic white families. For reasons of strategy, the Democrats also nominated two black men, including Reuben Pope. Pope was, Morgan said, a "white folks' nigger" who was nominated in the hope of dividing the freedmen. The end had always justified the means in the planter's vocabulary, he added, and although Pope "was a very bitter pill, considering the end to be gained, they could swallow him." They could even wrap Pope up "in the grand old flag and swallow the whole bundle." But in this, Morgan wrote, the old aristocrats exhibited "the same lack of correct knowledge of the *free* Negro's character as formerly they had done; for, while they reasoned that the freed people lacked discernment to enable them to see the hand of Esau in this arrangement, the fact was that the colored people knew old master so well they were on the lookout for just such tricks. The only feature of this trick that appeared to surprise them in the least was the old flag sugar-coating. The 'black folks' for so long had been witnesses of 'old mars'' contempt for the flag, that it had not occurred to them as within the range of possible events that the 'white folks' could so far deceive themselves as to suppose for a moment that its use for such a purpose would be accepted by anyone as evidence of real change of heart on the part of their former masters."

Reuben Pope and the flag failing, the Democrats challenged Morgan to a debate which was held at Dover Crossroads in the southern part of the county. Under arrangements previously agreed upon, Major Gibbs, who had a large plantation nearby, opened the discussion and was followed by his opponent, Albert T. Morgan, late colonel in the U.S. Army.

The audience on this day consisted of about five hundred black people — men, women, and children — and forty or fifty white men assembled in an open space in front of "the Crossroads white folks' church, from the front of which was [the] speaker's stand."

Politics was a serious business in this day and serious politicians came to political meetings ready to shoot as well as to shout. Running his eyes over the crowd, Morgan satisfied himself that many of the men — black and white — were armed. This was conspicuously obvious in the case of a raucous and mean-looking group of white men who had collected in front of the corner store across the street.

The major, handsome and self-possessed, began his speech by saying: "My colored feller citizens and friends." Having unintentionally informed his black auditors that they were not his friends, whatever their status as public persons, the major addressed himself almost exclusively to the "colored feller citizens." His "tone and manner," Morgan wrote, "were as gentle and persuasive as a turtle-dove's, but notwithstanding that, before he was half way through, considerable numbers of the colored folks had strayed off to the woods nearby or to the corner store over the way."

Nevertheless, the major's speech was not without interest. He told the black people that they knew him, knew his family, knew what he stood for. He was no stranger to them. Nor were they strangers to him. He could "appreciate their situation, their poverty, their distress." If they would only "t'ar them-selves away from their false leaders" and trust him, he could and would do a "heap more" for them than any stranger could.

Major Gibbs deplored the mean and despicable emotions that led some people, mostly Yankees, to look down on other people because of their color. Nobody "but Yankees had prejudice against the freed people on account of their color." Why even Fred Douglas, "the greatest black man that ever lived, and the man who made the radical party, had only a few days before been refused a seat at the table in a hotel up North, the same place where Colonel Morgan, their god, came from." Why, "they even hung colored folks to lamp-posts up North," up there "where Horace Greeley, the worst abolitionist that ever was, lived and published a newspaper—even in Massachusetts, where all the abolitionists came from, a state represented in Congress by a man who believed white men ought to marry nigros—the colored ladies, even in Massachusetts there was heap mo' prejudice and hard feelings against colored folks than in the South." He went on to say that he had no prejudice.

"No true Southerner had any prejudice against the color which God gave the nigros, and which they could no more help than they could fly." They "all knew his black mammy, Aunt Sally." Why! she had suckled him, and "he loved her to that day as much as his own dear mother, almost."

The major said, with much truth, that the Yankees weren't interested in black people. They never would have gone to war but for the tariff. All the Yankees wanted to do was to make "we all Southerners" pay them "a bonus for making the machinery and goods which the South was compelled to have from the North." Now, he continued, looking no doubt at Morgan, "they are paying these carpet-baggers to work on you all agin us." And, he added ominously, "it'll get yo' all into trouble, sho."

He urged the black voters to stand by the white men they had known all their lives, and boasted, somewhat contradictorily, that a majority of the men on his ticket were from the North — "the same place yo' god, Mawgin, come from" and were "just as good friends of the nig — of the colored people" as Colonel Morgan. He was pleased that his ticket included a black man — "a plain, honest, hard-working man like themselves." And, of course, they all knew "Reuben — Mr. — Mr. Pope." It was hard, Morgan commented, "for the major to say Mr. in that presence and in that connection, but he did."

Turning now to the opposition ticket, the major denounced it as a collection of adventurers and agitators — men who had no property and few qualifications. As for General Alcorn, why everyone knew that he had been one of the cruellest slave-owners in the South — "so cruel and inhuman that he had once punished a slave by castrating him." On the other hand, their candidate was *General Grant's own dear brother-in-law.*

In reply, Colonel Morgan said that although he hadn't lived in Yazoo as long as his opponent he was "tolerably well known" and he hoped they would know him better "after a while." He didn't want to make a long speech — he didn't want to weary them with a long recital "of what the major's party had done for the colored people," but he did want to show them what it had done for the white people of the state.

Speaking directly to the poor whites in the audience, he reminded them that they had "never had free schools, nor but few of any kind," that "the great slave lords" had appropriated all the benefits of the old system. They had even exempted owners of twenty or more slaves from conscription and had provided their conscript officers with blood hounds to be used in hunting down the poor whites who refused to be conscripted, and who ran away rather than fight for the protection of the slave-holder's right to own twenty or more Negroes. The major and his party would have to be judged by the record. In the light of that record, he begged them to "consider whether it would be possible for me or for my party to do worse."

Morgan admitted that Northern whites were biased. Northern prejudice was due, he said, to ignorance and the mystifications of Southern slaveowners. He hoped all that was over now and that there would be no prejudice anywhere against color.

Taking up another issue raised by the major, Morgan said that although Alcorn had been a large slaveowner, "he had long ago repented of that folly, and in proof of his sincerity had been for years standing squarely upon our platform, and that not only he but his former slaves and his neighbors all denied the charges of inhumanity which were now, for the first time, brought against him."

Morgan was surprised to hear the major praise Reuben Pope. Why, only two years before, the major's party had refused to vote at all because Reuben Pope and his people had been allowed the same privilege. He presumed there were many in the audience who had heard many of the major's party associates swear that they would die before they would go to the polls and "vote with a nigger." And now, this same party was "not only willing to vote alongside colored people, but also to vote for one; not only that, but actually favoring the constitution they had all the while been denouncing as a 'monstrosity,' a 'bundle of enormities'; not only that, they were now anxious to have for their governor the brother-in-law of the man they had unanimously all the while denounced as a butcher and as a tyrant, solely because he was the relative of President Grant." Morgan said his listeners would have to judge themselves of the true character of the Democrats' conversion.

This brought a chorus of approving amens from the black voters who had increased in number and were pressing close to the speaking stand.

To the evident approval of the new voters, Morgan denounced the contradictions in the major's speech and challenged the major to find any such inconsistencies in the record of his party. A voice from the crowd yelled: "Yo' don't own no land."

"Do all your candidates own land?" Morgan replied.

It was readily agreed that Reuben Pope didn't, and Morgan charged that a large number of the major white Democrats owned no land in the state. Challenged, he produced documents and read from the sworn statement of Major Gibbs, "made before a registrar in bankruptcy, that the only property he owned or controlled was a horse, saddle and bridle, saddle-bags, double-barrelled shot-gun, and a navy Colt's revolver!" This announcement, Morgan said, "authenticated by the seal of the court, produced a decided sensation, for my opponent resided upon a large and valuable plantation, which, however, shortly before going into bankruptcy, by some 'hocus pocus' had become the property of his wife; in name."

At this point, a white man, "half-witted or half-drunken," detached himself from the crowd in front of the store and elbowed his way "violently through the mass" until he reached a point directly in front of the platform. Having reached this point, he ordered the black people to curse Morgan.

"Tell 'im he's — hic-a-hic — liar; God damn him."

Morgan and the black people ignored the white man who continued to shout.

"Tell 'im he's a liar. God damn him."

When a black man asked the white man to keep still, the white man wheeled and shouted:

"You're a damned lyin' son of a bitch."

The black man made a motion as if to take the white man's arm and a white man in front of the store whipped out a pistol and fired. A group of black men drew pistols and fired back. There were, in all, ten to thirty shots. When the smoke cleared, the white man who fired the first shot was dead and one black man was seriously injured.

Under the circumstances, Morgan and his opponent agreed that it would be unwise to continue the dialogue, and the crowd dispersed. By nightfall, it was known throughout the county that black men and white men had tangled and that "the 'niggers' did not run, either." The leading white men, Morgan said, asked the sheriff to employ extra deputies to put down "the insurrection" and pledged the aid of "every good Democrat" if only he would "protect them against the nigros" who, it was feared, "having once tasted the sweets of self-preservation, would fly into all sorts of license unrestrained."

But the "insurrection" was over. The point had been made, and the election in Yazoo was orderly, quiet, and fair. The local and state Republican tickets were elected by overwhelming majorities.

The balloting in Yazoo County reflected a statewide trend. The Republicans defeated the Conservative-Democratic coalition 76,000 to 38,000 and carried the new constitution 113,000 to 900, but the Confederate disfranchisement clause was defeated. This was not, by any means, a purely Negro victory. An astonishingly large number of whites voted for the Republican slate which carried fifteen counties with white majorities. Despite that fact, white irreconcilables warned African-Americans that they were about to commit a "fearful crime against themselves and the superior race on which they depend for all that is valuable in life." To forestall "a crime against civilization," Democrats called for a day of prayer to God who, they said, had permitted Mississippi to become "an African province" and their children "to be held in Negro subjection" because of the sins of Mississippi whites.

If Mississippi was an African province, it was news to the native white governor, the native white attorney general, the native white treasurer, and the large number of native whites, including thirty Democrats, who were elected to the new legislature. It was obvious from the make-up of this legislature that the predominantly black electorate hadn't come to full consciousness of its position and power. Although African-Americans had massive majorities in thirty-three of the sixty-one counties, they were grossly underrepresented in the new legislature where they constituted less than two-sevenths of the total and less than three-eighths of the Republican caucus. Of the 33 senators (26 Republican), only five (three of them ministers) were black. Only 31 of the 82 Republicans in the 107-member house were black. But we must view these figures in perspective. Some of the richest Delta counties were represented by black representatives and senators, and the formidable Warren (Vicksburg), Adams (Natchez) and Washington (Greenville) County machines gave notice of things to come by sending all-black delegations. Equally significant was the fact that J. M. Wilson, a black representative, was elected from the white Democratic county of Marion.

Among the powerful voices in the Mississippi house during this period were John Roy Lynch, a youngish photographer from Natchez; Alexander K. Davis, a lawyer from Noxubee County; and Aaron Moore, a powerful Methodist minister and political leader in the Meridian area. In the senate were men like Hiram Revels, the conservative but able AME minister from Natchez; Charles Caldwell, the fearless former black-smith from Clinton; Robert Gleed, a well-to-do merchant from Columbus; and William Gray, a young Baptist minister from

Greenville and a fiery civil rights advocate who would soon be brigadier general of the Mississippi National Guard.

When, on January 11, 1870, the black senators and representatives sat down in the dilapidated old capitol in Jackson with the white newcomers and the white natives, an age died in Mississippi. Nothing indicates this more clearly than the speed with which the new representatives endorsed the Fourteenth and Fifteenth Amendments, two prerequisites for readmission to the Union. The vote for the Fourteenth Amendment was twenty-three to two in the senate and seventy-six to six in the house. The Fifteenth Amendment was endorsed unanimously in the senate and only one person voted against it in the house. These figures are striking, for there were thirty white Democrats in the assembly and an even larger number of native white Republicans.

Even more striking was what happened next. It was necessary for the legislature to fill two long-term U.S. Senate vacancies and to designate a person to complete the unexpired Senate term of Jefferson Davis, former president of the Confederacy. The Republican caucus decided with little difficulty to elect Adelbert Ames, the Union military commander, and Governor Alcorn to the long-term vacancies. The real contest came on the short term, which black Republicans demanded for a black man. Everybody's first choice, it seems, was James Lynch, the newly elected secretary of state. But Lynch's name was quickly scratched, for his election to the Senate would have required a new, expensive, and uncertain state election for secretary of state. After no little trouble, the caucus finally decided on Hiram Revels, an eloquent Methodist Episcopal minister from Natchez. Revels was born on September 27, 1827, in Fayetteville, North Carolina. Like many free Negroes of that period, he spent a period of forced exile in the free states, attending a Quaker seminary in Indiana and graduating from Knox College in Bloomington, Illinois. He then pastored churches in the Midwest and in the Border States and helped to organize a regiment of black Union soldiers. Once the victory was won, he returned to the South, settling in Natchez as a presiding elder of the Methodist Episcopal Church. It was here that he began his rise to fame and power, winning election to the Natchez City Council.

Heavy of frame, somewhat corpulent, with a protruding paunch, Revels was served by exceptional histrionic gifts and a striking presence. On the deficit side, it ought to be said that he was the very essence of the responsible Negro. In plain English, he was a timid, cautious, and conventional black man who later became an apologist for conservative Democrats.

Revels was conservative, but he was also lucky. He was elected to the state senate as a compromise candidate after a county convention deadlock between the two dominant factions of the Warren machine. On the first day of the session, Revels electrified the senate with a stirring prayer that made him a U.S. senator. When the black Republican caucus ran out of names, someone suggested the parson who had given the memorable invocation. This was perhaps a novel reason for electing a man to the U.S. Senate — but many have been elected for worse reasons. Thus it was that on January 20, 1870, the General Assembly of the state of Mississippi elected Hiram Rhodes Revels, then forty-two, to the U.S. Senate.

The election of a black man to fill the old Senate seat of Jefferson Davis appealed powerfully to the popular imagination, and Revels became an overnight sensation. The *Memphis Daily Avalanche* commented: "Seven cities contended for the honor of Homer's birth. How many will struggle for Revels' is yet a question. A week ago 5,000 people had never heard his name or if heard, it was only to be forgotten. Now it will be the subject of 500 "leaders" and when Revels reaches Washington the reporters of all the great journals will interview him. Happy Revels. He is of popular manners and speaks with great ease, fluency, and generally in good taste. In his intercourse with all classes he conducts himself with a decorousness that has won for him the regard of all his neighbors at home and of the members of the Mississippi senate of which he is now a member."

Some Democrats scoffed, calling Revels "a thousand dollar darky." To which a celebrated Northern correspondent replied: "I see in him a three thousand million Darky. I hear in his voice the thunders of Donelson, and Shiloh, and Vicksburg, and Gettysburg, and in his footsteps the tread of mightier armies than Napoleon marshalled for the conquest of Europe. The election of Revels is the net proceeds of war and bloodshed. He represents the assets and liabilities of the four years' struggle. He is the first fruits of Union and victory, whereof we have heard so much." Senator Simon Cameron of Pennsylvania added to the drama of the occasion by recalling that he had told Jefferson Davis on his departure from Washington in 1861: "I believe, in the justice of God, that a Negro some day will come and occupy your seat." Cameron said he was happy that the prophecy had come true. There were similar expressions of approval from other Republicans who nevertheless doubted that the Senate would seat Revels.

Modest and unassuming, Revels ignored the swirling national debate and entrained for Washington where he was lionized by blacks and whites. Washington's wealthy black elite, led by Dr. Charles Purvis and businessman George T. Downing, gave the senator-elect a royal reception at a series of lavish dinners and receptions. The climax of the Washington social season that year was an integrated party, hosted by white Radical John W. Forney, where the senator-elect received the blessings of President Grant and members of the cabinet.

When Revels presented his credentials to the Forty-first Congress on Wednesday, February 23, the galleries were filled to capacity, and the halls of the Capitol crackled with excitement. Democratic senators immediately raised objections and the debate continued for three days while Revels waited patiently in a lounge off the Senate chamber. Senator Willard Saulsbury, a Democrat from Delaware, opposed Revel's admission. He had, he said, little hope for America. He would, if possible, avert this threatened calamity; he would preserve to "our white posterity" this heritage bequeathed by noble white men to their white descendants. Revels, Saulsbury said, wasn't qualified; he didn't meet the test of citizenship. Nonsense, replied Senator Simon Cameron. Black people were citizens by a higher law—"that of having fought for and helped to save the Union." The Senate voted finally and Revels was admitted by a vote of forty-eight to eight. The people in the galleries rose as Revels walked down the aisle and was sworn in as the first black U.S. senator and the first black member of the U.S. Congress. Reporters, conscious of the weight of the moment, noted the precise time. It was 4:40 in the afternoon on Friday, February 25, 1870. Three weeks later, on Wednesday, March 16, Revels made his maiden speech, opposing the readmission of Georgia without proper safeguards for the black minority. His speech was well-received by an overflow crowd which filled every available space. "Never since the birth of the republic," the *Philadelphia Press* said, "has such an audience been assembled under one single roof. It embraced the greatest and the least American citizens."

With the seating of Revels and his white congressional colleagues and the passage of an act readmitting Mississippi to the Union on condition that it would never *never* disfranchise African-Americans, Mississippi Republican leaders turned their eyes to the task of reconciliation and Reconstruction. The range of problems bequeathed to the new regime was formidable. A new government had to be organized from top to bottom; a new code of law had to be created; a new public school system had to be organized. At that time, John R. Lynch wrote, there "was not a public school building anywhere in the State except in a few of the larger towns, and they, with possibly a few exceptions, were greatly in need of repairs. To erect the necessary school houses and to reconstruct and repair those already in existence so as to afford educational facilities for both races was by no means an easy task." It was also necessary, he said, "to reorganize, reconstruct, and, in many instances, rebuild some of the penal and charitable institutions of the State. . . . That this important work was splendidly, creditably, and economically done no fair-minded person who is familiar with the facts will question or dispute."

To make matters worse, the government was broke. When the Republicans took over the state, the treasury contained fifty dollars and the outstanding debts amounted to more than one million dollars.

In his inaugural address, on March 10, Governor Alcorn took note of these problems and urged Mississippians of all races and classes to forget the dead past. "The Northern Democracy," he said, "have overthrown the Southern Oligarchy! This is the measure of the fact accomplished by the action of the United States. . . ." The "muse of history," he added, "closes today a chapter of passion, bloodshed, and social revolution, and proceeds to write down the facts of this inauguration as the first event of a new chapter—a chapter which with her pen of light she heads by halcyon words of peace and hope." He was pleased by the support of the black people of Mississippi. "From me individually," he added, "the colored people of Mississippi have every reason to look with a profound anxiety for the realization of their new rights. In the face of memories that might have separated them from me as the wronged from the wronger, they offered me the guardianship of their new and precious hopes, in a trustfulness whose very mention stirs my nerves with emotion. In response to that touching reliance, the most profound anxiety with which I enter on the office of Governor of the state, is that of making the colored men the equal before the law of any other man—the equal not in dead letter, but in living fact."

Turning to the whites in the audience, Alcorn said: "The Union has brought us back, pardoned children, into its bosom. It bids us go forward this day, to the reconstruction of a government on the ruins left by our own madness. . . . And in approaching the duty made incumbent on us as representatives of a sovereign authority, our first work is to carry out in good faith the principles incorporated by the revolution just closed, in the letter and spirit of the constitution. . . ."

The Revolution was not closing; it was just beginning, as Alcorn and his white colleagues soon discovered. As in South Carolina, the new regime revolutionized government, enormously expanding the tentacles of the state administration and making massive adaptations in area and function. Mississippi Republicans also cleansed state statutes of racial distinctions and passed a stringent public accommodations law. The legislature declared that it was its intention to expunge from the record all laws "which in any manner recognize any unnatural difference or distinction between citizens and inhabitants of the state." On the debit side, it can be said that Reconstruction legislation in Mississippi, as contrasted with South Carolina, was woefully lacking in bread-and-butter content of direct interest to poor whites and poor blacks.

This was, in part, the result of the power and adroitness of Governor Alcorn who maneuvered skillfully to turn the Revolution to the advantage of planters and conservative commercialists. His legislative program (state aid to railroads and rich Delta planters, internal improvements) heavily favored conservative interests. And he used his enormous power to coopt or smash opposition. Under the constitution, he was empowered to appoint nearly all the state and county officers until the 1871 election. Senator Ames, who was already feuding with Governor Alcorn, said: "He could appoint this man a sheriff, that man a judge, that man county clerk, whoever he saw fit; and the members of the Legislature had their friends in office, and he could touch them to the quick in any part of the state," During his administration, Alcorn appointed a disproportionately large number of Democrats and conservative white Republicans. "So far as possible," historian Vernon Wharton said, "Alcorn avoided the appointment of Negroes." Northern-born white Republicans and some black politicians charged that Alcorn was "fixing up a party of his own (Whig) and using the Negro for a blind."

Alcorn's two-year stint as governor was, in fact, an extension of his skillful two-horse balancing act. Strategically, his plan was to give black people the form (a law) with one hand and to deny them substance (implementation) with the other. His was an absolutely brilliant piece of political artistry. For example: He was firmly opposed to any law that specifically barred black people from public facilities; but he was equally opposed to any law that specifically opened public facilities to black people. Hear him, now, as he denounces both legal segregation and legal integration in a message to the legislature. "If a mixture of the races be made the condition of participation in our public charities, no matter how you may regard the wisdom of the objection, that condition will act among the whites, to a very great extent, as a virtual exclusion. We must deal with this fact as we find it. While unwilling to recognize it to the extent of an absolute prohibition, in law, of a mixture of the two classes of pupils in the Institution for the Blind, or in the establishment for the Deaf and Dumb, I recommend in consideration of the acute sensitivities of those afflicted people, and on the general ground that an enforced violation of their opinions will but serve as a denial of their rights under the State Charities, that the supervisor of those Charities shall receive ample authority, in law, to exercise a wise discretion in the classification and keeping of the pupils of the two races." It was Alcorn's doctrine of "a wise discretion" which permitted *de facto* segregation in most schools. By organizing Alcorn University, which received the same annual appropriation ($50,000) and the same consideration as Ole Miss, Alcorn succeeded for a spell in throttling Negro demands for entry into the state university.

In the nature of things, men who ride two horses soon find that there is nothing beneath them but air. By the end of his

first year as governor, it was impossible for James Alcorn to
ignore signs that he was about to fall flat on his face. When he
opposed the state civil rights bill and the anti-Klan bill, black
legislators sprang into revolt and pushed them through the
assembly. When he unwisely attacked all white newcomers, he
sealed his doom by cementing a Negro-white newcomer alliance
that it should have been the aim of his policy to prevent.
Personal considerations also played a part. Men began to notice
and to comment on the fact that Alcorn made an excessive use
of the personal pronoun "I" and that he spoke rather too
frequently "of his large plantation and the very large number of
Negro slaves he had recently lost."

In the end, Alcorn was destroyed not by black men or white
newcomers but by native whites. In 1870-71, there was an
alarming increase in Klan violence in the state, particularly in
the eastern sections bordering Alabama. Republican leaders
were assassinated on the streets; churches and schoolhouses
were burned; masked men, some of them from Alabama,
thundered across the state, whipping, maiming, lynching. The
terrorist campaign reached a peak in March, 1871, with the
massacre of thirty black men in Meridian.

What was Alcorn doing all this time?

He wasn't doing very much. He decided on the worst of all
possible strategies in a revolutionary situation: he decided to
try to talk his way out, offering rewards for the white terrorists,
offering free transportation and jobs in *his* county to men and
women who could not live in freedom and dignity in *their*
counties. Alcorn wouldn't do anything; nor would he let
anyone else do anything. In an incredible political blunder,
he opposed a legislative resolution calling for federal intervention and sent a wire to the Mississippi congressional delegation
saying that "save [for 'some minor outrages'], Mississippi
presents an unbroken evidence of civil obedience and order."
A contemporary newspaper report noted that the "Mississippi
Republicans here lack confidence in the Governor and fear

that he intends to apostatize and join the Democrats, and that his dispatch is sent for political effect to aid in preventing passage of the legislation affecting the South now pending in Congress." Some Mississippi Republicans also charged that Alcorn was trying to gain "power and favor from the Democracy at the price of . . . the blood of his friends."

Thus stood James Lusk Alcorn as the fire of violence blazed.

The fire consumed him, burning away his last pillars of support in the black community. In disgust, black politicians turned from Alcorn to Senator Ames, who repeatedly denounced the "Mississippi outrages" and supported the federal Enforcement acts of 1870 and 1871. The passage of these bills provided the legal muscle which the federal government used to crush the 1870-71 insurrections in Mississippi, South Carolina, and other Southern states. More than nine hundred persons were arrested in Mississippi and 243 were tried and convicted in federal district court in Oxford.

Discredited by his equivocal policies, Alcorn resigned as governor in November, 1871, and entered the U.S. Senate to which he had been previously elected. He was succeeded by Lieutenant Governor Ridgely C. Powers, a Northern-born man with two large plantations and a post bellum plantation mentality. The interim Powers administration merely delayed the inevitable showdown between the white wing of the party, led by Alcorn, and the black wing, which was in search of a symbol and a standard-bearer.

At stake in this struggle was one issue and one issue only: Was black power to be real or nominal? Black leaders forced the issue by demanding a larger share in the decision-making apparatus. A radical black newspaper, the Vicksburg *Plaindealer*, said that too many Northern-born and Southern-born whites insisted on taking the offices although black people furnished the votes. This "thing," the *Plaindealer* said, "has played out." Black militants made their first move in 1872, electing John Roy Lynch, the twenty-four-year-old leader of the Adams County machine, speaker of the house. Lynch was a former slave who had been born near Vidalia, Louisiana, in 1847, to a planter and a black woman. Sold to a leading citizen of Natchez, he remained a slave until the federal occupation. After the war he attended night school, worked as a photographer's assistant, and dabbled in politics. A young man of great energy and charm, slender, fair, with quick bright eyes, Lynch was a formidable politician, quick on the stump, smooth and persuasive in the caucuses and corridors. Moderate and conciliatory, he soon attracted the attention of Ames and Alcorn, both of whom made special trips from Washington to persuade balky white Republicans that they should vote for him for speaker. Lynch performed his job with such dispatch that when he resigned to enter the U.S. House of Representatives, the Mississippi house, upon the motion of a prominent white Democrat, adopted a resolution thanking him for his "dignity, impartiality, and courtesy as a presiding officer."

John R. Lynch and his militant colleague, James Lynch, assumed leadership of the snowballing black power movement which led to bitter upheavals in the county and district conventions of 1872. John Lynch was successful in his drive to win nomination for Congress from the Natchez district, but James Lynch, who had a larger popular base, was isolated and defeated in the Vicksburg district by white Republican rivals who forced him into court on a charge of adultery and used the manipulated court proceedings to deprive him of the nomination. The bitter and revealing contest disheartened Lynch, who died a few months later, in December, 1872, of what some newspapers called "a broken heart." In a bitter editorial, a black newspaper said Northern-born whites and their black aides were primarily responsible for Lynch's death. "As with a magic wand," the paper said, "[Lynch] swayed and moved the masses whilst a candidate for the nomination. But it was snatched from him by the demon of corruption. He never recovered from the blow and when he fell, he fell a victim to the ingratitude of his own race.... Shame, shame upon the colored people that they permitted the most gifted orator of his race to be thus stricken down. James Lynch was killed by the carpet-baggers, and the whole race, as a political power, will soon be destroyed by the same instrumentality...."

The Lynch affair threw a revealing light on the Republican coalition of Mississippi. And in the light of that tragedy, black politicians re-examined their position and moved to the offensive, seizing party and convention posts in preparation for the 1873 campaign. Analyzing the situation some years later, Adelbert Ames said: "The demands of the colored delegates for state offices seemed to be irresistible, especially for lieutenant governor."

Since Ames seemed sympathetic to Negro demands, he was selected as standard-bearer of the dominant black wing in the 1873 canvass. Erect and handsome, with great piratical mustachios that drooped below his chin, Ames, then thirty-eight, was a native of Maine, a graduate of West Point, and a war hero who had won a Congressional Medal of Honor at Bull Run. An excellent administrator, one of the best examples of the much-maligned "carpetbaggers," Ames seemed genuinely interested in the plight of the freedmen. Unlike many Northern newcomers, he didn't patronize Negroes; nor was he susceptible to what A. T. Morgan accurately diagnosed as the newcomer's greatest weakness—the burning desire to "have the good opinion of Southerners." John L. McNeily, an anti-Negro chronicler, came to the same conclusion. Black people, he said, "had grown suspicious of their white emancipators, and with cause. In their hearts there were few of the Northern instruments of Reconstruction who did not despise and deride their own professions of race equality. The Negro was quick to detect the sham. In Ames, however, they discerned a genuine lack of all sentiment of race prejudice.... Carpet-bag rule was ameliorated to a degree by the desire of social intercourse with native whites. This was almost invariable, but Ames was an exception—he sought no favors and made no friends of them." It seemed then, Ames said later, "that I had a mission with a large M.... I believed that I could render [Negroes] a great service. I felt that I had a mission to perform in their interest, and I unhesitatingly consented to represent them, and unite my fortunes with them."

Because of his idealism and his repeated refusals to betray black people, Ames was an ideal candidate for the aroused black politicians who sensed their increasing weight in the world. This fact was emphasized by the Warren County Republican convention, the first county convention of 1873. The delegates came out for Ames for governor and demanded the posts of lieutenant governor, treasurer, and secretary of state for black men. The convention also nominated black men for county sheriff, both county clerkships and county treasurer. Urged by white delegates "to give the Anglo-Saxon a fair deal," black delegates endorsed racial ecumenicity by nominating a white man for assessor and for one of the four positions in the legislature.

The churning debate within the party exploded all over the landscape at the state Republican convention where black delegates denied renomination to two lukewarm whites and demanded three of the seven state offices, including lieutenant governor. The story, possibly apocryphal, is told of the militant Vicksburg delegates who reportedly climbed on desks, drew pistols and demanded the office of superintendent of education. However it was done, it was done. H. R. Pease, a conservative white newcomer, was pushed aside and T. W. Cardozo, an educated editor of uncertain reputation, was nominated for state superintendent of education. James Hill, the rising young politician from Holly Springs, was nominated for secretary of state. Hill, who was probably more powerful than any of his better-known contemporaries, was a native of Mississippi and the son of a distinguished white politician and a slave woman. A master of closed politics, Hill had great administrative and organizing ability. No orator, he shunned the spotlight and pulled strings from the wings. Born in Holly Springs in 1846, he educated himself and began his apprenticeship to power as sergeant-at-arms in the first Reconstruction legislature. In 1871, he was elected to the house. By 1872, he was powerful enough to promise the next U.S. Senate slot to his friend, B. K. Bruce.

Hill was a natural choice for the second position demanded by the black delegates. The real problem was lieutenant governor; for, behind the scenes, Republican strategists were planning a deal. The plan was for Ames to run for governor, serve a year or two and return to the Senate. This meant that the nominee for lieutenant governor would inherit the governorship. The problem here, of course, was the unanimous demand of black delegates for the position of lieutenant governor. Would Mississippi accept a black governor? Or, to put first things first, would the white power brokers accept a black governor? After feverish discussion, the white delegates said, yes, they would accept a black governor *if* the black man in question were Blanche Kelso Bruce, the shrewd, hardheaded political operator who had been born in slavery in Prince Edward County, Virginia, in 1841. Bruce, who attended Oberlin College, came to Mississippi in 1869 with no friends or prospects and only seventy-five cents in his pockets. A man of impressive appearance, broad-shouldered, heavy-set, erect, Bruce caught the eye of Governor Alcorn who made him sergeant-at-arms of the senate and then sent him to Bolivar County as assessor. Bruce improved on his opportunities, winning election as sheriff and buying a 1,000-acre plantation. More militant than Revels, Bruce refused to use the word colored, saying. "I am a Negro and proud of my race."

When the delegates approached Bruce with the deal that would have made him governor of Mississippi, he, unexpectedly, turned it down. He was running hard at the time for a U.S.

Adelbert Ames, a former
Union general, was elected
governor of Mississippi
in 1873.

Blanche K. Bruce was
first black man to serve
full term in the
U.S. Senate.

"TIME WORKS WONDERS."

IAGO. (JEFF DAVIS.) "FOR THAT I DO SUSPECT THE LUSTY MOOR
HATH LEAP'D INTO MY SEAT: THE THOUGHT WHEREOF
DOTH LIKE A POISONOUS MINERAL GNAW MY INWARDS." — OTHELLO.

In a Thomas Nast cartoon, Jefferson Davis,
former president of the Confederacy, reacts
to Hiram Revels, new occupant of his old
Senate seat.

Senate seat and was almost certain to get it at the next legislative session. "As between the Senatorship and the Governorship," John R. Lynch, a participant in the discussions, wrote,
"he chose the former, which proved to be a wise decision in
view of subsequent events." Since Bruce was unavailable, the
deal fell through, and Alexander K. Davis, the young senator
from Noxubee County, was nominated as a compromise candidate for lieutenant governor. Davis was an ambitious but
tactless young lawyer who had migrated from Shelby County,
Tennessee, in 1869. At the time of his nomination, he was party
boss in Noxubee County.

Before adjourning, the Republican delegates gave notice that
the tacit agreement not to push school integration was coming
to an end. The delegates resolved that "we recognize no distinctions as now existing by law in the rights of all children of the
State to equal privileges, and to accept such in all public schools,
colleges, or universities, and should any of said institutions of
learning deny to any child, on account of race or color, its equal
rights, we pledge ourselves to enforce said rights by appropriate
legislation, and we further pledge ourselves to the support of
our present institutions of learning, and our present educational
system as above explained."

During this time of mounting hope and pressure, the forces
of reaction were not idle. Stung to the quick by the open rejection of his party, Alcorn bolted and organized "the Republican
party of Mississippi" which waged a caustic and unsuccessful
campaign against the regulars. Alcorn was defeated 69,000 to
50,000 and even lost his own county which was dominated by
an intrepid black sheriff named John Brown.

The election of 1873 marked the highwater point of black
power in Mississippi. Black people won 55 out of 115 seats in
the house and 9 out of 37 seats in the senate—42 per cent of
the total. When the legislature met in January, I. D. Shadd of
Warren County was elected speaker of the house, and B. K.
Bruce was elected to a full term in the U.S. Senate. (Bruce

began his term on March 5, 1875, at a special session of the Forty-fourth Congress, and shortly afterwards made his maiden speech, energetically protesting the proposed removal of federal troops from the South.)

On the state level in 1873, black men served as secretary of state, superintendent of education, commissioner of immigration, commissioner of agriculture, and lieutenant governor. On Governor Ames' frequent absences from the state, Lieutenant Governor Davis moved into the governor's office and ruled with a firm hand. On one occasion, he fired the governor's private secretary, scratched a list of scheduled appointments, and appointed his own men.

The major black public servants on the state level in this period were: Hiram Rhodes Revels, U.S. Senate, 1870-71; Blanche Kelso Bruce, U.S. Senate, 1875-81; John Roy Lynch, U.S. House of Representatives, 1873-77, speaker, Mississippi house of representatives, 1872-73; Alexander K. Davis, lieutenant governor, 1873-76; James Hill, secretary of state, 1874-78; James D. Lynch, secretary of state, 1870-72; T. W. Cardozo, superintendent of education, 1874-76; I. D. Shadd, speaker, house of representatives, 1874-75.

It was during the Ames administration that Edward King, a white Northern reporter, visited Jackson to see how black power was working. Black people, he wrote, "lounge everywhere, and there are large numbers of smartly dressed mulattoes, or sometimes full blacks, who flit here and there with the conscious air which distinguishes the freedmen. I wish here to avow, however, that those of the Negroes in office, with whom I came in contact in Mississippi, impressed me much more powerfully as worthy, intelligent, and likely to progress, than many whom I saw elsewhere in the South. There are some who are exceedingly capable, and none of those immediately attached to the government at Jackson are incapable.... A visit to the Capitol showed me that the Negroes, who form considerably more than half the population of Mississippi, had certainly secured a fair share of the offices. Colored men act as officials or assistants in the offices of the Auditor, the Secretary of State, the Public Library, the Commissioner of Emigration, and the Superintendent of Public Instruction. The Secretary of State [Jim Hill], who has some Negro blood in his veins, is the natural son of a well-known Mississippian of the old *regime*, formerly engaged in the politics of his State; and the Speaker of the House of Representatives at the last session was a black man. The blacks who went and came from the Governor's office seemed very intelligent, and some of them entered into general conversation in an interesting manner."

On the local level, King found the same ferment and growth. Of Natchez, he wrote: "The present sheriff, the County Treasurer and Assessor, and the majority of the magistrates, and all the officers managing county affairs, except one, are Negroes. The Board of Aldermen has three Negroes on it. There is the usual complaint among conservatives that money has been dishonestly and foolishly expended; but the government of the city seemed, on the whole, very satisfactory." Once the center of ante bellum culture, Natchez at this point was a power center of the new regime. From here came the first black U.S. senator and Mississippi's first and only black congressman. Robert H. Wood, the scion of a free Negro family, served as mayor of this city which had a population of about nine thousand. Black voters had a distinct edge numerically, although black people constituted only one-half of the population. The black population seemed, King said, "to live on terms of amity with the white half." He saw black and white children playing together in the streets. Black hackmen, longshoremen, and public servants, he said, were "vociferously prominent."

What King saw in Natchez could be seen throughout the state during this period. Black men were sheriffs in Hinds, Issaquena, Monroe, Bolivar, De Soto, Coahoma, Washington, Holmes, Jefferson, Warren, and Claiborne counties. Black policemen abounded, and the police chief in Jackson was black.

There were numerous black chancery and circuit clerks, superintendents of education, and minor magistrates. It was not unusual in those days to empanel a grand jury of eleven black men and one white man. Sometimes, in fact, the entire panel was black. Vernon Wharton, a perceptive expert on this period, said that "many of the leading whites served willingly with the Negroes and found them generally kind-hearted, just, and honest."

Perhaps the best indication of black power on the local level was the make-up of the pivotal board of supervisors which exercised supreme legislative and executive authority on the county level. In Marshall, Yazoo, and Warren counties in 1873, three of the five supervisors were black. In Madison and Amite, four of the five were black. In Issaquena, all five were black. In addition, the members of the legislature, the sheriff, the clerks, the justices of the peace, and the constables in Issaquena County were all black. In that county, there were only two white public officials.

All this made an immense difference in the everyday lives of blacks and whites. Under the pulverizing impact of black power, racial lines cracked and in some areas disappeared. For the elite, anyway, there were open doors and open occupancy. In the capital city of Jackson, black politicians like James Lynch and James Hill lived in substantial homes on fashionable West Capitol Street. Hill, in fact, was a neighbor of J. Z. George, the former Confederate general and the reputed head of the Mississippi Klan.

In the circle of the powerful, power, not color, was the price of admittance. Both Alcorn and Ames entertained black officials at the governor's mansion. The anti-Negro Jackson *Clarion* reported on May 13, 1870, that "the mongrels [sic] adjourned to the executive mansion where a social equality orgy was celebrated; and the quarrels which had disturbed the 'eminent man' [Alcorn] and his carpet bag and African allies, were drowned in the flowing bowl. . . ."

Many things were drowned in the flowing bowl of power in this era. In parks, public places, and bars, there was free movement. There was also interracial dating and marrying. In 1870, Albert T. Morgan, the white state senator, married Carrie Highgate, and Haskins Smith, "a saddle-colored" member of the legislature, married the daughter of a prominent white businessman.

Some Mississippians thought the new order was permanent and acted accordingly. Consider, for example, the action of a wealthy Holmes County planter who had had seven children by six black women. In 1870, on his request, the legislature passed an act "making legitimate," according to the official record, "certain illegitimate children of James Anderson, residing in Holmes County, State of Mississippi, as therein specified in said act."

On all sides, there was a sense of widening horizons, of new possibilities and relations. To be sure, Reconstruction in Mississippi lacked economic content. But power is its own reward. A case in point is Robert Gleed, the state senator from Columbus. In 1873, he owned some 1,200 acres of land, four or five town lots, a home place, and a large store. Gleed was not an isolated example. At the time, black people in Columbus owned property worth $100,000.

From Natchez, from Vicksburg, from Jackson, from all points in the state, came similar stories of progress amidst struggle. According to an 1874 estimate made by Albert T. Morgan, then sheriff of Yazoo County, three hundred black people owned real estate in that county. The property ranged from small houses and lots in town to 2,000-acre tracts in corn and cotton. "Several of the colored planters," Morgan wrote, "were in quite independent circumstances. Their wives and daughters no longer worked in the cotton and corn fields. Each one owned a carriage, not always of the best pattern, to be sure, but ample for the family and sufficiently elegant in appointments for country uses.... Many more colored men owned live stock; horses, mules, cows, sheep, hogs, and chickens innumerable. The total value of the property of colored people of Yazoo at that date [1874] was not less than a million and a half dollars. They were in truth rising. Indeed, there was danger that 'our nigros' would, before long, 'own the whole country.' "

Buoyed up by economic gains directly related to political power, the horizons of black people expanded. New elements of meaning entered their lives, and commentators noted the emergence of the first of many "new Negroes." Morgan, for example, noted that Negroes "were demanding the same courteous treatment on the streets, in the stores, and at their homes for their wives, as common decency exacted for other ladies from the public, the merchants and his clerks, or callers at their residences".

Progress was not confined to the black community. Joshua Morris, the white attorney general, said the "people of Mississippi generally are improving now. I think that, notwithstanding they have had a great deal of misfortune, loss, and ruin throughout the State, resulting from the war, they are now substantially in a better condition than they were before the war.... The old politicians, though, will never get over it—never in this world."

While traveling in the state in 1874, Edward King saw neat new houses "scattered on hill and valley in every direction." He added: "Life and property are probably as safe at present as in any other State in the South. The [government] of Mississippi has not heretofore been of the best in respect to law and order; but the State seems to be now entering upon an epoch of peace and confirmed decency...."

There were, to be sure, loud outcries about high taxes and desperate men were hard at work manufacturing myths which would be swallowed whole by future writers, including, surprisingly, John Fitzgerald Kennedy who repeated [in *Profiles in Courage*] the story that reconstructed Mississippi was the worst state in the South. As a matter of fact, it was the best state. There is the testimony, first, of contemporary travelers. Alexander McClure said that "the Republican reign in this State was the best that has been known." There is, secondly, the testimony of James W. Garner and Vernon Wharton, the two outstanding authorities on Reconstruction in Mississippi. Both agree that there were no great frauds in Mississippi during this period. Garner wrote: "So far as the conduct of state officials is concerned, it may be said that there were no great embezzlements or other cases of misappropriation during the period of Republican rule." After diligent study, Garner could only find three cases of fraud on the state level. "The treasurer of the Natchez hospital seems to have been the only defaulting state official during the administration of Governor Ames. He was a 'carpet bagger' and the amount of the shortage was $7,251.81. The colored state librarian during Alcorn's administration was charged with stealing books from the library. The only large case of embezzlement among the state officers during the post-bellum period was that of the Democratic state treasurer in 1866. The amount of the shortage was $61,962." What Garner failed to mention is that the next embezzlement occurred during the administration of the white Democrats who "redeemed" the state from what they called "fraud and mis-management." The treasurer of that administration stole three hundred thousand dollars.

What I am concerned to emphasize here is that black power in Mississippi brought not ruin, but hope. By 1874, there were 75,000 students in school in that state, at least 50,000 of them Negroes. By that time, public buildings had been refurbished, welfare institutions had been established, and extensive im-provements—new sidewalks, pavements, gutters—had been made in counties and towns. By 1874, in short, Mississippi had entered the modern world from which it would soon secede. It was clear to most men in 1874 that it would take only a few more years to make the Revolution irreversible.

Could the Republicans hold on?

Watching the storm clouds gather in 1874, the shrewd A. T. Morgan expressed grave doubts. For one thing, the level of white desperation was rising, pushed by fears of Negro superiority, not Negro inferiority. "The marvelous fecundity of that race," Morgan wrote, "their wonderful progress in the science of politics, and their boundless ambition, as fully recognized by the leading minds among the enemy as by myself, and much more than by the people of the Northland, had completely changed the aspect of the *free* Negro question from one of doubt and sincere apprehension of his ability to survive, to one of the white man's ability to do so while in the presence of the Negro and while the conditions of existence were equal. The greatest minds in the State were divided on which would be the wiser policy for the white man, emigration and the abandonment of the State to the Negro, or a general arming of the white race with the purpose of checking by force the 'threatened supremacy' of the Negro race. To such persons these were the only alternatives."

So stood the white man on the eve of the storm.

And the black man?

In the schools, little black children were singing:

> *We are rising*
> *We are rising*
> *We are rising*
> *as a people.*

5

Black Governors,

White Sugar and Blood

On the night before the day of the installation of the first black governor of an American state, the streets of New Orleans crackled with rumor and intrigue. On this night, men, "full of benzene and patriotism," scurried from group to group, setting booby traps and political mines, preparing themselves against the coming of the day. Lights burned late in Carondelet Street offices; and, in the prestigious bar of the St. Charles rotunda, politicians leaned low over absinthe cups, whispering.

It was a warm, pleasant night, this Sunday in December, and there was an unusual amount of activity around the statehouse on Baronne Street which was surrounded now by federal troops who stood menacingly erect, bayonets gleaming. The massing of the federal troops, the hurried comings and goings, the agitated whispers, the general air of conspiracy and urgency: all this caused no end of excitement and speculation. On the waterfront, on Canal Street and Royal and Rampart and in Lafayette Square, men whispered to each other that trouble was coming.

It was — big trouble. A bloody struggle for control of the rich state of Louisiana was coming to a head. Two different election returning boards had certified the election of two different governors (one Republican, the other Democrat) and two different slates of legislators (one predominantly Republican, the other predominantly Democratic). Both sides had appealed to the courts and a federal judge had authorized the use of federal troops to forestall the menacing Democratic thrust. But all this was mere foam before the passing gust. This contest, as important and as desperate as any in the Reconstruction catalogue, was going to be decided not in the courts but in the legislature which was scheduled to meet in extraordinary session at noon on the following day.

By now, Sunday night, December 8, 1872, the complex legal issues had reduced themselves to terms the man in the streets could understand: a naked power struggle between two men, one white, one black, both young, both charming, both recklessly bold. Henry Clay Warmoth, the thirty-year-old white man, was a Union veteran and lawyer, an able, magnetic man who was, DuBois observed, "a born gambler, of unflinching courage, in causes both good and bad." Warmoth had been elected governor of Louisiana by a predominantly black and predominantly Republican electorate. But he had turned on his old friends and was acting now, in the dying days of his administration, with the Democrats. Using his vast powers of patronage and his dominant influence over one of the two election returning boards, he was one step away from success in his plan to certify the election of a Democratic governor and a predominantly Democratic legislature. But the exigencies of the situation required the support of the black lieutenant governor, P. B. S. Pinchback, who was then thirty-five. As presiding officer of the senate, Pinchback, in organizing that body, could make or break Warmoth by swearing in senators certified by either the anti-Warmoth (Republican) or pro-Warmoth (Democratic) factions. And what that meant in terms of *realpolitik* was that the state of Louisiana was in the hands of Pinckney Benton Stewart Pinchback.

It could have been in worse hands.

The son of a slave woman and a planter, handsome, charismatic, "not darker than an Arab," Pinchback was perhaps the best practical politician black America has produced. Like most of the black politicians of this era, he had been trained, to use his own words, in "the school of adversity," and he had fought his way "inch by inch, battling not only with poverty ... but contending all [his life] against opposition, fatigue, disaster and repeated failure." Born in Macon, Georgia, in 1837, he was the eighth of ten children of Major William Pinchback, a wealthy white planter of Holmes County, Mississippi, and his common-law slave wife, Eliza Stewart. The white planter freed his black family, and Pinchback and his brother attended Gilmore High School in Cincinnati. But when Major Pinchback died, the executors of his estate turned the black Pinchbacks away without a penny. Thus, at the age of twelve, Pinchback entered, he said, upon "life's rugged highway" with "naught but an indomitable will to live and succeed." For several years, he worked on steam boats on the Mississippi and Missouri rivers, tending cabins, waiting tables and assisting, so the story goes, one of America's most successful gamblers. When the war came, Pinchback served with distinction in the famous Louisiana Native Guards. He later resigned from the Union Army because of repeated incidents of discrimination and bias. With this experience behind him, Pinchback became a leading organizer of the Louisiana Republican party and served in the constitutional convention and the first state senate.

In the course of his rise from obscurity to power, Pinchback had acquired political style, a rich vocabulary, and deep insight into the passions and interests that move men. As a politician, he was noted for his uncompromising assertion of his individuality and personality. By temperament bold and assertive, he made no apologies for his color and insisted on the same rights and prerogatives as his white peers. It is no surprise, therefore, to learn that white conservatives honored him with their most telling adjectives: *dangerous*. Charles Nordhoff, a white Northern reporter said: "Now, Pinchback understands organization. He has at this time a propagandist of his view in many parishes, and it is said that he means to make himself, if he can, master of the colored people." Pinchback had both the gifts and the deficiencies of the practical politician. He lacked, especially in the opening phases of Reconstruction, the idealism the hour required. And he sometimes failed to see that the fabled art of the possible is the art of making some things impossible. Pinchback played the game of politics by the white man's rules, but there were limits beyond which he would not go, as we shall soon see.

As a leader of the Louisiana Republican party, Pinchback held or claimed more offices (state senator, lieutenant governor, *de facto* director of the New Orleans schools and police force, governor, U.S. represensive and U.S. senator) than any other black man in American history. "I confess," he said once, "I like to be on the winning side." For almost four years now, Pinchback had been on the winning side, serving as "second man" to Governor Warmoth. While aristocrats and millionaires waited in anterooms, A. E. Perkins wrote, "this shrewd and adventurous politician sat with the governor behind closed doors, making and unmaking laws and men." Now that the issue was the making or unmaking of the governor, Pinchback assumed the inscrutable posture that made him, in the opinion of a Democratic paper, "one of the best poker players in America."

If, as Stanley Loomis has said, the test of a statesman is the warmth with which he is able to embrace his enemies, Pinchback was a statesman of the highest order. Although he had been closely associated with Governor Warmoth, he said he was neither an admirer nor a subordinate "of that gentleman." In fact, Pinchback considered himself an equal, if not a major

partner, in the Warmoth-Pinchback machine. Governor Warmoth, he said, "always acknowledged he couldn't get along
without me."

It was close to midnight on this Sunday when Warmoth
recognized that he couldn't get along without Pinchback in the
coming confrontation. So, swallowing pride, Warmoth accom-
panied C. A. Weed, conservative proprieter of the *New
Orleans Times*, to Pinchback's home where, according to Pinchback, the governor made a most unusual offer. Pinchback said
he would sleep on the matter and reply the next morning. (He
said later that he gave this equivocal answer in order to draw
the governor out and trap him.) When dawn came with no
reply from Pinchback, Warmoth made an uncharacteristic
blunder. He sat down in his quarters in the St. Charles Hotel
and wrote a letter, signed it, and sent it by messenger to
Pinchback. Pinchback, smiling no doubt, sat down, scribbled a
reply and hurried to the senate, where he rode roughshod over
the opposition and installed an anti-Warmoth body.

With two or three thousand men milling restlessly in the
streets outside and with six or seven senators on their feet
shouting for recognition, Pinchback handled himself with the
ruthless efficiency that made him a dangerous enemy. Wielding
a quick gavel, he refused to recognize anyone and announced:
"The time has come to organize. The secretary will call the roll
of the old senators." As the words resounded in the hall, the
Warmoth supporters recognized with horror what Pinchback
was going to do. He was going to swear in the old senators; and
these senators, once certified, were going to rule on the credentials of the contestants. Since the old senators were overwhelmingly anti-Warmoth, the Warmoth supporters raised strenuous
objections. All over the floor now, men were on their feet,
screaming and waving sheets of paper. But Pinchback was
suddenly deaf and blind. Turning to the secretary, he said: "As
soon as the names of the senators-elect are called they will each
of them come forward and be sworn."

W. L. McMillan: I desire—
Pinchback: The chair will entertain no motion until after the calling of the roll.
H. J. Campbell: I—
Pinchback: The chair will hear you as soon as the roll is called.

As soon as the roll was called, Pinchback cited the authorities for his ruling. Then, with exquisite timing, he played his trump card, telling the senate that a conspiracy was afoot to overthrow the state government. In tones of aggrieved indignation, he accused Warmoth of awakening him at midnight and trying to bribe him by offering fifty thousand dollars and the right to name "any number" of state officials in return for a pro-Warmoth senate. In support of this charge, which created consternation in the statehouse, Pinchback read Warmoth's letter. Then, in thunderous tones, he read the reply in which he spurned the offer and vowed to do his duty "to his nation, his party, and his race."

The two letters doomed Warmoth.

Before adjourning that afternoon, the house of representatives impeached Warmoth "for high crimes and misdemeanors in office" and the senate organized itself into a court. That same afternoon, Pinchback, "surrounded," reporters said, "by quite a crowd of well-wishers and adherents." walked across the passageway to the office of the secretary of state where he signed the oath of office as governor in place of the impeached and suspended Warmoth. A contemporary newspaper report says a white Louisiana native, Associate Justice J. C. Taliaferro of the state supreme court, administered the oath of office in an "impressive voice, while the bystanders stood with uncovered heads, and P. B. S. Pinchback was then governor in place of H. C. Warmoth. . . ."

As soon as the ceremony was over, men dashed outside and screamed the news to the throng in front of Mechanics Institute, the temporary state capitol. By five o'clock, the *New Orleans Republican* was on the streets with an EXTRA. By nightfall, it was known as far north as New York that Louisiana had "a nigger governor."

It is a measure of the mood of the times that this news "produced no marked sensation," as a reporter noted, "except among the politicians." There were some raised eyebrows and some fulminating against "the audacious Negro intruder," but most whites took the thing in stride. Calls for a monster mass rally flopped, and attempts to panic the business community failed. In fact, state securities "stiffened toward the close of day," and state warrants advanced a point. Later that night, the stirring news and warm weather brought out on promenade large crowds. Some of these strollers stopped at the Varieties Theatre and saw *A Conjugal Lesson*. Others stood about in little knots discussing the first proclamation of "His Excellency, the Acting Governor." In this, his first public message, Governor Pinchback urged a quick trial for Warmoth, a thorough investigation of election frauds and a modification of "repressive laws."

Reviewing the fast-moving developments, the St. Louis *Globe* told its readers that the events of the day "read as good as a play." The same thing can be said of the whole Louisiana Reconstruction drama, which was reflected in microcosm in the intrigue, daring, and turbulence of the act of December 9, 1872.

To understand this act and its relation to the larger play of which it was a part, to understand "the big trouble" that followed and how Louisianians reacted to their black governor, to understand, above all, whether the play taken as a whole was a tragedy or a comedy, one must back up five years now and consider the backdrop and the chain of causes.

In its externals, the Reconstruction drama in Louisiana presents a confused and disorderly picture of petty disagreements, corruption, massacres, midnight assassinations, and endless *coups d'état*. But behind these externals we must see the larger realities that moved men and shaped the disagreements they had, as well as the terms in which they debated those disagreements. The real realities were brutally simple: sugar, cotton, bread, and gold. It was for these things and over these things that men struggled, and because Louisiana had more of some of these things than her neighbors and promised more, the struggle there was more intense and more desperate. In sum, then, the stakes were higher in Louisiana, and men were willing to pay more and to kill more to insure that the power of the state was used for them instead of against them.

The politics of division paid more in Louisiana, and there was more to divide. A boot-shaped agricultural bonanza, veined by the Mississippi and Red rivers and hundreds of streams and bayous, Louisiana was luxuriantly rich in natural resources and was of preeminent importance as a terminal of commerce and trade. From the alluvial parishes (counties) along the Mississippi and Red rivers came hundreds of thousands of bales of cotton which were supplemented by the rich yield of the cane fields in the Sugar Bowl in the south. Both the cotton and sugar were produced by black men who constituted the dominant human resource in the rich sugar and cotton parishes: Carroll, Concordia, Madison, Tensas in the northeast; Bossier, Caddo, De Soto, Natchitoches in the northwest; Assumption, Ascension, St. Mary, Terrebonne in the Sugar Bowl west of New Orleans. In some of these parishes blacks outnumbered whites by eight and nine to one. And the rich black Sugar Bowl area was the cohesively militant power base of the Radical Reconstruction regime. Most of the poor whites, on the other hand, were clustered on the oak and pine poor white land to the North. Louisiana's social structure reflected the basic divisions in the land. The cotton country of north Louisiana, for example, was Protestant; the sugar-oriented south, which had been ruled by both the French and Spanish, was Roman Catholic.

A counterpoint of clashing worldviews, Louisiana had, in 1870, 364,000 black citizens and 362,000 white citizens. Neither the black nor the white group was homogenous. Centuries of institutionalized amalgamation had produced tens of thousands of white black men and black white men. The "white" group included Creole descendants of the French and Spanish settlers as well as Cajuns, Acadians, Italians, Anglo-Saxons and *Cachumas:* "whites" with a dash, as Creoles put it, of *café noir* — black blood. On the other hand, the black group included black Creoles and thousands of "slim Negroes" who talked French, an English visitor observed, "with the grimace, vivacity, and repartee of Parisians."

Half-French and half-Anglo-Saxon, half-Protestant and half-Catholic, half-white and half-black, Louisiana had long been a cauldron of social tensions. And all these tensions found concrete form in the mortar and lacy grillwork of New Orleans which provided the stage on which the drama of Reconstruction in Louisiana unfolded. When Pinchback assumed power in Louisiana, the commercial and political life of the state revolved around New Orleans' Canal Street which, Robert Somers, a Reconstruction visitor, described as "a broad, noble thoroughfare, with ample carriage ways and banquettes for pedestrians on either side, and a dais in the middle, partly carpeted with grass, on which all the city cars have a common rendezvous — a street of fine stores and warerooms, where any stranger has a key at hand to all parts of New Orleans." At the corner of Canal Street, on the riverfront, was the Custom House, which plays a pivotal role in this story as a backdrop and symbol. The Custom House at this time was the second largest (after the U.S. Capitol) structure in America. A huge pile of Maine granite, with a gaunt and vacant interior and a still unfinished roof, the Custom House was the center of federal initiative in Louisiana. It contained not only the custom house but also the post office and federal courts and the offices of the U.S. marshal and other Republican power brokers. Nearby, "amidst acres of sugar barrels and cotton bales on one hand and a forest of ships on the other," hundreds of black longshoremen processed the material that made New Orleans the largest cotton mart in the

South. Visiting the city in 1874, Edward King was struck by the activity on the levee. "About these boats," he wrote, "closely ranged in long rows by the levee, and seeming like river monsters which have crawled from the ooze to take a little sun, the Negroes swarm in crowds, chattering in the broken English characteristic of the river-hand. They are clad in garments which hang in rags from their tawny or coal black limbs. Their huge, naked chests rival in perfection of form the works of Praxiteles and his fellows. Their arms are almost constantly bent to the task of removing cotton bales, and carrying boxes, barrels, bundles of every conceivable shape and size; but whenever there is a lull in the work they sink down on the cotton bales, clinging to them like lizards to a sunny wall, and croon to themselves, or crack rough and good-natured jokes with one another. . . ."

The wealth the black longshoremen handled and, behind that, the wealth of the water and of the fields it fecundated and of the muscular black bodies who tore that wealth from the ground and bundled and moved it: these things structured New Orleans, socially and architecturally. Canal Street, the main artery, shot straight up from the levee into the loop of the city. Branching off from one side of this street were the narrow and picturesque streets of the French Quarter. On the other side of Canal were St. Charles Street, and the St. Charles Hotel, where Governor Warmoth lived; Carondelet Street, where big cotton and sugar factors, including businessman P. B. S. Pinchback, had their offices; and Baronne Street, which was dominated by the statehouse. Although the Reconstruction governments were predominantly Republican, the city of New Orleans (140,000 whites, 50,000 Negroes) was predominantly white and Democratic, a fact that gave rise to no end of turbulence and disorder.

The great city of New Orleans had been brilliant and lawless under the rule of whites, and it was brilliant and lawless under the rule of blacks and whites. The city suffered, moreover, from a late Parisian adolescence. At the drop of a campaign slogan,

men would take to the streets and shoot it out behind barri-
cades. In 1860, the *New Orleans Delta* said: "For seven years
the world knows that this city, in all its departments, Judicial,
Legislative, and Executive, has been at the absolute disposal of
the most godless, brutal, ignorant and ruthless ruffianism the
world has ever heard of since the days of the great Roman
conspirators."

From this vantage point, we can see plainly that Reconstruction in Louisiana was merely a continuation at a higher level of
desperation of a pattern of violence to which Louisianians had
become accustomed. It was a continuation, too, of the desperate
economic struggle that undergirded the Civil War. This struggle was, in essence, a contest between big planters and Northern commercialists. After the war, this contest assumed in
Louisiana the form of a struggle between powerful white
Southerners (big planters of cotton and sugar and their professional and business allies) and the large number of white
Northerners, many of them Union veterans, who flocked to the
state in search of cotton and sugar and the blessings that these
staples bestowed. To get these blessings, of course, it was
necessary to control the instruments that controlled the black
cotton-pickers and cane-crushers from whom almost everything
flowed. For the simple fact of the matter was that the black
population was the prop of the whole social order. Without the
black man, there could be neither sugar nor cotton nor gold.

To the victor, then, would go control of the black man and
the spoils produced by the sweat and blood of black men;
would go also what was but another name for the same
thing — the instruments of the state which defined work, land,
wages, education and the real relations between man and man.

A complicating factor in the duel between Northern-born
and Southern-born white men was the presence in Louisiana of
one of the largest groups of free Negroes — some twenty thousand — in the South. Among this group were descendants of the
original settlers and proud scions of the black men who fought
with Andrew Jackson in the defense of New Orleans. Edu-

cated, for the most part, and well-to-do, Louisiana free Negroes entered into a direct and open contest with the whites who claimed the right to lead the more than three hundred thousand freed slaves. Free Negroes, however, operated under severe historical handicaps. Some spoke French and some spoke English; some were Roman Catholic, some Protestant. Many, moreover, had unrealistic notions about their own special place in the complicated Louisiana pecking order. It is a point of immense and ironic significance that the aristocratic free Negroes were soon outdistanced in the race for power by newcomers and freedmen skilled in the vocabulary of mass mobilization. The best representatives of this group were newcomers like Pinchback and dauntless former slaves like Oscar James Dunn.

The point at issue here is the basic and recurrent motif of Reconstruction: the triangular contest between Northern-born and Southern-born whites who wanted to use black people for their own interests, and the desperate attempt of black people to use themselves for their own interests. The struggle of Louisiana freedmen falls into this basic pattern, with two crucial differences. In other states, black leaders attempted, for the most part, to control the chief executive by indirect means. In Louisiana, black leaders repeatedly reached for the main prize. In other states, black leaders moderated their opposition to equivocal whites for fear of destroying the party and paving the way for Democratic control. In Louisiana, black leaders demonstrated repeatedly that they, like Samson, were willing to pull down the whole edifice if only the men who used them and betrayed them could perish in the ruins with them.

It was apparent from the start that Louisiana was going to play by a different set of ground rules. When time came to select decision-makers, the state Republican party split into two factions, the Pure Radicals and the Plain Radicals. In essence, the Plain Radicals represented the interests and aspirations of Northern newcomers, federal officeholders, and the free Negro elite. Faced with a predominantly black electorate (eighty thousand black voters and forty thousand white voters in 1867), the Plain Radicals hailed black power but urged "moderation and discretion" in its use. Among the most talented proponents of this policy were William Pitt Kellogg, a former Illinois lawyer who was allied with Custom House interests through his job as collector of the port of New Orleans; S. B. Packard, the heavy-set U.S. marshal who represented the large number of federal officeholders in and around the Custom House; and Henry C. Warmoth, a native of Illinois with a poor white Southern background.

One must set the stage carefully to understand what happens next—and one must focus a large spotlight on Henry Clay Warmoth who was both the villain and the catalyst of the piece. Warmoth, as Dunn very astutely observed, was "preeminently the prototype and prince of the tribe of carpetbaggers. . . ." All the subdued shades and tints we observed in the portraits of Scott of South Carolina and Reed of Florida were etched in bold contrasts in the character of Warmoth, who was the distilled essence of the adventurer on the make. Let it be said at once that Warmoth was a superbly talented adventurer. But this only compounded the problem. For the skills of the adventurer and the skills of the social revolutionary, which is what the hour required, are antipathetic. The social revolutionary is characterized by drive, daring, and a willingness to sacrifice almost anything or almost anyone for an overriding social purpose. What characterizes the adventurer, on the other hand, is precisely the lack of social purpose. The adventurer is willing to sacrifice almost anything or almost anyone in order to achieve a private passion.

Like all adventurers, Warmoth sought power for power's sake. Like Robert Scott of South Carolina, like Harrison Reed of Florida, Warmoth had no interest in the fate of black men who risked their lives in order to give him power, save as their fate served his own passion for elevation and control. Shrewd, cool, hardheaded, with devastating insight into the weaknesses of men, Warmoth was as singular a mixture of brilliance and rapacity as the Reconstruction era produced.

Born in Illinois in 1842, he studied law and entered the Union Army where he became a lieutenant colonel at the age of twenty-three. He left the army in a cloud of controversy and settled in New Orleans, where his audacity and striking address made him a leader of the Republican party. In 1865, Warmoth's sensitive antennae told him that the black people of Louisiana were the coming power and he unhesitatingly adopted their cause, demanding ballots and instant integration. Intrigued, black people gave him their votes and Warmoth became, at the age of twenty-six, political master of the state of Louisana.

From the beginning, Warmoth was opposed by the radical blacks and whites who gathered around J. T. Roudanez, a wealthy, Paris-trained black doctor who established America's first Negro daily, the bilingual *New Orleans Tribune*, and called for a far-ranging program of plantation cooperatives and a black-dominated government. This group, which was called the Pure Radicals, has been strangely neglected by historians, possibly because of its consciously left orientation, which touched at crucial points the unfolding insights of the radicals of the Paris Commune. The Pure Radicals represented, in some respects, the most advanced segment of radical thought in America at that juncture. They demanded "an entire renovation of the political element" and "a truly democratic system of labor." Deeply influenced by radical currents in Europe, the Pure Radicals sought "a plan of credit for the people" and said: "...we cannot expect complete and perfect freedom for the working men, as long as they remain the tools of capital, and are deprived of the legitimate product of the sweat of their brow." The *Tribune* called for a complete extinction of the planter class. "The planters are no longer needed in the character of masters," the paper said. "But they intend still to be needed as capitalists, and through the necessity of moneyed

Abraham Lincoln school for freedmen reflected the sudden
change in the fortunes of black people in Louisiana.
Reconstruction in Louisiana was turbulent, chaotic.

The first Negro daily newspaper in America, the
New Orleans Tribune, was founded by a wealthy black
doctor, J. T. Roudanez, who championed radical political
and economic program.

help, to retain their hold on the unfortunate people they have
so long oppressed. It is that hold that every friend of justice
and liberty is bound to break. As capital is needed to work the
plantations, let the people themselves make up this capital. Our
basis of labor must now be put on a democratic footing. There
is no more room, in the organization of our society, for an
oligarchy of slaveholders, or property holders."

By using the power of patronage and by manipulating the
fear of radicalism, Warmoth and the Plain Radicals routed the
Pure Radicals who wanted, critics said, "to go beyond the true
rewards of victory." In the constitutional convention, Pure
Radical demands for land reform were quashed, although party
leaders found it expedient to endorse constitutional provisions
on public accommodation and school integration. The Plain
Radicals won the second and decisive test of strength when
Warmoth defeated the black Pure Radical candidate, Francis
Dumas, in the close race for the gubernatorial nomination. The
Plain Radicals followed up this victory by expelling six Pure
Radicals from the Republican party. In a gesture of conciliation, two black men, Oscar J. Dunn and Antoine Dubuclet,
were nominated for lieutenant governor and treasurer, respectively. The Pure Radicals refused to support Warmoth and
threw their support to the Independent Republican candidate J.
C. Taliaferro, a native Louisianian, who was trounced in the
general election by a vote of 64,000 to 38,000. When the new
legislature met, black politicians constituted about half of the
101 representatives and about seven out of the thirty-six
senators. These figures are rough estimates because the extraordinary melange of black white men and white black men made
a precise account impossible. ·

Pure Radicals lost the first round of the contest, but they had
the last, bitter laugh. For Warmoth made an abrupt and
unexpected turn to the right after his inauguration on July 13,
1868. In his inaugural address, he lectured black people on
"virtue and education," "honesty and sobriety," "industry and

obedience to the law." He urged his black supporters not to intrude themselves socially upon the white people. As for the new government, he said it should pursue "a resolute and manly [but] moderate and discreet" program. What did this mean? "Let legislation," Warmoth explained, "be kept as much as possible in harmony with the sentiments of the whole people. It is better that the course of legislation should rather fall behind than to outstrip the popular wishes and demands."

When Warmoth followed up this declaration by vetoing a public accommodations bill which made it a crime to refuse service to black people, the Pure Radicals regrouped behind Lieutenant Governor Oscar J. Dunn, a former house painter and plasterer. A shrewd, self-educated, unimpeachably honest man who struggled furiously against black and white betrayers of Reconstruction, Dunn was one of the stock characters in the Reconstruction drama. Unlike the theatrical Warmoth and Pinchback, he was a plodding, slow-moving man who was regarded by all his contemporaries as "incorruptible." He had been born a slave in Louisiana and had escaped. He had also served as a captain in the Union Army from which he resigned in a protest against segregation and discrimination. He was forty when the war ended, "a fine-looking, portly man," Warmoth said, "brown of skin, and of extraordinary dignity and poise."

With Warmoth teetering on the edge of outright collaboration with anti-Negro forces, Dunn skillfully rallied black Radicals. He also received substantial support from moderate freedmen and powerful Custom House politicians who were alarmed by Warmoth's tendency to appoint conservative whites and bootless adventurers to important state and party posts. By 1871, the black lieutenant governor was the leader of the state party and the front-running contender for the gubernatorial nomination.

Dunn and his group said Warmoth had "sold out his radical principles to the Democrats." At that time, Warmoth was being openly wooed at lavish dinners in the Canal Street mansions of

leading Democrats. Moreover, as he tells us in his memoirs, he
relied heavily on the advice of anti-Negro leaders like Dr.
Newton Mercier, "who was perhaps the first man in social life
in New Orleans"; Herbert P. Mason, a former member of
General Robert E. Lee's staff; and General Richard Taylor, a
planter and former slave owner. All this naturally alarmed
Warmoth's old friends who said he was trying "to get into high
society." Warmoth replied heatedly that his opponents were
trying to set up an all-black government in Louisiana. He was
fighting, he said, against "the spirit of Santo Domingo."

In the first two years of Republican rule, both the Dunn and
Warmoth factions subordinated this sharp internal struggle to
the larger demands of renovating the institutions of the state. In
Louisiana, as in South Carolina and Mississippi, the Republicans inherited social anarchy. "I found," Warmoth wrote, "the
State and City of New Orleans bankrupt. Interest on the State
and City bonds had been in default for years. . . . Our public
roads were mere trails. . . . New Orleans had but four paved
streets. . . . There was no money in either state or city treasury." New Orleans, he added, "was a dirty, impoverished, and
hopeless city, with a mixed, ignorant, corrupt, and bloodthirsty
gang in control. It was flooded with lotteries, gambling dens and
licensed brothels. Many of the city officials, as well as the police
force, were thugs and murderers. Violence was rampant. . . ."
    The immediate need was money, and Warmoth raised it, not
always in the approved Wall Street manner. There was also a
need to spend money, and Warmoth spent it, not always
wisely. A new and vastly expanded state apparatus was
created; an integrated school system was organized; levees were
built and improved; and millions of dollars were pledged, often
unwisely, for railroads, levees, roads, and other social capital.
    Another need, more urgent, was public order. As soon as the
Republican regime was installed, reckless white men organized

an open revolt under the leadership of the Knights of the White Camellia, a Klan-like terrorist organization. In a brutal campaign of terrorism, which claimed the lives of more than a hundred black and white Republicans, the terrorists suppressed the black vote in the 1868 Presidential campaign and carried the state for the Democrats. Alarmed, the Republicans counterattacked, passing a militia law and a series of election and registration measures which gave the governor extraordinary power. The governor, for example, was empowered to appoint registration and constabulary officials in all parishes; and a returning board, with the governor as the dominant member, was empowered to throw out the votes in parish elections marked by fraud and violence. These acts, passed in the legislative session of 1870, checkmated the terrorists for, in a sense, it was more important now to count the votes than to cast or suppress them. It quickly became apparent, however, that the election and registration acts also checkmated Warmoth's Republican opponents, for Warmoth's power of appointment and certification under the new laws made him almost unbeatable in a statewide canvass. The worst fears of the anti-Warmoth faction were realized when Warmoth proposed and pushed through a constitutional amendment that made him eligible for a second term.

With the passage of this amendment, the tempo of events picked up. Anti-Warmoth Republicans now came out into the open under the Dunn banner. The first skirmish was fought at the August, 1870, Republican convention where Dunn defeated Warmoth by a vote of 54 to 43 in a contest for convention president. When Warmoth retaliated by joining Democrats in a move that deprived Dunn of his power of appointment in the state senate, both sides abandoned the amenities and girded for the open warfare that dominated the state in 1871. Dunn saw his chance and seized it in the spring of that year when Warmoth injured his right foot and crossed the state lines to recuperate at a Mississippi resort. As soon as Warmoth crossed the state line, Dunn installed himself in the executive chambers and proceeded to discharge the duties of governor. Looking back on the situation many years later, Warmoth wrote: "He [Dunn] made removals of officers, appointments to fill vacancies; granted pardons and reprieves to criminals in the penitentiary, and exercised all the functions of a Governor. It tickled my enemies very much. The Democrats liked to point to what had come to the proud people of Louisiana in having a Negro for Governor, and some of the Democratic press did not fail to say that they preferred a 'nigger' Governor to a carpetbagger."

What disturbed Warmoth even more were clear signs that the Republicans were planning to impeach him and make Dunn a regular resident of the executive chambers. To forestall this move, Warmoth ordered crutches and hurried back to New Orleans to face his detractor at the August, 1871, Republican convention. Arriving late, he found Dunn and his supporters in complete control of the physical arrangements and the all-important list of delegates. With a flourish, the governor bolted the Dunn convention and organized a second convention in Turner's Hall. Public business ground to a halt, Canal Street stores closed and thousands milled in the streets as the white governor and the black lieutenant governor fought for control of the party. Attempts to effect a compromise failed, and the two groups of Republicans elected different state presidents—Dunn for the regular Republicans and Pinchback for the Warmoth group—and proceeded to read each other out of the party. Pinchback, then a leader of the Warmoth faction, said later that he was collaborating with the governor in order to defeat him. "I had a good many friends under Warmoth in office and was comfortably housed myself," he said. "I concluded that I would drive along with him until I could get a convenient jumping-off place." What Pinchback failed to mention is that both he and Dunn were seeking the same prizes: the governorship or the U.S. Senate. But Dunn had a head start and he pushed his suit for all it was worth, telling Horace Greeley in an 1871 letter: "There are 90,000 voters in this state, 84,000 of whom are colored. In my judgment, a fair and untrammeled vote being cast, nineteen-twentieths of the Republican party in the state, including a majority of the elective state officers and all of the Federal officers, with a few exceptions, are opposed to the administration of the present state executive." Dunn accused Warmoth of "crimes against his party and his people" and added: "We want for ourselves, and for all the people of all parties, better laws on the statute-book, and better men to administer the same, and we are persuaded that neither of these wants will ever be met so long as the present executive exercises any material control over the politics of Louisiana." At the same time, Dunn appealed to the black voters of Louisiana. Stressing the importance of the forthcoming state convention, he urged the election of "good, honest men that will look out for the interests of the colored man, and not be duped by the money or the promises of Governor Warmoth, and above all do not elect as a delegate any of his officeholders, who being under obligations to him for position, will be compelled to support his policy." Dunn added: "We have a great work before us, and in order to be successful we need the aid and cooperation of every colored man in the State. An effort is being made to sell us out to the Democrats by the Governor, and we must nip it in the bud...."

It is not altogether clear how Dunn and his followers intended to "nip [the Warmoth threat] in the bud." But the evidence suggests that the Dunnites intended to impeach Warmoth and install Dunn in his place at the opening of the legislature. A little more than a month before the opening of the legislature, on November 22, 1871, Dunn, then forty-six, died suddenly at his residence on Canal Street. Dunn partisans charged that their leader had been poisoned. A. E. Perkins, a modern investigator, said four physicians signed a certificate saying Dunn's death was due to "congestion of the brain."

Perkins added: "But Dr. Warren Stone, one of the examining physicians, in an additional statement said death was due to excessive vomiting."

However that may be, it is certain that Dunn's death benefited several politicians, among them Henry Clay Warmoth, who immediately called a special session of the senate, ignoring the house of representatives which was dominated by men who wanted to impeach him. With the troublesome house out of the way, Warmoth engineered the election of Pinchback to the position of president of the senate. This made Pinchback *de facto* lieutenant governor. It also made it highly unlikely that the Dunnites would impeach Warmoth and elevate Pinchback, a political enemy and a Warmoth man, to the governorship. Thus fortified, the governor launched a blitzkrieg offensive, ousting his opponents in the house and seizing control of that body. The ousted legislators, most of them black, organized a second legislature in a room over the Gem Saloon on Royal Street and issued a call for a trial by combat:

TO ARMS! TO ARMS!! TO ARMS!!!
COLORED MEN, TO THE FRONT!

Warmoth's SLAVES at the Mechanics' Institute pretended to-day to expel Antoine, Adolph, Burch, Wilson, Kearson, Williams, Tureaud, Geddis, Johnson, Laurent, Kenner, Harper, Harry Lott, and other colored members of the house of representatives. Warmoth will next attempt to remove Ingraham and Antoine from the Senate

Rally, on SATURDAY, at 10 o'clock, at the corner of Rampart and Canal Streets, and let those who have trampled on your rights as freemen and citizens tremble until the very marrow of their bones shakes. Let the cry be,

DOWN WITH WARMOTH AND HIS THIEVING CREW.
RALLY! RALLY!! RALLY!!!
LIBERTY OR DEATH!

In the midst of this frantic skirmishing, the U.S. military commander wired Washington for instructions. "For the last three days," he said, "peace has been maintained solely by the display of the United States troops, and a contest for the Statehouse is at this moment only averted by my placing troops near that point, with definite orders to prevent riot. The difficulties between the contending parties are as far from a solution as ever, and the members representing the two factions in both houses are so nearly equal and so bitter that the collision, if it be allowed to come on, must be a very disastrous one."

This was hardly an exaggeration, for on Sunday, January 21, 1872, the anti-Warmoth forces broke into an armory in Algiers and seized arms. The next day, several thousands assembled at the Gem Saloon and were preparing for an assault on the state capitol when word came that the U.S. government would intervene to protect the Warmoth legislature. Disheartened, the insurgents dispersed, and Warmoth, sensing his advantage, moved to the attack, skillfully and ruthlessly crushing the revolt.

In the weeks that followed, Warmoth used every instrument to intensify his hold on power. He tightened his grip on the electoral machinery by appointing dubious whites from New Orleans to important posts in the Black Belt parishes. He also increased pressure on state officeholders, who were required, according to contemporary reports, to give Warmoth undated resignations as a price of appointment. The effectiveness of all this can be gauged by the plaint of an old black man who was defeated for office in a Black Belt parish. "Is it possible," he asked, "I have no vote come out of that box? 'Fore God, I know I vote for myself."

Meanwhile, on the national scene, a group of Liberal Republicans denounced Reconstruction and seceded from the national Republican party. The split on the national level led to a series of splits in Louisiana, where Warmoth began to drift toward the right while Pinchback sought a reconciliation with the regular Republicans. As the internal squabbles rose to new heights of bitterness and intensity, Warmoth desperately dou-

The black governor,
P. B. S. Pinchback, was
a leading figure in the
political struggles of the state.
Pinchback was installed
as governor after the
impeachment of
H. C. Warmoth.

Oscar James Dunn, a
former slave, served as
lieutenant governor of
Louisiana from 1868 to
1871. He was party leader
in the state until his
sudden death in 1871.

bled his bets, offering the state machinery to the Democrats for, a Democratic editor said, "social recognition, oblivion for the past, and future respect, with an equal showing for political honors." Whatever the price, the offer was accepted and Warmoth endorsed John McEnery, the anti-Negro Democratic candidate. Pinchback promptly abandoned his demands for the governorship and delivered the Pinchback wing of the party to the now-dominant Custom House machine. The Republican coalition fielded a slate of five black and three white candidates headed by William Pitt Kellogg, the Illinois-born U.S. senator, and Caius César Antoine, the black collector of the port of Shreveport. Pinchback was nominated for congressman-at-large.

The campaign, which was marked by a concerted program of terror and intimidation by Democrats, was climaxed by a famous railroad race between Pinchback and Warmoth. In the middle of the campaign, both men found themselves in New York City at the same time. While walking down Broadway, Pinchback happened to see the governor and the two men chatted for a while and promised to meet again that night for a "bird dinner." Pinchback continued to the Fifth Avenue Hotel where he described the Louisiana situation to Senator Harry Wilson of Massachusetts and Senator Zachariah Chandler of Michigan. The situation, as Pinchback described it, was grave. Warmoth, he said, was now acting with the Democrats and, with his control of the electoral machinery, was in a position to throw the state to the Democrats. The only hope was a law passed by the last legislature which deprived the governor of his control over the electoral process. But, said Pinchback, it was unlikely that Warmoth would sign the bills. As the talk continued, it developed that Pinchback, not Warmoth, held the key to the situation. For in the absence of the governor, he, as lieutenant governor, could legally exercise all the powers of the governor. And if he could reach Louisiana and sign the bills while Warmoth was still out of the state, "the entire machinery of registration and elections would be changed, and the chances of the Republicans carrying the state doubly magnified." Chandler and Wilson urged Pinchback to start for Louisiana immediately, saying that "the control of the state, and possibly of the Federal government was involved."

Pinchback started immediately, leaving New York that night on the Pennsylvania Railroad. But his failure to appear for dinner aroused the suspicions of Warmoth who checked the train stations and determined that Pinchback had left for New Orleans. Realizing the implications of that step, he immediately wired Major E. A. Burke, a leading Democrat of New Orleans, "to find a way to keep Pinchback out of Louisiana." The powerful Democratic machinery of the South immediately went into action. A special train was placed at the disposal of Warmoth who left New York in hot pursuit of Pinchback. Democratic strategists also wired special instructions to railroad agents and Democratic clubs in every county through which Pinchback's train was scheduled to pass. Pinchback was told later that "every railroad entering New Orleans from the North was picketed for miles from the State line and the orders were to prevent my entrance into the State in advance of the governor if it required the sacrifice of my life."

Oblivious of these elaborate and ominous preparations, Pinchback speeded south, losing six hours in Pittsburgh "on account of no trains running on Sunday," and six hours in Cincinnati because of a missed connection. By now, only a few hours separated Pinchback and Governor Warmoth who was traveling on a special, "rattling along at the rate of forty, fifty, and even sixty miles an hour where the road would stand it." The race would have been close at any rate, but Warmoth and his Democratic allies weren't taking any chances. When Pinchback's train pulled into Canton, Mississippi, about eleven o'clock at night, Pinchback was awakened by a white man who asked: "Are you Governor Pinchback?" Before Pinchback could answer, the man said: "Your Excellency, there's a telegram for you in the station. It's very important and, as you would probably want to answer it immediately, it would save trouble for you to come and get it there."

"Have I got time?" Pinchback asked.

"Oh, yes" the man replied, "we'll hold the train for you."

Pinchback dashed into the station and realized immediately that "something was wrong." In telling the story later, he said the man "seemed to be in no hurry to hand me the pretended dispatch, and his face had a sinister expression upon it. On reaching the door in my attempt to return to the train I found it closed and locked on the outside. This confirmed the suspicion already aroused, and I made a desperate attempt to regain the train by bolting through the window. It was too late. I saw only the rear end of the train disappearing around the curve in the road fully a mile distant." The next morning Warmoth's train lumbered into Canton with Warmoth, a "triumphant expression upon his face," standing on the front platform of his special car. Warmoth had won the first round, but the contest was not over.

After the voting on November 4, both Kellogg, the Republican candidate, and McEnery, the Warmoth-Democratic candidate, claimed a majority, and the contest shifted to the returning board which split along Warmoth and anti-Warmoth lines. The net result, as we have seen, was the impeachment of Warmoth and the elevation of Pinchback to the governorship. Warmoth bitterly contested Pinchback's assumption of power, but he seemed unable to summon his old audaciousness. In one last fling, he ousted a key state court judge and certified the election of one of his adherents who immediately issued an injunction forbidding Pinchback to exercise executive power. Pinchback coolly countered by pushing through the legislature in one day a bill that abolished the court. Thus, in one stroke, he made the court, the troublesome judge, and the injunction disappear into thin air.

Pinchback said once that he had tagged along with Warmoth because "I wanted to see what his plans were so as to defeat him." If so, Pinchback proved an apt pupil. Moving swiftly, he occupied all the trenches of power and capped a virtuoso performance by appointing a Confederate hero, Major General

James Longstreet, commanding general of the Pinchback militia. On that same day, Wednesday, December 11, 1872, he issued two proclamations, declaring the rump "Warmoth legislature" illegal and affirming his purpose to uphold the constituted authorities and to enforce the laws of Louisiana.

Before long, Governor Pinchback was *de facto* and *de jure* master of Louisiana. On Thursday, December 12, he received the following telegram from Washington.

Department of Justice
December 12, 1872

Acting Governor Pinchback,
New Orleans, Louisiana:

Let it be understood that you are recognized by the President as the lawful executive of Louisiana, and that the body assembled at Mechanics' Institute is the lawful Legislature of the State, and it is suggested that you make proclamation to that effect, and also that all necessary assistance will be given to you and the Legislature herein recognized to protect the State from disorder and violence.

(Signed)   GEO. H. WILLIAMS
Attorney-General

Equally important in the total scheme of things was the recognition Pinchback received from New Orleans Democrats. It was necessary for Democratic officeholders to have their commissions signed by the governor. But which governor? Significantly, the Democratic officeholders of New Orleans decided that Pinchback, not Warmoth, was the real power in the state. On Wednesday, December 18, according to a dispatch in the *New Orleans Republican*, "Mayor Wiltz and the new Democratic Administration . . . called on Governor Pinchback in the Gubernatorial parlor to get their commissions. After a cordial adieu the city officials then withdrew. They did not look as though they were 'oppressed' or humiliated but seemed quite jolly."

Pinchback, who had a bitter and ironic sense of humor, was

pleased by the behavior of New Orleans Democrats. He said later that he told the black secretary of state that "all applications for commissions from the city of New Orleans should be made directly to me.... I did that with the view of seeing whether Judge Abell and other gentlemen, prominent and notorious Democratic candidates, would recognize me as the Acting Governor of the State, and each one of these gentlemen came in person to the office and received his commission from me, and the press of the day will show that courtesies passed between us. Those judges thanked me for my courtesy, and they said, 'We bow to the powers that be.'"

Pinchback held that power for thirty-six days, from December 9, 1872, to the inauguration of Republican Governor W. P. Kellogg on January 13. During this time, he appointed several officers, including a state supreme court justice, signed legislative acts, addressed the legislature and issued public proclamations. Pinchback, who did not have a false sense of modesty, said later that he singlehandedly added four years to the life of the Reconstruction regime in Louisiana.

As the new year began, Governor Pinchback tightened his grip on the government machinery. He was in his office, a black newspaper said, "night and day," receiving streams of suppliants and advisors. He was also busy behind the scenes, supervising moves that isolated the "Warmoth legislature," which was meeting at Lyceum Hall. On Friday, January 3, supporters of the Warmoth legislature held a mass meeting to express opposition to the "Pinchback government." On the same day, Governor Pinchback issued an Executive Address in which he warned the white Democrats that there were limits to dissent. "Not content with all these outrages against American citizenship," the governor said, "these foiled and defeated leaders of a minority, when thwarted by the majesty of the law as construed and enforced by an honest and independent judiciary, State and Federal, now propose, through a man pretending to be Governor-elect, and a Legislature pretending to be elected, to organize and operate a government in direct conflict with and in violation of the dignity and peace of the existing government of the State of Louisiana and of the United States. We recognize the right of free discussion and of free assemblage of the people. They may lawfully meet, not only to memorialize the authorities to redress wrongs, to perpetuate rights; not only to criticise and censure their servants, wherein they may deem them derelict, but even to denounce them for wrongs, real or imaginary; but when any class of men, with an undetermined and unascertained official status propose to meet and organize a law-making department and inaugurate an executive and exercise governmental functions in the presence of and in conflict with the existing established authorities, such parties are revolutionists, and guilty of treason against the State, and are disturbers of the peace, and must be dealt with as such." He added:

"I am prepared, as the acting executive of Louisiana, to permit, without let or hindrance, a faction of her citizens to indulge themselves as fully as the largest personal liberty may require, and the financial embarrassment and social disquiet incident thereto must belong to them, but when their action becomes organized and suggests and prompts violations of the law, and obstructions and antagonisms to the authority of the State in the exercise of its legitimate functions, it cannot for a moment be either ignored or overlooked, but must be met and suppressed. It is my duty as Executive not only to quell mobs and insurrections, but to prevent, by the prompt and vigorous execution of the law, the inception of such riots and disturbed conditions. I do not propose that such a state of things shall be inaugurated in the State of Louisiana as will make it necessary for the national authorities to declare martial law therein and take possession thereof, however much this deplorable issue may be sought and desired by the few ill-advised, shortsighted, and self-seeking men who are laboring to that end."

The main issue at stake here was the determination of the

In a major Reconstruction military battle, the integrated
Louisiana state militia meets the assault of the
revolutionary White League on the streets of
New Orleans.

Struggling for power, Democrat L. A. Wiltz
makes an unsuccessful attempt to take over
the speaker's chair in the Louisiana house.
Democrats made repeated attempts to
overthrow government.

white Democrats to inaugurate a Democratic governor and
legislature in defiance of the state and federal courts. Pinchback
warned the Democrats that he would use the "whole force of
the State" to prevent the inauguration of "the pretended
Governor." He was dissuaded, however, by federal officials
who feared an all-out racial war. These officials told Pinchback
that the best method of handling the dissenters was to ignore
them. Although Pinchback admitted the weight of this argument, he continued to prepare for a total confrontation, pushing
through the legislature an act "to suppress riotous and unlawful
assemblies, and to define the duties of the officers of the State
in regard thereto, and to punish officers and others for neglect
or refusal to discharge and perform duties imposed upon them
by law." This was followed by an act which authorized the use
of the state militia for that purpose.

During the days that followed, the new governor played his
cards with consummate skill and turned over the Republican
machinery intact to the new governor, W. P. Kellogg. At the
inauguration on Monday, January 13, Pinchback delivered a
"farewell address" in which he noted that he had performed his
executive duties "in the face of bitter antagonisms of race when
the temper of the times was unfriendly to a charitable judgement and the quiet execution of the laws." In addition, he said,
"some of the parties acting in conjunction with me and from
whom I expected support have not only failed to give me a
hearty support in the discharge of my delicate duties but have
indulged in hypercriticisms upon what they have pleased to
call my indiscreet exercise of power." He continued in the
following vein:

"Holding my position only for a few weeks and under
circumstances embarrassing in the extreme, it was neither
possible nor desirable for me intentionally and for my own
purposes or otherwise to do either unwise or unjust or ungenerous things toward the people of Louisiana. My time of service
and my administration with its mistakes and whatever of good

I have been able to impress upon it is now before the country and I am content that the people, irrespective of party, and when the passions of the hour have passed, shall render the verdict upon my official acts."

Turning to the white governor-elect, Pinchback said: "I now have the honor to formally surrender the office of governor, with the hope that while you will administer the government in the interest of *all* the people, your administration will be as fair toward the class that I especially represent as mine has been to the class that you represent."

In tribute to his skill, the grateful Republican legislators elected Pinchback to the U.S. Senate. Since he had already been elected to the House of Representatives, he went to Washington with the unique distinction of being both a congressman-elect and a senator-elect. Pinchback was a new experience for the U.S. Senate which had, like every other American institution, two standards of judgment — one for white men, another for black men. Not only in the Senate but in every other center of power in Washington, black men of power were expected to be purer, quieter, *whiter* than their white peers. They were expected, above all, to meet the white man's idea of what a black man ought to be. These were the ground rules, and Hiram Revels, who preceded Pinchback, played by the rules. But what was the world's most exclusive club to do with Pinchback, who not only refused to stay in his place but denied by his words and deeds that white or black people had any particular place?

For three years, the U.S. Senate grappled with that question. Almost the whole of one extra session was devoted to the problems posed by the credentials of the senator-elect from Louisiana. Pinchback, it should be noted, didn't make it easy for his white supporters. He refused to beg or bow, saying: "Sir, I demand simple justice. I am not here as a beggar. I do not care so far as I am personally concerned whether you give me my seat or not. I will go back to my people and come here again; but I tell you to preserve your own consistency. Do not make fish of me while you have made flesh of everybody else."

In his flamboyance and in his uncompromising insistence on a single standard for black and white men of power, Pinchback resembled the twentieth-century maverick, Adam Clayton Powell Jr. And the national uproar and the white-backlash bigotry that surrounded Senate considerations of his case in the 1870's were eerily similar to the consideration of the Powell case by the U.S. House of Representatives in the 1960's.

During the anguished, drawn-out proceedings, Pinchback became a national celebrity. Washington women, intrigued by his "Brazilian" good looks, went out of their way to meet him, and Pinchback stories made the rounds. The correspondent of the *New York Tribune* composed a ditty in honor of the controversy:

> *Pinch, brother, pinch with care,*
> *Pinch in the presence of the senataire.*

We catch a glimpse of Pinchback and the embattled senators in a dispatch from the Washington correspondent of the New York *Commercial Advertiser*. Thomas C. McCreery, the Democratic senator from Kentucky, according to this dispatch, was saying privately that he would give "that nigger some sleepless nights before he gets his seat." Other senators were communing with their consciences and their constituents. And all the while Pinchback was gliding "around the Chamber like a bronze Mephistopheles, smiling sardonically, and buzzing his supporters." The *Commercial Advertiser* reporter felt that the matter hinged largely on color. "Aside from a political view of the question," he wrote, "Pinchback's presence in the United States Senate is not open to the smallest objection, except the old Bourbon war-whoops of color. He is about thirty-seven years of age.... His features are regular, just perceptibly African, his eyes intensely black and brilliant, with a keen, restless glance. His most repellent point is a sardonic smile which, hovering continuously over his lips, gives him an evil look, undeniably handsome as the man is. It seems as though the scorn which must rage within him, at the sight of the dirty ignorant men from the South who affect to look down upon him on account of his color, finds play imperceptibly about his lips." The reporter went on to say that Pinchback's manner was "reserved but polite, exhibiting a modesty rarely seen in a successful politician—a model indeed of good breeding to those Texas and Louisiana Yahoos who shout 'nigger, nigger, nigger' in default of common sense or logic. Mr. Pinchback is the best dressed Southern man we have had in Congress from the South since the days when gentlemen were Democrats...."

After an interminable debate, the Senate refused to seat Pinchback who promptly charged racial prejudice. Pinchback opponents denied the charge, citing "election irregularities" and charges of fraud, which were never proved.

Embittered by the ordeal and by the fact that twelve Republican senators voted against him, Pinchback concluded that idealism was dead in America. He charged that the North was about to abandon the black man and said the black man had to make a deal with the Southern white man—before it was too late. Black people, he said, were between "the hawk of Republican demagogism and the buzzard of Democratic prejudices. The aspirants for position in our party threaten us with excommunication if we do not follow every jack o'lantern who raises his feeble light, and the Democrats invite us to annihilation if we turn away from these Republican jack o'lanterns." Black people were damned, he said, if they did and damned if they didn't. "Truly," he concluded, "ours is a great risk."

If all this was not clearly seen by black people, it was beginning to be clearly felt. On the local level in Louisiana, there was a great deal of disillusionment and despair. Nordhoff met a black man in a country parish who told him that the

Republicans were just as bad as the Democrats. "And if we put our own color in," he added acidly, "somebody comes along and shoves money in their pockets, and makes them forget their own people."

This disillusionment was the beginning not only of reform but of wisdom. It was the beginning, too, of another intra-party struggles which raged until the final overthrow of Reconstruction in Louisiana. In 1874, for example, black Republicans cursed and attempted to attack Republican Governor Kellogg when he appeared on the floor at a parish convention in New Orleans. Pinchback and other black leaders accused Kellogg and Packard of trying to organize a White League in the Republican party. In that same year, a committee of black Republican leaders, led by Pinchback and P. G. Deslonde, charged that the integrity and capacity of black men were "ignored in the councils of the party, while our manhood and citizenship are not infrequently humiliated by those whom we have exalted to power. There is a species of mystery, so far as we are concerned, about the plans of the campaign and the policy of the State Administration, which denies to every colored man in this commonwealth, not even excepting the lieutenant governor, the secretary of state, the superintendent of public education, and the state treasurer, all participation and knowledge of the confidential workings of the party and government." Not satisfied with this state of affairs, black Republicans moved to oust their allies. By 1875, the black thrust was straining the party fabric to the breaking point. "Under the inspiration of Pinchback and other ambitious colored leaders," Nordhoff reported, "they [black people] begin to grasp after all the offices. 'We have the majority,' they say, 'we cast the votes; the offices belong to us; we do not need you....'"

Meanwhile, things were going from bad to worse on the state level. For several months in 1874, the state had two governors and two legislatures. When the federal government tipped the scales in favor of the Republicans, the Democrats withdrew to the bayous and killed hundreds of blacks and whites in brutal massacres at Colfax, Coushatta, and other Black Belt centers. Failing to gain power with this tactic, Democrats became open revolutionaries. A series of seizures of parish courthouses was climaxed on Monday, September 14, 1874, by a *coup d' état* in New Orleans. A congressional committee negotiated a compromise, which gave the Democrats a majority in the house of representatives and the Republicans a majority in the senate; but the compromise failed to satisfy the Democratic insurrectionists who continued to snipe at the Kellogg government.

Under strong pressure from angry black insurgents within the party and conservative whites without, Kellogg moved belatedly to eliminate the widespread corruption which involved both parties, both races, and all classes. Although this corruption was not peculiar to the Republicans or the Louisiana of that day, it provided a campaign issue for white supremacists who accused black people of stealing millions of dollars and "lavishing them upon abandoned white women." Actually, as a congressional committee pointed out, "the prime movers" in corruption in Louisiana (and elsewhere) were "wealthy, influential, and highly respectable Democrats." Warmoth, as usual, put it in blunter terms. He told a delegation of bankers lobbying to protect their interests that "these much-abused members of the Louisiana legislature are at all events as good as the people they represent. Why, damn it, everybody is demoralizing down here. Corruption is the fashion."

Governor Kellogg made a small dent in the Louisiana fashion by initiating sweeping reforms that saved the state millions of dollars. During the first two years of his administration, the state debt was reduced, by funding, from twenty-five to fifteen million dollars; state taxes were reduced from 21½ to 14½ mills, and state expenditures were drastically slashed.

Despite the revolutionary turbulence, which precluded either brilliant or orderly government, the Reconstruction regime made a large, if largely symbolic, difference to Louisianians. During this period, cotton-pickers, cane-crushers and dock-workers were stimulated to challenge their environment. It is significant that there was a large amount of labor unrest in the state in this period. Not only in the cities but also on the plantations, men and women dropped their implements and demanded working conditions and wages commensurate with the new image they had of themselves. Traveling in the state in 1875, Charles Nordhoff, a conservative white Republican, remarked on the "large number of colored mechanics" in New Orleans. Elsewhere in the state, he saw black men working as masons, carpenters, shoemakers, blacksmiths. In the towns, he said, "a considerable number of Negroes own their own homes." He added: "All have a strong desire to own small lots of land."

Under the umbrella of black power, a small but significant number of black people climbed a rung or two of the economic ladder. Some laborers managed to climb into the artisan class, and some artisans managed to withstand the strong challenge of white workers who wanted to take their votes so they could take their jobs. In New Orleans, powerful black politicians like Pinchback and C. C. Antoine discovered that access to political power is access to economic power. By virtue of their political position, several black politicians made small fortunes as real-estate operators, cotton factors, and directors of corporations.

There were also striking gains in the field of education, as indicated by the passage of the most sweeping anti-segregation provisions ever enacted in the educational field in America. "Be it further enacted," the school law said, "[that] any teacher of any public school, who shall refuse to receive into any school any child between the ages of six and twenty-one, who shall be lawfully entitled to admission into the same . . . shall be deemed guilty of a misdemeanor, and, upon conviction thereof, shall be punished by a fine of not less than one hundred dollars nor more than five hundred dollars, and by imprisonment in the parish jail for not less than one month nor more than six months; and all such cases shall have preference before other criminal cases upon the docket of the court before which they shall be brought; and such persons so offending shall also be liable in an action for damages by the parents or guardian of the child so refused."

During this period, most children attended segregated schools, but a large number learned their letters in integrated classrooms. In fact, a larger proportion of the school population—at least one-third—attended integrated schools in New Orleans between 1868 and 1877 than attend integrated schools in New York City and Chicago today.

There was sustained and bitter opposition to the integrated schools. It was necessary, for example, for policemen to escort Governor Pinchback's children to the exclusive boys' high school at Magnolia and Carondelet where organized gangs made their lives miserable. "They were good enough niggers," one of the ringleaders said, "but they were still niggers." Later, in December of 1874, white Democrats stormed an interracial girls' high school and removed all girls who were identifiably black. Protected by state and city police, the black girls returned to the school which they attended until the end of Reconstruction.

A substantial number of Louisiana whites tried to evade the provisions of the school law by founding and supporting private white schools. Louisiana churches and Northern philanthropists enthusiastically supported this movement. The Peabody Fund, for example, was a major opponent of integrated schools. Most of its funds in the South went to white children who refused to attend integrated schools. The Peabody Fund and other foundations also supported private white schools. "Great numbers of private schools," Edward King noted, "have sprung into existence, especially in New Orleans, where the predominant religion is Catholic; and the Germans have shown their fear of mixed schools by establishing special schools for their children."

Private schools notwithstanding, the integrated Louisiana school system could claim substantial achievements. In 1872, the school superintendent reported, with some exaggeration, that "the right [of integration] thus bestowed by the highest law of the State and recognized by every school act passed since the adoption of the Constitution, *has been vindicated with such prudent firmness as to be no longer questioned.*" The superintendent admitted that most students attended segregated schools. "Yet in many of the schools white and colored pupils may be seen together, and where this exists it is not too much to say that the latter are treated with greater kindness by their fellow pupils than, under similar circumstances, they would be in many Northern cities."

Black power also brought the blessings of public visibility. Visitors remarked often on "the polite but consequential" black policemen who could be seen not only in New Orleans but also in the country parishes. There were also black sheriffs, and black men dominated some of the police juries (county commissions). There was, also, at least one black mayor: Monroe Baker of St. Martin.

During this period, black people elected two congressmen — only one, Charles Edmund Nash, was seated — and the following black men held state offices: P. B. S. Pinchback, governor, thirty-six days, 1872-73, and lieutenant governor, 1871-72; Oscar J. Dunn, lieutenant governor, 1868-71; C. C. Antoine, lieutenant governor, 1872-77; P. G. Deslonde, secretary of state, 1872-76; Antoine Dubuclet, treasurer, 1868-79; W. G. Brown, superintendent of education, 1872-77. Scores of black men served in the General Assembly which contained on the average about seven out of thirty-six in the senate and about half of the 101 members in the house.

The first question put to a visitor in these days, according to journalist Robert Somers, was: Have you seen "the Negro

Legislature"? Somers went to see the integrated legislature of Louisiana and reported: "There were a few carriages, and some knots of people round the door of the Mechanics' Hall, in which the Legislative Body sits. The lobbies were crowded with Negro men and lads 'from the country,' with a sprinkling of more whites and sharp-visaged townsmen; and Negro women were selling cakes, oranges, and lollipops up to the door of the Chamber of Representatives. Within the Chamber itself were seated in a semicircle round the Speaker's chair, with little fixed desks and drawers full of papers before them, a body of men as sedate and civilized in appearance as a convention of miners' delegates in Scotland or the North of England. On close inspection, a few Africans were visible, but yellow men seemed to predominate. The Senate differed little in general aspect or composition, but was presided over by Lieutenant-Governor Dunn, a really black man as far as could be seen in the shadows, and was being addressed by an honourable white Senator of an intellectual cast of head and face, who appears to have gained more notoriety than all the rest by marrying a black woman. There is no supreme law of taste, and Negro suffrage and love together combine to produce occasional startling effects."

Black suffrage and love together combined to produce a great many startling effects in reconstructed Louisiana. Though marred by imperfections, bled white by terrorists and betrayed by friends, black and white, the Reconstruction regime still reached plateaus of democracy men now living have never known. To be sure, the gains in education and humanism were balanced by grave defects in administration. But despite its imperfections, the Reconstruction regime was better by far from the standpoint of democracy than any other government in the state in the hundred years preceding 1867 or the hundred years that followed 1867.

6

The Minor States:

The Vote Revolt That Failed

W HEN, ON JANUARY 9, 1967, the Georgia legislature yielded to the U.S. Supreme Court and admitted a black
man previously excluded,* it added yet another postscript to
Hegel's dictum that history repeats itself twice—the first time
as tragedy, the second time as farce.

Most of the Georgia legislators knew little of Hegel and less
of Henry McNeal Turner. Few, if any, of them realized that
they were repeating, with only slight variations, the gestures
and words of men who lived one hundred years ago. But
history had anticipated their bad faith by writing similar
headlines once before, not only in Georgia but also in Alabama
and Florida and Arkansas.

Almost one hundred years ago, the Georgia legislature was
in the business of expelling black men for militancy, *Negritude*,
and speaking out of turn.

Almost one hundred years ago, Alabama whites were
executing absurd maneuvers in a desperate attempt to avoid the

*The legislature had barred Julian Bond because of a militant statement in opposition to
the Vietnam war.

278

implications of the federal voting rights bills of the 1860's and 1870's.

Almost one hundred years before the showdown on the Edmund Pettus Bridge, the real Edmund Pettus was fuming in his Selma law office while black *and* white men tramped through the Selma streets, singing a harshly militant "We *Have* Overcome."

> *The white man's day has passed*
> *The black man's day has come at last.*

Thus history plays its little tricks, confirming not only Hegel but also Santayana, who said once that men who cannot remember the past are condemned to repeat it.

We caught a glimpse of that truth in previous chapters by tracing the ascending curve of black power in South Carolina, Mississippi, and Louisiana, the three states where the face of black authority was open, direct, and compelling. Let us turn the canvas now and look at the gray areas of power — the twilight states where black voters had large influence but little decision-making power.

In terms of political muscle, these states range themselves on a descending scale, with Florida and Alabama representing a middle tier of power, followed by Arkansas, Texas, Georgia, North Carolina, and Virginia. It has pleased historians to stress the powerlessness of the black voters of these states. But all things are relative, including power. In point of fact, the "powerless" black voters of some of these states had more real power ninety years ago than the black voters of any contemporary state, with the possible exception of New York. The black citizens of Arkansas, for instance, were a distinct minority; yet Arkansas passed a civil rights bill of such severity that it would not be possible to pass it today in either New York City or New York State. Moreover, the black minorities of the white-dominated states sent proportionately more black men to their legislatures than any contemporary state.

Black people constituted about 45 per cent of the population in three of the minor states (Florida, Alabama, Georgia), one-third or more in three other states (North Carolina, Virginia, Texas) and one-fourth in Arkansas. Because of the distribution of the male population and the disfranchisement or apathy of some whites, the black share of the vote was even higher: 59 per cent in Florida, 49 per cent in Georgia, 47 per cent in Virginia, 45 per cent in North Carolina, 37 per cent in Alabama, and 26 per cent in Arkansas.

Black people had the votes, but, as we have said here often, it takes more than votes to make power. Power in Western democracies is made by votes plus desire, will, consciousness, organization, money, and action. Fresh out of slavery, with few lawyers and professionals and almost no money, the black populations of the minor states were at a distinct disadvantage in the scramble for power. Black voters learned fast and they produced an extraordinary crop of indigenous leaders, but time and the times were against them.

In politics, as in love and war, a good beginning mortgages the ending. Realizing this, conservatives struck hard at the very beginning of Reconstruction, confusing the goodhearted, intimidating and murdering the bold. In point of fact, Reconstruction never got off the ground in several states, including Virginia and Texas. In these states, a counter-coalition of conservative Democrats and conservative Republicans isolated black and white radicals during the constitution-making process. Aided by a murderously effective Ku Klux Klan campaign, the counter-coalition soon reduced the huge black electorates to virtual impotence. Of overriding importance here is the fact that the black populations of the minor states were in the minority. Even in Florida, where there were sixteen thousand black voters and eleven thousand white voters, the white population was in the majority in thirty-one of the thirty-nine counties.

Lacking the dense majorities and the demographic dispersion

of states like South Carolina and Mississippi, the black electorates of Florida and other states were at the mercy of circumstances. In order to make their potential power real, black voters had, of necessity, to form coalitions with either poor whites, rich whites, or Northern whites. Elements of all these groups entered into coalitions with black voters. But the price of coalition was white domination. In all instances, this policy was rationalized as a strategic necessity. Then, as now, black people were told that it was better to make haste slowly, thereby permitting biased whites to assimilate the reality of black power bit by bit. When black voters demanded a larger share of decision-making power, they were told that the survival of the coalition depended on the invisibility of Negroes. A Texas Negro politician reported: "The white men here say that if we put a colored man in the field that the radicals will lose the race." What this meant in practice was that the black voters in Texas and other states furnished the lion's share of the vote and got the lamb's share of the spoils.

There is a passage in A. A. Taylor's account of Reconstruction in Virginia which is illuminating in this general connection. "There was usually," he wrote, "factional strife between the Negro political leaders and the prominent white men in the party. The Negro spokesmen boldly asserted that the whites were in the party not because they were interested in human rights, nor because they had any serious thoughts as to improving the conditions of the Negroes. What they wanted, the Negroes maintained, was merely to hold the offices and exploit the Negro for their own personal benefit. In practically all of their nominating conventions, therefore, there usually ensued a fracas of such bitter nature that even after the matter had been apparently adjusted there were left wounds which were too serious to be healed before the time of the approaching election. Knowing more about political manipulation than the Negroes had had the chance to learn, the whites in the party generally unseated and counted out sufficient delegates to nominate their

candidates, usually white men. If they saw they were about to
be defeated in a convention, they would sometimes withdraw
from the legally constituted body and organize as a faction,
claiming legality through some technicality decided upon be-
forehand for such an emergency and worked out in a would-be
legal style. When the claims of these two groups came before
the central or State committee, the candidates nominated by
the majority of the constituents of the Districts would be
ordered to give way to those of the [white-dominated] machine.
If the Negro candidates refused to give way, they were charged
with destroying the party and giving aid and comfort to the
enemy."

With such friends, black people needed few enemies, a truth
underlined by the fact that Reconstruction was soon undermined in the twilight states. Radical reconstruction lasted less
than three years in four states (Virginia, Georgia, North Carolina, Texas) and less than six years in Alabama and Arkansas.
Though handicapped by a constitution that discriminated
against Black Belt counties, the Negro voters in Florida
managed to hold on for nine years.

Florida and Alabama, the two twilight states where black
voters waged the strongest fight, provide vantage ground for
consideration of two major approaches to the problems and
perils of coalitionship. Both states were poor, rural, underdevel-
oped. But Alabama, unlike Florida, had a large and relatively
articulate poor white population and was in the take-off stage
of commercialization. The state, at that time, contained more
than nine hundred thousand persons — 562,000 white, 437,000
black. The largest city in the state was Mobile (40,000), followed by Montgomery (10,000), and Selma (7,000). Birmingham was still a gleam in the eyes of English and Northern
investors who were just moving in for maximum exploitation of
the mineral riches of the northern counties. This region and the
pine barrens of the southeast were inhabited largely by poor
whites. The old aristocrats and the former slaves held the

cotton-rich soil in the middle. Selma, a busy cotton mart, was a symbol of Black Belt power. Robert Somers, who visited the city in January, 1871, was impressed by what he saw. "There are," he wrote, "many fine buildings, several large yards for storing cotton, and two or three broad streets of shops and warerooms where most accessories and many articles of luxury may be purchased. Two-thirds of the men of business are Germans, many of them of Hebrew extraction. The Jews have settled largely in Southern Alabama, and what with Negroes and colored people, and German and Jewish names, there is a foreign air about Selma." Black people outnumbered white people in Selma and other Black Belt centers, but white people had a comfortable margin on the state level.

The white margin was smaller in Florida, the poorest and smallest of the reconstructed states, with a population of only 187,000 (96,000 whites, 91,000 Negroes). Most of the state was uninhabited. Miami and Miami Beach were wildernesses of "mangroves, seagrapes, and scrub palmetto, infested with snakes and mosquitoes," and Daytona Beach was waiting for white and black Republicans to give it life. A visitor from the twentieth century would not have found Florida altogether strange. There was the cigar industry at Key West and the abiding obsession with Cuba, which was then embroiled in controversy with Spain. One reads with interest that "refugees in Key West" were organizing armed expeditions against Cuba. The white population in the area around Key West and in the older, cotton-oriented section of the north was small and dispersed. Two-thirds of the black population, on the other hand, was concentrated in the half-dozen cotton counties in north central Florida.

With different material bases, Florida and Alabama neces- sarily presented different political silhouettes. In Florida, the coalition rested on the shaky foundation of two competing groups of Northern-born whites. In Alabama, the coalition was based on a remarkable entente between poor blacks and poor whites. In both Florida and Alabama, the coalition moved through two phases: a phase of outright white domination, followed by a rising tide of black expressiveness.

The first phase in Florida was an extension of the bitter convention fight which led, as we have seen, to the expulsion of black radicals and the drafting of a constitution which was frankly designed to prevent the heavily populated Black Belt from dominating the state. From that point until the end of Reconstruction in Florida, the black wing of the party and the two competing white wings were at daggers drawn. The dominant white wing was led by Harrison Reed, a minor-league Warmoth, who was a former publisher of a Wisconsin paper. Small, slight, bespectacled, with a large bald head, a huge bushy beard, and a talent for manipulation and control, Reed organized a conservative coalition which isolated and contained the relatively small black delegation (19 of 76) to the first legislature.

With black interests underrepresented and feuding whites occupying the corridors of power, black leaders were confronted with large problems of strategy. Although the black interest never reached a dominant position in the coalition, an increasingly restless black electorate forced increasingly large concessions. The state capital was located in the predominantly black county of Leon, and a favorite tactic of black Floridians was to assemble in the rotunda of the capitol and denounce white and black "traitors." A leading force in this campaign was the Negro church, particularly the African Methodist Episcopal Church. At an AME conference in 1871, black ministers called for boycotts and intensified political education. The conferees resolved "that our social sympathies are warmly towards those who help us in material and mental aggrandizement, by affording us willingly opportunities for the acquisition of this world's goods and mental culture; and that our patronage rightfully belongs only to those who patronize us as far as occurs in the ordinary course of fair business." The conferees also said "that those steamers, railroad companies, merchants, and others who treat our people so disgracefully from sheer hatred, malice, and prejudice, are not worthy of our support [and that] our people as much as possible should be advised to ship their produce, and make their purchases by and from those who treat them fair." As for biased white newspapers, the black ministers said they "should be beautifully let alone."

A series of none-too-nonviolent demonstrations gave point to this message and forced the appointment of Jonathan C. Gibbs, a Dartmouth-educated Presbyterian minister, to two state cabinet posts. As secretary of state (1868-71) and superintendent of education (1872-74), the tall, lean, circumspectly militant Gibbs made an ineradicable mark on the state, giving concrete form to the bill "to establish a uniform system of public education." A white historian said he was "probably the most outstanding character in the early life of the Florida public school system." Despite that fact or perhaps because of it, Gibbs lived in a climate of terror. When Judge Mifflin Gibbs of Little Rock visited his brother in Tallahassee, he found him living "in a well-appointed residence, but his sleeping place in the attic resembled, as I perceived, considerably an arsenal." The black Florida cabinet officer told his brother that "his life had been threatened by the 'Ku Klux.'" Like Oscar Dunn of Louisiana, Gibbs died suddenly after attending a political banquet. It was said that he was poisoned by political enemies who feared his growing power.

Another beneficiary of the developing political consciousness of the Florida electorate was Josiah Thomas Walls, a Virginia-born free Negro and a former sergeant major in the Union Army who was nominated for Congress after black politicians threatened to wreck the Republican convention. The only black man to represent a whole state as congressman-at-large, Walls was elected three times and unseated twice in contested election cases. He was a large citrus farmer and an early Florida booster. In Congress, he distinguished himself by his efforts to improve the economy of the state.

On the local level, hundreds of black politicians participated

Henry McNeal Turner
was a leader of radical
forces in the
Georgia legislature.

Josiah T. Walls of Florida
was the only black man
to represent an entire state
as congressman-at-large.

White lawyer appeals to an integrated jury in reconstructed Southern state. Black men also participated in government as constables, sheriffs, magistrates, mayors.

J. W. Hood was a leading figure in Reconstruction politics in North Carolina.

in government as sheriffs, constables, tax assessors, school superintendents, and magistrates. At least one black man, Matthew M. Lewey of Newnansville, served as mayor of a town.

No less important was the strong public accommodations act which black Republicans pushed through the legislature in the face of the determined opposition of white Republicans. The bill provided "that no citizen of this State shall, by reason of race, color, or previous condition of servitude, be excepted or excluded from the full and equal enjoyment of any accommodation, advantage, facility, or privilege furnished by innkeepers, by common carriers, whether on land or water, by licensed owners, managers, or lessees of theatres or other places of public amusement; by trustees, commissioners, supervisors, teachers, and other officers of common schools and public institutions of learning, the same being supported by moneys derived from general taxation, or authorized by law, also of cemetery associations and benevolent associations, supported or authorized in the same way." Violators of the law were required to pay the victim $100 and were subject to fines of not less than $100, or more than $1,000, and imprisonment for not less than thirty days and not more than one year.

This was also a period of phenomenal growth for the state. Florida had never constructed a creditable system of charitable and penal institutions, and the Republicans plowed new ground, opening an insane asylum at Chattahoochee, and constructing or refurbishing welfare institutions in Tallahassee and other towns. By 1876, 28,444 pupils, one-third of them black, were attending 676 schools. At that time, the educational law provided that each county was entitled to send as many students free of charge to the state universities — one in Gainesville and one in Tallahassee — as it had representatives in the legislature.

The Republicans did not reglect Florida's economic interests. New railroads and improved water transportation opened up the state and stimulated agricultural and industrial production.

By 1876, the citrus industry was assuming commercial importance and thousands of tourists were streaming to the state.

In 1869, Governor Reed extended premature congratulations
to Floridians on their strides toward freedom. "Throughout our
beloved state," he said, "opposition to federal authority and
republican government has ceased, and all classes of people
yield obedience to the laws. The newly-enfranchised citizen of
color sits side by side with his white fellows in the cabinet, the
halls of legislation, the jury-box, and on the boards of commissioners—occupies the magistrate's chair, and executes the
decrees of courts, without exciting violence or occasioning
asperity. The change since your last session [of the legislature]
is marvelous, and calls for grateful recognition."

In different circumstances, and with a different base of
power, the black voters of Alabama made similar gains, sending
three Negroes (J. T. Rapier, Benjamin Turner, Jeremiah Haralson) to Congress and scores of Negro politicians to the state
legislature. To the dismay of General Edmund Pettus and
other conservatives, two of the three black congressmen represented the predominantly black Selma district.

What makes the Alabama story even more remarkable is the
fact that Reconstruction in Alabama was neither black nor
Northern. Alabama white men were in control of the government, and the two Radical Republican governors were northern Alabama white men. It has been estimated that at least
twenty thousand Alabama white men actively supported the
Republican party in that state.

The situation in Alabama was complicated by the presence
of a large number of Northern and Southern commercialists
whose primary interest was the fabulously rich mineral section
around the new town of Birmingham. In time, the thrust for
freedom on the part of poor whites and poor blacks was
crushed by the passion for coal and steel. But before that
happened, Alabamians made their first tentative, toddling steps
toward a democratic state.

Urged on all sides to remember the tender sensibilities of

the white Republicans of northern Alabama, black voters bided
their time for two years, sending a substantial delegation of
twenty-seven members to the first legislature and electing
sheriffs and minor officers in Dallas (83 per cent Negro),
Lowndes (83 per cent), and other Black Belt counties. Beginning
in 1870, Black Belt politicians upped the ante, demanding a
larger slice of power on the state level. A white Alabamian
stepped aside and Rapier, a wealthy cotton planter, was nominated for secretary of state. Although Rapier and the Republican
ticket went down to defeat, the Negro demand for parity increased apace and reached partial fulfillment when the Republicans returned to power in 1872.

Tall, dark, and well-educated, Rapier took the lead in the
campaign. "Nothing short of a complete acknowledgment of
my manhood will satisfy me," he said. "I have no compromise
to make and shall unwillingly accept any." In the same spirit, a
black politician from Mobile announced that he intended to
drink in white bars, ride on white streetcars, and dance in
white ballrooms. From other politicians came demands for
integration of the University of Alabama and an acceleration of
the pace of desegregation. A black minister from Jackson
county urged caution, saying he wanted to hold onto north
Alabamians "until their stomachs grow strong enough to take
Civil Rights straight"; but G. S. W. Lewis, a state representative, said he was tired of waiting for his rights. "Hereafter," he
said, "we intend to demand [our rights] and we are going to
press them on every occasion and preserve them inviolate if we
can. The day is not far distant when you will find on the bench
of the Supreme Court of the state a man as black as I am, and
North Alabama can help herself if she can." This orchestra of
protest reached a crescendo with the convening in 1874 of an
all-Negro equal rights convention which demanded first choice
of political nominees in Black Belt counties and a proportionate
share of offices in white counties.

One result of the rising expectations of black voters was a

sharp increase in the number of black officeholders. John Carroway, a black editor from Mobile, served as speaker of the house and Peyton Finley was elected to the state board of education. By 1874, thirty-five Negroes (26 per cent of the total) were serving in the Alabama state legislature.

During this period, Montgomery County was represented in the legislature by two white men and three black men, and Perry County was represented by one white man and two black men. In Sumter County, the sheriff and solicitor were black and the white registrar was married to a black woman. Roderick Thomas was judge of the criminal court in Dallas County and Negroes were serving on city councils in Selma and other cities. Black policemen were common. General James H. Clanton, the head of the Alabama Klan, said: "I see Negro police — great black fellows — leading white girls around the streets of Montgomery, and locking them up in jail." In some Alabama counties, the majority of the supervisors were black.

It was during this period of heightened hope and heightened determination that Edward King, a white Northern reporter, visited the state. He found the state capitol in Montgomery "surrounded with the usual number of Negroes, old and young." In the capitol itself, "the colored legislators [were] lounging about the lobbies, waiting for the session to begin. . . . There were a good many among them who were lightly tinctured with Caucasian blood, and all were smartly dressed and aggressive in their demeanor.

"In the House of Representatives the colored members appeared to have voluntarily taken seats on one side of the House, and the conservatives, who were in like manner assembled on the other, were overwhelmed by a deafening chorus of 'Mr. Speaker!' from the colored side, whenever they proposed a measure."

Such was the spirit of aggressive black citizens in the first Reconstruction of Alabama. Very different was the case in other states where conservatives managed to blunt the edge of black

Electioneering in a minor state, a black politician defines
the issues at a plantation meeting.

Alabama Congressman
James T. Rapier was a
militant advocate of
equal rights.

Mifflin Gibbs was elected
to the post of municipal
judge in Little Rock,
Arkansas.

Jonathan Gibbs, who was
brother of Mifflin Gibbs,
held two state cabinet posts
in Florida.

hope. In Georgia, for example, black citizens were soon shunted to the back streets of power. As soon as the military occupation ended, the dominant native whites expelled twenty-seven black legislators who were deemed ineligible because of their race. The four Negroes who remained in the legislature were so fair that the investigating committee decided it would be inexpedient to probe into their origins.

As it turned out, the expulsion of the black legislators was a monumental blunder. A wave of protest rolled across the country, and Henry McNeal Turner, the first black chaplain in the U.S. Army and a future AME bishop, arraigned his colleagues in a memorable speech on the house floor.

"Cases may be found," he said, "where men have been deprived of their rights for crimes and misdemeanors; but it has remained for the State of Georgia in the very heart of the Nineteenth Century to call a man before the bar and there charge him with an act for which he is no more responsible than for the head which he carries upon his shoulders. The Anglo-Saxon race, Sir, is a most surprising one. No man has ever been more deceived in that race than I have been for the last three weeks. I was not aware that there was in the character of the race so much cowardice, or so much pusillanimity. . . .

.   .   .   .

"It is very strange, if a white man can occupy on this floor a *seat created by colored votes*, and a black man cannot do it. Why, Gentlemen, it is the most shortsighted reasoning in the world. . . .

"If Congress has simply given me merely sufficient civil and political rights and made me a mere political slave for Democrats, or anybody else—giving them the opportunity of jumping on my back in order to leap into political power—I do not thank Congress for it. Never, so help me God, shall I be a political slave. . . . You have all the elements of superiority upon your side; you have our money and your own; you have our education and your own; you have our land and your own, too. We, who number hundreds of thousands in Georgia, including our wives and families, with not a foot of land to call our own — strangers in the land of our birth; without money, without education, without aid, without a roof to cover us while we live, nor sufficient clay to cover us when we die! It is extraordinary that a race such as yours, professing gallantry, chivalry, education, and superiority, living in a land where ringing chimes call child and sire to the Church of God — a land where Bibles are read and Gospel truths are spoken, and where courts of justice are presumed to exist; it is extraordinary, I say, that with all these advantages on your side, you can make war upon the poor defenseless black man."

It *was* extraordinary, and Congress refused to readmit the state until it readmitted Turner and his Negro colleagues. But the freedom of action of the black legislators was severely limited in an atmosphere of violence dominated by conservative Democrats and conservative Republicans. Within a year, Georgia became the first of the reconstructed states to re-establish white Democratic control.

Before the curtain that lifted for a moment dropped, black voters elected two members of the Atlanta City Council and sent Jefferson Franklin Long, a thirty-four-year-old Macon tailor, to the U.S. Congress. Black men also held other state and federal positions in Georgia, and black legislators sat in the legislature until the twentieth century.

The same situation obtained in the Border States where the bubble of power soon burst. By artifice, violence, and intimidation, the white leaders of North Carolina, Virginia, Texas, and Arkansas hedged the black electorate with formidable obstacles which minimized the impact of black power. Too far outnumbered to influence government policy materially, black politicians and their supporters voted and held office; but they were used generally as a means to someone else's end. Perhaps the best indication of the state of power in the Border States is the share of legislative seats: 9 per cent in Texas, 11 per cent in Arkansas, 13 per cent in North Carolina, and 16 per cent in Virginia.

In Virginia, as in other minor states, black legislators attracted a great deal of attention. Visiting the Virginia legislature in the fall of 1870, Robert Somers counted several black delegates. One of the legislators, he wrote, "was a pure Negro, very well attired, and displaying not more jewellery than a gentleman might wear; while another, who seemed to have some white blood in his veins, was a quite masculine-looking person, both physically and mentally." In the senate he identified "two coloured Senators among the number, quite black, but senatorial enough, and like men who in Africa would probably have been chiefs." He added: "In the Lower House the coloured delegates mingled freely with the other members, but in the Senate these two sat in a corner by themselves. Yet they seemed to take a cordial interest in the proceedings, and manifested all sympathy with the Senators who addressed the House."

Of the Border States, only North Carolina sent a black man to Congress (J. A. Hyman) in the period under discussion. A black man, Dr. J. D. Harris, was an unsuccessful regular Republican candidate for lieutenant governor in Virginia, but only Arkansas had state cabinet officers: W. H. Grey, commissioner of immigration; J. C. Corbin, superintendent of education; J. T. White, commissioner of public works.

Cabinet officers and congressman apart, the right to participate in government was meaningful, and it yielded important gains. Largely because of the black electorate, public school systems were started in the minor states. And at great cost in terms of financial manipulation, railroad systems were constructed, and Alabama, Georgia, and Florida were started on the road to industrial development. Although democracy was done to death in the minor states by privilege, guile, and superior firepower, these were permanent contributions no amount of distortion can blot out.

Black people gained, too. Because of the black legislators and black sheriffs, many men lived who otherwise would have died and many ate — and well — who otherwise would have hungered.

Power matters, and even a little power helps.

It meant something then — and it means something now — to be in trouble with white folk and to have a black judge and a half-black jury. It meant something to people to be in need and to have a friend in power who needed them.

There were friends in power then. From Texas to Virginia, black men made and executed laws, levied taxes, ran school systems and participated in the vital decisions of the community. In some instances and in some communities, black influence was decisive. In Petersburg, Virginia, for example, Edward King discovered that black people "were largely represented in the Common Council, and sometimes had a controlling voice in municipal affairs." At the time of King's visit, both the commissioner of streets and the engineer of the board of waterworks were Negroes. "The white citizens," King added, "have readily adapted themselves to circumstances, and the session of the Council which I attended was as orderly and, in the main, as well conducted as that of any Eastern city."

In the time of which we write, one could find cities and counties like Petersburg in Texas, Arkansas, North Carolina, Georgia, Alabama, and Florida. To be sure, black people did not have maximum power in these states. But they did have some power. And the difference between having some power and having no power is the difference, as millions now know, between bread and no bread, between a job and no job, between life and a living death.

Politics, Harold Lasswell has said, is the science of who gets what, where, when, and how much. In this period, in these states, black people got something. If what they got was not as much as they should have gotten, it was a great deal more than they would have gotten had they been on the outside looking in.

7

Society "Turned Bottom Side Up"

IT HAD NEVER HAPPENED before, and it has never happened since, in America.

Seeing it in the flesh, James Sheppard Pike recoiled in horror. Black men and black women, he wrote, were lording it over "haughty" Anglo-Saxons, the black men proud in their skin, the black women scornful of fields and kitchens, both black men and black women assuming new roles that undermined basic assumptions of the white dispensation. It was, Pike reported, a society "suddenly turned bottom-side up," with the black people on top and the white people on the bottom.

It seemed to Pike, as it seemed to other white reporters who visited the South during the Reconstruction era, that by strange ways and incompletely the old precept had been fulfilled and the greatest, much to their surprise, had become the least. Nothing in Pike's past life had prepared him for such a turnabout; nothing had prepared him for the spectacle of black men sitting in the crimson plush Gothic seats of power with their feet on the rich mahogany tables. A lifetime of devotion to "liberal" causes had prepared Pike for the traditional handout to needy and properly deferential blacks. But

298

where — in what institution, in what school, in what church — could he have prepared for what he saw now: black people in charge, *running things*, and white people, "cowed and demoralized," accepting "their positions with a stoicism that promises no rewards here or hereafter." It was monstrous, Pike said; and he was right. It is always monstrous when the poor, the downtrodden, and the disinherited present their bills at the bar of history.

In a violently anti-Negro book, Pike admitted that his "pride of race was incontinently shocked." Black power in South Carolina, he said, had created a society that was "a testimony against the claims of Anglo-Saxon blood." It was "the dregs of the population habilitated in the robes of their intelligent predecessors." It was "the slave rioting in the halls of his master, and putting his master under his feet."

Other Northern white reporters, less hysterical perhaps, but no less white-oriented, echoed Pike. Edward King saw a city hall "controlled by blacks, and the magistrates, the police, and the representatives in the Legislature [were] nearly all Africans." He saw, he said, sights terrible to behold. "The lands have been taken from [the whites], and the Negro rules over both them and their lands. He and his fellows dispose not only of the revenues of Beaufort [South Carolina], but of the State. The idle and vicious of his race huddle together in gorgeous parlors, once decorated with elegant furniture, purchased by the planters with the proceeds of slave labor." In New Orleans, Charles Nordhoff saw similar sights. He even saw "men who were slaves but ten years ago, and began life with nothing at the time, now driving magnificent horses, seated in stylish equipages, and wearing diamond breastpins." Of like tone and tenor was a *New York Herald* story which carried the following headline:

> The Beggared Chivalry Sulky but Industri-
> ous — Poor Whites Miscegenating and
> Robbing Hen Roosts — Rich Nig-
> gers Running Legislatures

We know now that what white reporters saw in the South in the 1870's was distorted by the defective lenses of white supremacy. But the very violence of their language betrays the fact that they were looking at the beginning of a real revolution that fissured Southern society at every level. Let us go back in time to that brave black world, supplementing the observations of biased whites with contemporary reports from black partici- pants, noting, as we travel, the changes black power wrought in the everyday lives of the people. By and large, commentators have focused on the legislature and the statehouse, forgetting that politics is not the petty manipulations of the few, but the day-to-day struggles of the many. When politics is real, thou- sands of people change. When politics is serious, millions change. Indeed, a real change in politics—that is to say power relations—changes everything, including sex, birth, and death. For the simple fact of the matter is that power is a precondition of the human. Without power, men cannot be men—and if men cannot be men then women cannot be women. In the Recon- struction period, when for a very short time power was black— or at least off-white—black men were men and black women were women. And in the wake of that revolutionary (for America) change, a whole society was hurled suddenly from its old combinations, to crash tumultuously together, seeking new ones.

A visitor from contemporary Africa or Asia would not have felt out of place in the new society. In the large, the recon- structed South presented a face not unlike the faces of the rising societies of Africa and Asia, with a tiny black political elite (and a small white economic elite) at the top, and the great masses of people, black and white, huddled together at the bot- tom, close to the earth. At a superficial glance, it seemed that not much had changed with the overwhelming majority of black people who still lived in one- and two-room huts and followed the sun, working from first light to dusk. For the many, life was still hard. But then life had always been hard, and now, for the first time, there was hope. The yeast of power was lifting the top layers as well as the bottom layers of the black group. One observes with interest that reporters noted an intense exhilaration among the black people of that era. They felt they were presiding at a new era in the history of man. They felt the millennium was around the next turning. They could *see* facts (black governors, black sheriffs) that justified the hardness and the sacrifices of their lives. Materially poor, they were spiritually rich, for there were no boundaries to their hope.

In visualizing the contours of this society, it is best perhaps to begin with the poor, for bread is of the essence of politics and changes or lack of changes in the bread-getting syndrome condition every other aspect of men's lives. As we have said often, the real tragedy of Reconstruction was the failure to link bread and ballots through meaningful land reform. The grand outcome of this failure was a divergence of the political and economic axes. Ultimate political power (in many instances) was black, but ultimate economic power was white. And what this meant in the reconstructed South was that political power had to rapidly convert itself into economic power or go to the wall.

As in Africa and Asia today, the attempt to effect this metamorphosis (which is the real, perhaps the only, point of politics) was protracted and painful. The failure of land reform forced the great mass of black people into a form of peonage, the sharecropping system. The discipline of hunger replaced the discipline of the whip, and it became a settled point of planter policy to prevent black people from acquiring land. This was accomplished by shamefully manipulating share-cropper accounts, which were kept by the planter, and by siphoning away surplus capital at the plantation store. This is not the place to discuss sharecropping in detail, and the point of these generalizations is to stress that this policy could not succeed without the shield of state power, without control over lien, land, and wage legislation and the judges and administrators who interpreted these laws. So long as black people retained at least partial control over these vital matters, they could not be excluded from the perquisites of power: franchises, contracts, jobs.

Black people were not unaware of the economic value of political power, and they used their leverage in the legislatures and courthouses to push themselves up. In South Carolina and other states, Republican legislatures passed tenancy legislation to protect tenants against arbitrary disturbances. Bills were also passed "to enable indigent persons to obtain credit," and state agencies were created to look out for the interests of the poor. On the local level, Republican justices of the peace (many of them black) and predominantly black juries frequently ruled in favor of renters and sharecroppers in the constantly recurring disputes over wages, liens, and lands. The Radical Republican tax policy also created a climate of expectancy and hope in the black community. One could see the results of this policy in every arena of the economic life of the South. It was not unusual in that day for black men to own and manage plantations of a thousand acres or more. Some of these big planters were politicians like Blanche Kelso Bruce and James T. Rapier, who discovered that politics pays in more ways than one; others were bold farmers who fought their way into the entrepreneurial class by ingenuity and sweat. To be sure, the big black planters, like the big white planters, were few and far between. But the fact that they existed at all a few years after slavery is significant. The big black planters were the *avant garde* of the black entrepreneurial class which died with the death of black power. In their brief time in the sunlight, they stimulated other black men who slowly and painfully accumulated enough dollars to buy a mule and a few acres of land. There are no reliable figures on Negroes who acquired land in this period.

but indirect evidence suggests that the number was considerable. Travelers reported examples of successful independent farmers in almost every county. By the mid-seventies, according to Charles Nordhoff, the black people of Georgia owned "nearly 400,000 acres of farming real estate, besides city property." Contemporary observers reported similar thrusts toward farm ownership and economic independence in Virginia, South Carolina, and other states. Speaking on the floor of the South Carolina house of representatives in 1870, Reuben Tomlinson said: "If we could get together the statistics of the laboring men who have during the past year become land owners through their own exertions and industry, we would be perfectly astounded."

Alarmed by the sharp rise in the number of independent black farmers, white planters organized combines to protect their economic interests. In some cases they refused to sell land to Negroes. Some planters also entered into conspiracies to fix wages and to blacklist obstreperous workers. But this policy was hampered by the inability of white planters to use the state power to support their economic interests. Courts scrutinized planter complaints with great care and sometimes refused to order the arrest of workers who offended white planters. Encouraged by the impartiality of the state, many workers fought back with sit-down demonstations and strikes. In many instances, black workers refused to make a contract for the next year or to leave the plantation. There were also several cases of dissatisfied workers expressing their resentment by burning fields, barns, and houses.

Black economic interests were also defended by labor conventions which were organized in every Southern state. In 1870, a Mississippi labor group urged Negroes not to work as laborers and suggested that they refuse to pay more than $1.50 per acre for farm land. Three years later, the Colored Labor Convention of Alabama urged the abolition of sharecropping and demanded a uniform system of written contracts. The

Alabama convention said the interests of "the laboring masses" would best be served by working for a fixed amount of wages per annum, payable monthly.

Because of the white boycott, farms available to black people were generally on inferior or indifferent land. Situated thus on marginal land, with inadequate financial backing, many black farmers were sitting ducks for economic adversity. A series of bad crops, the depression of 1873, and the hostile economic environment forced many Negroes to return to sharecropping. Some gave up hope and made no further effort, but others persisted and made enviable records. Benjamin T. Montgomery, who bought Jefferson Davis' baronial plantation at Davis Bend, Mississippi, was, according to leading white conservatives, one of the best planters in Mississippi. Montgomery's cotton won all the prizes at the famous Cincinnati Exposition. The example of Montgomery and other independent farmers and planters led the Florida African Methodist Episcopal conference to pass the following resolution.

Whereas labor is the basis of all wealth, and wealth is an absolute necessity of civilized society, and a peaceful condition of society....
Resolved by the convention of ministers and laymen of the Methodist Episcopal Church of Florida, that we congratulate our people upon the rapid progress they have made in the past six years, and upon the increase of mixed industry, homesteads, and small farms in opposition to the ruinous plantation system, and [we consider] those together with the increase in school houses and churches, and also the deposit of nearly three million dollars in the savings-banks, as a greater pledge of our progress to the friends of freedom throughout the world than can be found in the house of any people who sprang from as lowly a condition as ourselves....

Economic progress was also reported in Southern towns where black workers virtually monopolized work on the wharves and in the building trades. Contemporaries saw black men at work in tobacco factories in Virginia and phosphate plants in South Carolina. It was reported that most of the teamsters were black and that black masons and carpenters were more than holding their own. Although most black urban workers were unskilled, it seems that there was a higher percentage of black skilled workers in the 1870's than in the 1960's. Indeed, it has been estimated that of the 120,000 skilled workers in the South at that time at least 100,000 were Negroes.

At that time and for many years afterwards, black people were the social wealth of the South. The Southern railroads and other public and quasi-public works were built almost entirely by black laborers. In a rare moment of objectivity, the Jackson *Clarion* admitted that black workers were the main producers of the South. "The Negroes of the South," the *Clarion* said, "are its wealth. . . . The South, without the Negro, for a generation at least, would be a wilderness and a waste." The new labor system provided the rural masses with a modicum of purchasing power which, in turn, supported consumer goods. Travelers reported that the men with "the Negro trade" were getting rich.

Sensing their own increasing weight, black men moved into the mainstream of the economy and rapidly developed small businesses (restaurants, blacksmith shops, barber shops, general stores) which served both black and white. Particularly aggressive in this effort were black women who sold vegetables, candy, and pop in open-air markets in almost every city of any size.

On a higher level, black men were busy converting votes into dollars. Richard J. Cain, the South Carolina congressman, was one of the biggest and most resourceful real estate operators in the Charleston area, and James Hill, the slender Mississippi secretary of state, was a big businessman deeply engaged in land and real estate deals. Like the big operators of today, the big operators of the Reconstruction period made money as a result of political connections. Beverly Nash, the powerful South Carolina senator, landed a lucrative contract to furnish bricks for the state penitentiary; and his colleague, Henry

Hayne, was granted an equally lucrative contract to furnish fuel for the penitentiary. It is not without significance that both Nash and Hayne were on the board of trustees (Nash was chairman) of the penitentiary.

Some of the big deals of this period were tainted by fraud and favoritism, but most were the inevitable by-product of power. Power over roads and bridges and public works, the power to tax, the power to give or withhold contracts and franchises—what is this if not the power to make some men rich and to keep others poor. With something approaching amazement, black men discovered that there was money in power. On the precinct and county level, Republican power brought the first touch of embourgeoisement to thousands of ordinary black people. The sheriff's office operated on the fee system and the jobs of several county sheriffs were estimated to be worth more than twenty thousand dollars a year. Black men held some assessors' posts which were worth more. In addition to the perquisites attached to the posts of county supervisors, school superintendents and justices of the peace, black people reaped financial benefits from the relatively minor (for that day) patronage posts of policemen and state militiamen.

Power paid other dividends. A. J. Ransier, lieutenant governor of South Carolina, and F. L. Cardozo, state treasurer, were among the major stockholders and directors of the Greenville and Columbus Railroad, and P. B. S. Pinchback and other politicians were among the incorporators and directors of steamship companies, oil corporations, phosphate factories and banks. In an allied development, black lawyers handled major corporate accounts and were much sought after by rich industrialists seeking tax benefits and franchises from the Republican governments. Robert Brown Elliott, South Carolina's most powerful black politician, operated in the mainstream of money, and his law partner was a conservative white Democrat.

Other by-products of power were independent corporations

like the Mount Alto Mining and Land Company of Virginia. African-Americans also organized numerous producer and consumer cooperatives. In South Carolina and Louisiana, black cooperatives bought and ran large plantations. In Baltimore, Richmond, Charleston, and other cities, cooperatives bought land and homes which were sold to members in small parcels at reasonable prices. An outstanding example of cooperative enterprise was the Chesapeake, Marine, and Dry Dock Company which was organized by Negro caulkers, carpenters, and mechanics after they were excluded from work on Baltimore docks. The excluded workers bought a shipyard and marine railway, and the company was soon doing more repair work than any other firm of its kind in the city.

The black cooperatives were expressions of a heightening and transformation of the consciousness of black people whose sense of themselves as members of a specific group broadened and became clearer. Reconstruction awakened in millions hopes and aspirations they did not know they had; and these hopes and aspirations came to shape new standards of judgment. Black laborers, excluded from the new labor movement, formed their own national labor organizations. Black Christians, confined to separate pews and excluded from the structure of government of white churches, withdrew and formed their own churches and church associations. There was also a proliferation of fraternal organizations and embryonic insurance associations. Many of these new institutions, particularly the churches and rifle clubs or militias, were closely allied with the black man's quest for power. Charles H. Pearce, a Tallahassee AME minister, said: "A man in this state cannot do his whole duty as a minister except he look out for the political interests of his people." An oblique tribute to the effectiveness of black ministers came from a Wilkinson County, Mississippi, white man, who said: "It is a fact, demonstrated by experience, that the combination in one Negro, of preacher and politician, is always dangerous to the peace of the community."

Fruits of power, free schools, attracted adults and children. Political power in the Reconstruction period brought many tangible benefits to masses of black people.

Howard University was one of several black institutions
of higher learning constructed during this period.
The Freedmen's Bureau played a major role in
founding Howard.

From one end of America to the other in these days, black people were busy building institutions that were dangerous to the peace of biased white men. It appears from the evidence that the level of consciousness of the black people of the 1870's was higher than the level of consciousness of black people of the 1960's. Black people then never seemed to tire of each other, and at the drop of a hat they would assemble in the thousands for picnics, parades, and excursions. "They had a passion," John De Forest wrote, "not so much for wandering, as for getting together." Edward King added in the same vein: "The Virginia Negro has almost the French passion for fête-days."

During this time of hope and rising racial consciousness, black people pre-empted July 4th and other national holidays. On the Fourth and on Emancipation Day, Southern Negroes took over the streets of major Southern towns. Drums booming, flags flying, they surged through the streets in massive pageants of power. Edward King viewed such a parade in Virginia. The streets, he wrote, were filled "with stout men, decently clothed, and their wives and sweethearts. . . . Each was talking, vociferously; officials, in flaming regalia and sweating at every pore, rushed to and fro; bands thundered and urchins screamed."

Since politics was real, since it was an activity that corroborated reality and promised to change reality, black people gave to politics the kind of attention their children and grandchildren would give to entertainment and religion. The rhythm of life was the rhythm of the political year which began with mass meetings in churches, courthouses and fields, and built to a stirring climax on election day. It was not uncommon to see a thousand black people on foot or on horseback, trekking to and from meetings. Nor was it unusual for a field hand or a laborer to tap unsuspected reservoirs of talent and rise to the top of the political heap. Observers noted that black people showed an "extraordinary aptitude" for "learning political forms." To chair a meeting or to stand up in a political gathering and make a motion: this was the height of many men's ambitions in that strange and clamorous period.

On election day, the big day of the year, every precinct became a huge picnic ground. Black people came to the polls in large groups a day in advance and camped out like soldiers on the march. They set up large tables and consumed huge quantities of lemonade and stronger beverages. Communing thus, they discussed the issues of the day and traded political information. This camaraderie extended through election day when almost all courthouse yards and courthouse squares were thronged with Negroes. When, at last, the voting was done, the crowds returned to the plantations, rejoicing in freedom.

But this was not the end of the participation of the people in the political process. Black people flocked to the courts and other public places to watch trials and discuss the issues of the day. Thousands filled the galleries and windows of the legislature and expressed their pleasure or displeasure with cheers and hisses. From January to December, the black electorate lived in a primary relationship with power. They liked the feel of it. They liked to be in close proximity to the buildings (courthouse, statehouse) that symbolized power. "Around [these buildings]," King noted, "are always lounging crowds of Negro men and women, as if they delighted to linger in the atmosphere of government and law, to the powers and responsibilities of which they have lately been introduced."

What did black power mean to the average black man?

How did it enter his life?

To the average black man, black power was a shield against hostile white power and a key to locked doors. It was a key, among other things, to manhood and womanhood. Shielded by power, both men and women demanded the respect due men and women. They refused to give way, give in, or take orders. They demanded the same respect for their wives and children as public opinion demanded for white women and white children. James D. B. De Bow, a white editor, made a trip to

the South two years after the war and observed that some
Negroes "retained their old-time courtesy, but a majority of
both men and women are evidently staggering under the
weight of their own importance, and were ludicrously inflated
and pompous."

Black men were especially sensitive about the symbols of
slavery, and refused to answer the old slave bells or work in
gangs under an overseer. Certain symbols (hats, walking canes),
which were *verboten* in the slave era, now became positive
symbols of manhood and womanhood. Clothing also served as
an outward manifestation of a change in status, and black men
splurged on canes, scarves and swallow-tailed coats.

It was considered dishonorable for a black man to let his
women and children work in the fields. The new dispensation
apparently pleased the women, for they were everywhere the
most vocal and aggressive champions of the Radical Republican
regime. Reporting from South Carolina, Robert Somers wrote:
"The Negro women are now almost wholly withdrawn from
field labor [and the] children who were made available under
slavery for industrial purposes are being more and more
absorbed by the schools."

Not only children but grown men and women were
absorbed by the schools. The whole race, observers said,
wanted to go to school. Reporters saw black people studying
everywhere—on the wharves, in the fields, in the kitchen. It
was not unusual to find three generations—a grandmother, a
mother and a daughter—sitting on the same bench in the same
classroom. One old Negro man told his teacher: "I'm jammed
on to a hundred, and dis is my fust chance to git a start."

Aided by Northern philanthropists and the Freedmen's
Bureau, black men constructed their own schoolhouses. "In
every village of the South," Tourgee reported, "was erected one
or more of these rough wooden buildings, consisting only of a
roof, rafter, walls and floor of undressed plank. The minimum
of cost and the maximum of space were the objects kept

constantly in view, and usually attained beyond all question. These houses became to the colored people what the court of the temple was to the Jews — the place of assembly and worship, as well as instruction. They were usually unsectarian; and it was no unusual spectacle to see two or three denominations worshipping in the same house, while the school was under the management and control of still another."

Because of black power, black people in many areas had better schools than white people. The Republican regimes were also very liberal in providing scholarships and free textbooks. Nordhoff said "the colored people [of Louisiana] are generally better supplied than the whites with free schools."

The new schools rapidly became major community centers rivalling the church in importance. Parents maintained a close watch over the curriculum and visited the schools often to hear their children read and recite. A. A. Taylor, the black historian, wrote: "They were all eager to hear the essays, declamations, and recitations of these developing youth. So popular became education among the Negroes that parents who kept their children at home to work were generally branded as unworthy citizens."

In many cases, black people decided who could teach and what they could teach. Black men controlled the entire educational system of several Southern states, and on the local level real control was often invested in predominantly or wholly Negro boards. White teachers often had to pass a board of examiners composed wholly or in part of blacks, and black parents often exercised their right to veto native white Democrat teachers. Many black parents demanded black teachers for black schools. On one occasion, Richmond, Virginia, parents used statistics to prove that scholarship and attendance records were higher in schools staffed by black teachers.

In New Orleans and other cities, black and white children attended the same classes in the same schools. George W. Cable, a white Southerner, visited an integrated school in New

Orleans and observed: "... I saw to my great and rapid edification, white ladies teaching Negro boys; colored women showing the graces and dignity of mental and moral refinement, ladies in everything save society's credentials; children and youth of both races standing in the same classes and giving each other peaceable, friendly, effective competition; and black classes, with black teachers, pushing intelligently up into the intricacies of high-school mathematics."

Black and white people also mingled in "peaceable, friendly, effective" competition in bars, railroad cars, and places of public amusement. An anonymous white South Carolinian, writing in the *Atlantic Monthly*, said: "The Negroes, however, are permitted to, and frequently do, ride in first-class railway and in street railway cars. This liberty at first encountered much opposition from the railroad conductors and white passengers, and led to several fights, expulsions, and lawsuits. But it is now so common as hardly to provoke remark. . . ." There was also mingling in residential areas. Black men with money lived in "white" sections, and white politicians and white schoolteachers, male and female, often lived in Negro neighborhoods. Some whites developed such a preference for Negro life that they were almost lost to the white race. They were referred to and sometimes referred to themselves as "white niggers." According to Walter J. Fleming, some white politicians became *de facto* Negroes, speaking, he said, of "us Negroes," and "we Negroes." When Alabama Republicans defeated the Democrats in 1872, a white Radical shouted: "We Negroes have beat 'em."

With the barriers down and power looking the other way, there was considerable mingling and marrying at all levels of society. From press and pulpit there were frequent denunciations of disorderly houses openly patronized by men and women of both races. It was necessary for the Klan to whip some white women to keep them from Negro dances and to maim and murder some white men to keep them from legalizing their love for black women. But in defiance of the law (in white-dominated states) and the Klan (in black-dominated states), intermarriage continued. Particularly galling to diehard Southerners was the decided preference some white men of power showed for black women. Governor Franklin J. Moses Jr., the South Carolina-born Republican, was not the only high-ranking official to give public notice of a preference for blacks over blondes. White papers repeatedly denounced "Yankees" for walking the streets with black women on their arms. There were even louder outcries when politicians and ordinary citizens legalized their preferences.

The most celebrated interracial marriage of this season occurred in Mississippi where Albert T. Morgan, the white state senator, crossed the color line and legalized his love for the stunningly beautiful Carrie Victoria Highgate, a native of Syracuse, New York, who had settled in the state as a missionary and teacher. Morgan tells us in his memoirs that he was smitten with admiration for the black beauty when he saw her for the first time at the school she operated in Jackson. Two years passed, however, before all obstacles—including an anti-miscegenation law—were removed. As soon as the Mississippi legislature passed a bill, authored by Morgan, which legalized interracial marriages, Morgan approached his brother Charles. It was rumored at the time that Morgan was deeply involved with an attractive Mississippi white woman, and Charles Morgan, an ardent Radical, received the news with something less than enthusiasm. But Albert Morgan persisted, without identifying his bride-to-be.

"Have I your consent," he asked, "to marry the only girl in this wide world that I care a 'tinker's bauble' for. . . .?"

"My consent?" Charles Morgan fenced. "Why, you're of age, man. As you make your bed, you must lie, you know."

"Yes, I've heard that remark before, and shall doubtless often hear it again. But you promise not to disown me, do you?"

"Ye-e-a-s. Yes, I'll promise, but . . ."

"Look me in the eye, old polecat," Albert Morgan said, "I am anxious to see how you take it—there, steady now! You are *mistaken*, my brother! God willing, I am going to marry a 'nigger' schoolmarm."

God had no objections. More significantly, in the context of the time, the Mississippi legislature had no objections. And so, on August 3, 1870, Morgan and his bride were married in Hinds County, Mississippi. They began housekeeping in Yazoo City after a hectic wedding trip which included ejection from a bus in Louisville, Kentucky, and the printing of a variety of vulgar stories by Northern newspapers.

If we credit casual observers, there were more marriages of white men to black women than of white women to black men. But the evidence is far from conclusive. The *New York Herald* reported after a North Carolina survey: "The rich white says that his poorer brother has lost all self-respect, that his women take up with Negroes (which is a sadly frequent fact, at least out here)."

Despite the difficulties, Othellos and Desdemonas continued to pursue each other. A. A. Taylor offered one explanation of the intermarriage boom. "The recognition of the civil rights of the Negroes," he wrote, "and their increasing prestige in the economic and political spheres . . . counteracted the proscription of those who intermarried. Poor white women sometimes chose Negro husbands because these men of color were more wealthy and influential than the available males of their own race. Probably the most interesting of all was that of R. T. Coleman in Cumberland County [Virginia]. He was the owner of a large farm and acquired considerable property of various kinds. He was remarkable in that he distinguished himself as a horse trader, a politician, a preacher, and the husband of three white women. They were short-lived, but he was business-like enough to have them insured to the amount of $1,000 each. When he married the third time there was a specific law against such persons even living as husbands and wives in Virginia. But he evaded the law by marrying in the North and establishing his wife in a separate home a few yards from his. He was not disturbed and enjoyed the highest respect of both races."

There was everywhere a sense of the opening of new vistas. At the top level of the new society, all barriers—sexual, social and economic—crumbled in the crucible of power. The black elite—wealthy professionals, politicians, and merchants—moved in the ambience of a world that had almost forgotten color. They exchanged home visits with powerful white politicians. They were in and out of the Exchange Hotel in Montgomery, the City Hotel in Tallahassee, and the St. Charles in New Orleans. They were in and out of the offices of the powerful and were forever rushing off to very important conferences in New York and Washington.

The new men of power lived in the best sections of town and drove big landaus with blooded horses. The black lieutenant governor of South Carolina had a white governess for his children, and other black men of power were served ably by white servants and aides. Then, as now, the pleasures of the powerful were predictable (wine, fast women, and faster horses) and expensive. William J. Whipper, the powerful South Carolina legislator, was a horse fancier with a talent for oratory and flamboyant entertaining. On one occasion, the well-to-do attorney hired a ship to carry his Charleston friends to a little party he was holding in Beaufort. Viewing the whole thing with a jaundiced eye, a white South Carolinian wrote: "The legislators and others in their high society are first-class swells.... The Negroes of the wealthier set naturally imitate all the social customs of the whites, paying homage to the ladies, preventing females from working, sending the children to school, living in fine houses, employing servants, supporting a good table, and keeping carriages, and horses."

No one lived better or attracted more attention in this period than the celebrated Rollin sisters who played a role in the South Carolina revolution not unlike the role played by Madame Roland in the French Revolution. Handsomely educated, fiercely independent, and ravishingly attractive, the five Rollin sisters were the daughters of a Frenchman and a black woman. At the end of the war, they became wholehearted partisans of the new order and developed political skills of the highest order. The oldest sister, Frances, married William J. Whipper, the powerful state senator. And the single sisters — Charlotte, Katherine, Marie Louise, and Florence — ran a radical salon where the leading members of the South Carolina directorate gathered and acquired identity.

Only the naïve were scandalized by the political maneuvering of the quintet. For, as a conservative reporter of the *New York Herald* said, in "periods of transition and choosing, as, for instance, during the French and our own Revolutions, and as in the case of the late Paris Commune, women of tact, pluck, education and experience have always governed masses of men. France had her Madame de Tencin, Madame du Deffond, Madame de Genlis, her Theresa Cabarrus and her Madame Roland. The War of Independence produced such women as Mrs. Robert Morris and the heroic Moll Pitcher.... And South Carolina is not to-day without her feminine celebrities, albeit they may not be of the orthodox and Caucasian shade of skin." This reporter, who had "heard of the famous sisters... but had never seen them," was granted an interview in June, 1871. Let us go with him to the white frame house with a large piazza on a fine, tree-shaded street back of the capitol in Columbia. The reporter made his way up the flight of steps to the front door of the "Rollin mansion" and pulled the bell handle. "In a few moments," he wrote, "I heard light footsteps tripping through the hall and the door was opened to me by a beautiful girl, in a graceful, cool white robe. I thought of the old Scotch ballad as I looked upon this girl —

> *Oh, she's fair and she is rare*
> *And she is won'drous bonnie,*
> *There's none wi' her that can compare*
> *I love her best of ony.*

"The girl [he continued] was about fifteen years of age, having a figure moulded in the best outlines. Her face was that peculiar hue which comes from the admixture of pure white blood with the mulatto, and results in the quadroon. Her eyes were almost almond-shaped, lustrous as moonlight; her teeth were white and shapely; a warm red blush mantled her olive cheeks, and a smile played around the dimple in her chin."

This reporter represented the most vehemently anti-Negro newspaper in the North. But his political bias was shattered, temporarily, by the beauty of Marie Louise Rollins. With some confusion, we can imagine, he managed to state his business and was ushered into a parlor, on the left of the hall, "which had an open window looking out on a garden" where there was a fountain "whose waters were plashing [sic] in the dying sunset."

But it was Marie Louise, not the sunset, which entranced the *New York Herald* reporter. And his eyes followed her as she moved about the room "arranging the music on a fine piano, which occupied a corner of the room." The room also contained, he noticed, a large center table which was covered with books and magazines, a copy of Bryon, "half-open, a number of the *Atlantic*, with a volume of Gail Hamilton works and another of Louisa Alcott".

At this point, the reporter's reverie was disturbed by the rustle of a trailing dress. "A "female form entered" and he was face to face with Charlotte Rollin, "the Madame de Tencin of South Carolina." Charlotte Rollin's figure, he noticed, was not "devoid of grace and suppleness," although "not so correct in outline as that of Marie Louise." Her hair, he said, was "just a little and but a very little kinky" and she had "the skin of a mulatto, slightly freckled."

Lottie Rollin, as she was called, came directly to the point. She had been deceived and misquoted by white reporters and she was more than a little suspicious, and with cause, of the intentions of the *New York Herald* reporter. The reporter answered that he would never abuse her confidence. That settled, he was invited into another parlor, across the hall,

Market women at an open-air store in
South Carolina. Sidewalk markets were dominated by
black merchants in many parts of the South.

A large crowd attends Emancipation celebration in Washington, D.C. The political year was marked by many celebrations and parades attended by thousands.

which was hung with choice pieces and engravings" and decorated with handsome furniture, including "a well-stored bookcase." There were also, he noticed, several portraits of a white state senator from Colleton who was later identified as Katherine Rollin's fiance.

While the interview was in progress, Katherine Rollin, a "tall and slender young lady, attired in black silk, with large black eyes, and long straight hair behind," returned from a reception at the governor's mansion, and the fourth sister, Florence, wandered in from the back of the house. The four sisters then interviewed the reporter.

"Are you fond of poetry?" Lottie Rollin asked.

"Yes, Marm."

"I am personally fond of Byron," Lottie Rollin continued. "What a dear reckless fellow he was, to be sure. His "Corsair" and his "Childe Harold" are so beautiful."

Lottie Rollin went on to say that she loved "Miss Browning above all the poets," and that she also liked Whittier because he was "the poet of human liberty and the rights of mankind."

The reporter confessed that he was "rather astonished at the knowledge of the poets displayed by these young girls, who are despised by the white race of the old *régime* in South Carolina." He was told that "two of the girls had been educated at Dr. Dio Lewis's School, No. 20, Essex Street, Boston" and that Louise had attended a convent school near Philadelphia.

It appears from the interview and from other evidence that the Rollin sisters, like Madame Roland, had little understanding of the deeper currents of the Revolution. In the course of the interview, the sisters, who were aligned with Governor Robert Scott, made disparaging remarks about W. J. Whipper, their brother-in-law, and Robert B. Elliott, the rising black leader. They also, if the reporter can be believed, tried to separate themselves from the great mass of black people by stressing their free Negro lineage. In evaluating this statement, one must consider the source—the *New York Herald*—and the fact that the sisters expressed a definite black nationalist strain, saying defiantly: "As for the State of South Carolina, of which we are natives ... the rebels will never get it back into their hands while there are ninety thousand votes cast by the black race at our elections."

The powerful lived differently, and they died differently. In this era, flags flew at half-mast when powerful black men died, and all public offices were closed. U.S. senators and governors served as pallbearers and some Southern whites, out of grief or self-interest, found it expedient to sit in attendance. The funeral of Lieutenant Governor Oscar J. Dunn was one of the most colorful of its kind in New Orleans. And when James Lynch, the Mississippi political boss, died, the legislature, by joint resolution, appropriated one thousand dollars for the purpose of erecting a monument over his remains. He was the first and probably the last Mississippian, black or white, so honored. In an ironic gesture, Lynch was buried in Greenwood Cemetery with Confederate heroes and other well-known whites. Black men of power were also buried in "white" cemeteries in Selma, Columbia, New Orleans, and other Southern cities. When the tide of black power receded, the bones of some black men were dug up and reburied in "Negro" cemeteries.

How did whites react to all this?

What were they doing all this time?

Some Southern whites were marching, willingly or unwillingly, with the dominant power. As for the rest, they were trying, to the best of their ability, to pretend that nothing had changed. Withdrawing from public life, this group plunged into the past. Walter F. Fleming said: "I knew an old man who refused for several years to read newspapers, so unpleasant was the news."

Some whites found the tensions unbearable and openly adopted revolutionary postures of violence. Others packed their bags and went West. Edward King met a typical irreconcilable on a steamer bound for Texas. The white man said: "I hain't

nothin' agin a free nigger but I don't want him to say a word to
me. The world's big enough for us both, I reckon. We ain't
made to live together under this new style o' things. Free
niggers and me couldn't agree."

Other whites who couldn't agree with free Negroes withdrew into private shells and looked back in anger and frustra-
tion. James Pike was shaken by the apathy of the South
Carolina whites. The average white man, he wrote, was reticent
and reserved in the face of black power. "Having been, as he
considers, doomed by the revolution, he sits haughtily tranquil,
wrapped in reserve, save when he ventures to predict the
downfall of the Republic, and to lament the despotism under
which he asserts that he is kept. He is fond of gloomy horo-
scopes."

In his study of Reconstruction in South Carolina, Professor Joel Williamson reported two typical responses to black
power. A white lawyer who had fled the state chided a friend
who had remained: "Well, Dick, you have a charming Supreme
Court in S.C. now—a contemptible scallawag occupying the
seat once adorned by O'Neal and Dunkin, and two carpet
baggers (& one of them a *Negro*) in the seats once graced by
Wardlaw & Withers. How do you feel before such a Bench?
When you address such creatures as 'your Honors,' don't the
blood boil or grow chill in your veins? And how can you say
'Gentlemen of the Jury' to a panel of loathsome, leather-headed
negroes?" Another white South Carolinian, an inmate of the
insane asylum, wrote a similar letter to a minister in an
unsuccessful attempt to evade the authority of the black
regents. The white ministers advised the white inmate to read
the Holy Bible. The inmate replied—"If the stupid Negroes
who act as Regents of this Institution had read the Bible as
much or as long as either my wife or I have done, they would
not need when sitting as a board on Such Cases as mine, to ask
the Stupid and insulting questions that some of them now do
when exercising their brief authority While I appear before

them." The issue of black authority also posed delicate problems in Mississippi. Postmaster H. R. Pease was stopped on the streets of Vicksburg by "one of the most respectable citizens" who said in a loud voice: "I hear, sir, by God, that you are going to appoint a damned nigger to be a clerk in your post-office!" Pease replied that he certainly was going to appoint a black clerk. "Then, sir, I tell you it's a damned outrage, and this community won't stand it, sir!" Pease replied coldly, "You will have to stand it."

Aristocrats postured and pretended, but they also accommodated, for it is impossible to ignore power. To quote the white South Carolinian of the *Atlantic Monthly* article again; "It is esteemed disreputable among the whites to Mr. a Negro, though, of course, it is frequently done when a man has a bill to lobby through the legislature or other favor to request. The same remark will apply to touching the hat."

By the mid-seventies, more and more whites were touching their hats. By that time, black people were more secure in their new positions. They knew, by then, that they had been victims of a cruel mystification, and that they could operate the levers of power as well as white people. No longer apologetic, scornful of false friends and hard-eyed foes, they demanded an acceleration of the social revolution. A Mississippi white man said: "The Negroes are crazed and drunken with their new sense of power." And with that new sense of power came a sharpening of racial consciousness and racial pride. One could see in almost every field, in almost every street, the dawning of a new sense of self-respect and peoplehood. Some black people even rose to the conception of the Southern states as unique expressions of the black personality. A hostile witness, Edward King, said: "The Negro is not especially anxious to see immigration come in. The spirit of the race is strong within him. He is desirous of seeing the lands in the Commonwealth in the hands of his own people before the rest of the world's poor are invited to partake. He is impressed by the idea that

South Carolina should be in some measure a black man's
government, and he is jealous of white intervention.... The
black man lets the Africa in him run riot for the time being. He
even dislikes to see the mulatto progress; and when he criticizes
him, it is as if he were necessarily inferior." There were still
vestigial remains of the slave conditioning. "But the full
blacks," King said, "are gradually beginning to assert themselves, and certainly in South Carolina and in many other
sections, they have as much pride of race as the haughty
Caucasian."

It was to reverse this dawning sense of peoplehood that
Southern whites staged the violent counterrevolution that we
shall consider in the next chapter. But the counterrevolution
did not blot out a fact that Sir George Campbell, a perceptive
English writer, noted in 1879. "During the last dozen years," he
wrote, "the Negroes have had a very large share of political
education. Considering the troubles and the ups and downs
that they have gone through, it is, I think, wonderful how
beneficial this education has been to them, and how much these
people, so lately in the most debased condition of slavery, have
acquired independent ideas, and, far from lapsing into anarchy,
have become citizens with ideas of law and property and order.
The white serfs of the European countries took hundreds of years
to rise to the level which the Negroes have attained in a dozen.

8

The First White Backlash

NOTHING WAS LEFT to chance.

The assassins — highly placed aristocrats and their poor white allies — huddled in dimly lit rooms in Clinton, Mississippi, and decided that Charles Caldwell had to die. He had to die because he was black, because he was powerful, and because the black power he personified stood between the assassins and absolute control of the state.

In that day and age, black politicians were usually shot down in broad open daylight in the county square. But Charles Caldwell was no ordinary politician. He was strong, he was fearless, he was a dead shot — and nobody wanted to meet him face to face. It was decided, therefore, that one of the few white men Caldwell trusted would lure the black politician into Chilton's store for a friendly Christmas drink. The white man would then maneuver Caldwell to a fixed position before the open window. The two men would clink glasses in the traditional Christmas toast and at that precise moment a white marksman, situated across the street, would blow Caldwell's brains out.

Nothing, as I say, was left to chance. It was all planned deliberately and carefully in the Christmas season by the good Christian burghers of Hinds County, Mississippi.

Charles Caldwell, a former state senator who had helped to draft the constitution and who was now a top officer of the state militia, was no fool. He knew he was marked for death. He had been warned time after time not to walk the streets alone. But such warnings carried no weight to a man of Caldwell's temperament. He was no child, he said; nobody was going to tell him what to do; nobody was going to keep him from walking the streets of his home town. Thus it was that on Thursday "in the Christmas" in 1875 that Caldwell brushed aside the pleas of his wife, Margaret Ann, and walked toward the center of Clinton, a sleepy little town near the state capital. It was late in the afternoon and long shadows lay athwart the deserted streets. Everyone, it seemed, was inside celebrating the Savior's birth. How was Caldwell to know that men were preparing another crucifixion? How was he to know that hard-eyed men with loaded guns were following his every step?

Caldwell walked on, unaware of the watching eyes, and met, quite by accident it seemed, his old friend Buck Cabell. The two men had known each other for a long time. They "never knowed anything against each other," Mrs. Caldwell said later, "never had no hard words." Presuming on this old friendship, Cabell insisted that Caldwell join him in a Christmas treat. Caldwell said "no, he didn't want any Christmas." Cabell was offended. "You must take a drink with me," he said. "You must take a drink." So saying, the white man took his black friend by the arm and escorted him into Chilton's cellar. Witnesses said later that the two men "jingled the glasses, and at the tap of the glasses, and while each other held the glass, while they were taking the glass, somebody shot right through the back from the outside of the gate window, and Caldwell fell to the floor."

People came running now from all directions and the wounded man was soon surrounded by men with rifles and pistols. Gasping for breath, bleeding profusely, Caldwell pulled himself painfully to a sitting position and ran his eyes, disdainfully, over the assassins—community leaders, judges, politicians, men of substance, men he had known all his life. Caldwell asked someone to drag him outside in the open air. He said he didn't want "to die like a dog closed up." When they had taken him outside, Caldwell asked a white preacher to drag him home so he could see his wife before he died. The assassins, smelling death, moved in quickly for the kill, shouting, "Dead men tell no tales." With one last painful effort, Charles Caldwell pulled himself erect, smoothed the wrinkles in his blood-stained coat and said: "Remember, when you kill me you kill a gentleman and a brave man. Never say you killed a coward. I want you to remember it when I am gone."

The assassins opened fire. Caldwell crumpled and his body was "grotesquely turned completely over by the impact of innumerable shots fired at close range."

Dying thus, in astonishment and agony, with the massed skill and wealth of the white community arrayed against him, Charles Caldwell characterized an age in which men voted with dirks and Winchester rifles. Political significance apart, in his life and death one is brought face to face with the human dimensions of the violent counterrevolution which overthrew Black Reconstruction in the South and dealt American democracy a massive blow from which it may never recover.

No one knows how many Charles Caldwells died during this desperate white time. But conservative estimates run into the thousands. Albion W. Tourgee, a white Republican who experienced the counterrevolution in the flesh, said: "Of the slain there was enough to furnish forth a battlefield, and all from those three classes, the Negro, the scalawag, and the carpetbagger,—all killed with deliberation, overwhelmed by numbers, roused from slumber at murk midnight, in the halls of public assembly, upon the river-bank, on the lonely woods-roads, in simulation of the public execution, tortured beyond conception." And the wounded? "Ah!" Tourgee wrote, "the wounded in this silent warfare were more thousands than those who groaned upon the slopes of Gettysburg."

It was in this manner, with these methods, with these weapons, that the white South was won.

In a development comparable to the political paroxysms of contemporary Latin America, Asia, and Africa, white Southerners hurled themselves with a bloody spasm against the ramparts of black power. The struggle, which was waged by political assassination, midnight massacres, and repeated *coups d'état*, raged for more than ten years and completely changed the political climate of America.

It was a cruel and unequal struggle.

Black people fought back with whatever they could lay hands on, but all the high ground and most of the resources were in the hands of their adversaries who were backed, moreover, by powerful forces in the North. Protected by these powerful forces, protected by Northern newspapers, U.S. senators and representatives, the Democratic party and the new labor movement, the Southern counterrevolutionaries pressed their campaign from a nexus of strategic positions. They owned the land, they owned the tools, they owned the banks and newspapers; and they were determined to own the only things that stood between them and absolute control: the state apparatus and the black laboring population.

What we have to deal with here is not a local or episodic movement but a South-wide revolution against duly constituted state governments, led by the leading white men of the South, the Sartorises as well as the Snopeses, the old planters as well as the rising class of bankers, merchants, and lawyers. At a series of interstate meetings in Nashville, New Orleans, and other centers, these men decided to use any and every means to topple the new Republican governments and reduce the black populations to second-class citizenship. They drew up coordinated plans and designated targets and objectives.

Funds for guns and cannons were solicited from leading planters, industrialists, and merchants. Significantly, a substantial
portion of the war fund came from Northern industrialists and
businessmen.

From the beginning, the white conspirators based their plan
on a destruction of the new coalition of African-Americans,
poor whites, and Northern newcomers. As for executing the
plan, the scheme was to isolate black people from their allies
and kill or drive out all Republican leaders, black or white,
Northern-born or Southern-born.

As soon as the first Republican governments were inaugurated, the counterrevolutionaries sprang into action, using
internal subversion, civil disobedience, and Big Lie propaganda
techniques in a concerted effort to deny the new governments
the money they needed to operate. Tax strikes were organized,
and chambers of commerce and boards of trade told Wall
Street bankers that prosperous whites would never pay what
they called "the bayonet bonds" of the new governments. Since
white conservatives controlled the leading white newspapers, it
was relatively easy to create a hostile environment which made
it difficult, if not impossible, to raise money on the securities
market. In 1871, for example, Governor Harrison Reed of
Florida charged in an official proclamation that "men of high
standing and influence" were "seeking to bring the laws into
contempt" and "encouraging seditious sentiments toward the
government" by telling citizens that they did not have to pay
taxes.

Artfully spreading confusion and dissension, the counterrevolutionaries abandoned the orthodox methods of presenting a
case to the public, and relied almost entirely on corruption and
secret influence—bribery, the systematic entertainment of
Republican leaders like Chamberlain of South Carolina and
Warmoth of Louisiana, and the manipulation and distortion of
the news. They also made excellent use of spies and double
agents. Some white men entered the Republican governments

with the express purpose of destroying them. Others bribed Republican legislators and told. Still others accepted positions in order to keep the new governments from going too far. One of the more celebrated double agents of the period was the Northern white man who became an assistant to the black secretary of state in Florida in order to get inside information and to sabotage the administrative machinery.

This tactic was facilitated by the terrible innocence of the new men of power, who made the suicidal mistake of trying to conciliate their enemies by giving them important state positions. In every Southern state, the circuit and supreme courts were in the hands of native white Southerners with conservative backgrounds. It was relatively easy, therefore, for counter-revolutionaries to tie the governments in knots with skillfully waged wars of injunctions and mandamuses.

Subversion from within was facilitated also by the ambivalence of white Republican leaders, most of whom had no real interest in black people and little real faith in democracy. Like most men of their place and time, they looked down on poor men — black and white. Most of them, moreover, had a desperate desire for social acceptance by their enemies. The grand outcome, as Albert T. Morgan very astutely observed, was that most white Republicans "went forward with their work as though their first duty was to consult the enemies of the system."

Boring from within with Trojan Horse techniques while maintaining strong pressure from without, white conservatives sapped the energy and initiative of the new governments but failed to topple them. This was a distinct compliment to the sophistication of black voters who clung to the Republican regimes despite well-financed efforts to bribe or mystify them into a coalition against their fundamental interests. Faced thus with a determined and cohesive black bloc, white Southerners fell back on their first line of rapport with black men — violence. At a Southwide summit conference at Nashville's Maxwell

House in May, 1867, the white elite of the South organized the paramilitary Ku Klux Klan and selected Nathan Bedford Forrest, a former slave-dealer and Confederate general, as grand wizard. At a similar meeting in 1868 in New Orleans, the Knights of the White Camellia came into being. Among the many offshoots of these revolutionary trunks were the Society of the White Rose, the Pale Faces, Red Shirts, and a Mafia-like Louisiana group called the Innocents. Most of these organizations were allied with the regular Democratic party organizations. Indeed, in some cases, the Democratic organizations had their own "secret service committees" which were charged with the responsibility of "silencing" black and white leaders.

Under whatever name, the terrorists' organizations had one fundamental purpose: the restoration of white control and white domination of black people. Since black power or the possibility of black power stood between white people and the control of the black population, the Klan and other terrorist organizations were organized specifically to destroy black power and to create conditions that would make it possible for white men to exploit black men socially, politically, and economically.

Why did white men want to control black people?

Why did they want to exploit them?

They wanted to control black people because the arithmetic of the situation made it necessary to control black people in order to control the state and the wealth (cotton, sugar) that the state and black people created. Contrary to the popular impression, the main complaint of the prosperous leaders of the terrorists was not race, but property. They claimed that the government was being used to favor the interests of poor people — black and white — at the expense of the rich. Badly scared by the various measures in support of labor tenants, white employers of black labor, especially landowners, became the major supporters of the Klan. These men defined their tasks, at least privately, as the restriction of the political and

A modern artist depicts the assassination, in December, 187 of Charles Caldwell, Mississipp political leader.

Political tactic of white terrorists was lampooned in a contemporary cartoon. Terrorists seized state governments by suppressing the Negro vote.

Ku Klux Klansmen, captured in a
Reconstruction riot at Huntsville, Alabama,
were sketched by a *Harper's Weekly* artist.

economic power of black labor. Lewis E. Parsons, who had served as Democratic governor of Alabama before switching to the Republicans, told a congressional committee investigating Ku Klux Klan violence, that the fundamental purpose of the Klan was to control the black man "and also to control his labor." It came to be understood, he continued, "that in this way Negroes might be made to toe the mark again, to do the bidding of the employer, to come up to time a little more promptly, and do more work than they would otherwise do. It also soon became apparent that in this way the Negroes could be deterred from voting, as they naturally would." One thing, in other words, led to another. The white conspirators wanted to take the black man's ballot so they could take his bread. They wanted to depoliticize the black man so that they could dehumanize him.

It was the control of the state and its instruments of violence, it was the power to name and the power to define, the power to keep down and the power to push up — it was *power* and power alone that had enabled white people to control black people for 250 years. Only power, only brute force, *only violence*, in the last word, can separate man from man and man from woman. In the absence of the massed violence of the state, in the absence of community-wide sanctions supported overtly or covertly by the police and the army, man will recognize man and man will, above all, recognize woman. The Ku Klux Klan was an ominous recognition of that fact; it was a continuation of the long red line of violence that is the color line in America. Edwin L. Godkin, publisher of the *Nation*, recognized that fact when he said that the whole South before the war was a huge Ku Klux Klan. Godwin need not have been so geographically specific. The whole of America before Appomattox was a huge Ku Klux Klan. Slavery was violence against black people by the American state which authorized individuals and their agents in three articles of the U.S. Constitution to violate the personalities and the bodies of African-Americans. During the seventy-six-year period from the ratification of the Constitution to Appomattox, violence became white America's only rapport with black Americans. Not only in the South but also in the North, the white mob and, behind that, the police force and the Army guaranteed the alienation of every black-white relation. And whenever the state could not, for any reason, provide the level of violence necessary to keep black and white Americans in their places, extra-governmental terrorist organizations came into being to discipline not only black people but also white people. The Klan came into being to provide the violence of separation. It came into being to organize the extra-governmental force necessary to make the state once again the principal engine of violence against African-Americans.

Control: that was the issue. On no other subject, except property, which is another form of control, were the white conspirators so venomous. William W. Davis, the conservative chronicler of Reconstruction in Florida, said: "When the Negro justice issued writs and warrants or tried minor cases, when Negro legislators went to Tallahassee to dominate with their white confederates the making of state laws, when Negro county commissioners took their seats beside white men, when Negro jurors sat in judgement, when Negro rowdies with jeering crowded away the white voters at the polls, when Negro tax officials put up for sale property forfeited because the white owners could not pay taxes, when Negro posses hunted with guns for white offenders, when Negro constables arrested whites and dragged them to jail, when Negro politicians and their friends proclaimed in public meetings the arrival of racial equality, political and social, and tried to clinch their assumptions with laws concerning hotels, theatres, and railway cars—when these outward and visible signs of the Africanization of social institutions came under the eyes of whites, many individuals—rich and poor (most were poor), ignorant and enlightened—spoke and did things in a frenzy of race passion against the black. It made little difference how successful the black might have been in his elevated position." Pejoratives apart, Davis captured here the frenzy of race passion that seized white insurrectionists confronted by layers of black power that helped black people not only to control themselves but also to control some whites. According to a contemporary visitor, there was the same frenzy in South Carolina where white people were incensed by the "parading more than enough of Negroes as senators, as policemen, as militia, as the armed forces and the dominant power of the state." According to a North Carolina conservative, the Klan was formed to destroy the image of black authority. "I do think," he told a congressional investigating committee, "that the common white people of the country are at times very much enraged against the Negro population. They think that this universal political and civil equality will finally bring about social equality; there are already instances in the county of Cleveland in which poor white girls are having Negro children. Such things as these are widening the breach between these two classes of our population. The white laboring people feel that it is not safe for them to be thus working in close contact with the Negroes...."

As this quotation indicates, the Klan movement was fuelled also by the irrational power of the habit of hate. White people wanted to control black people because they had always controlled them and because the subordination of all black people to all white people had become a psychological need to some men. Keeping black people down gave meaning and dignity to their lives. It compensated them for their defeats and failures. It also—though this was not said openly—protected them from the competition of men to whom they attributed superhuman sexual and social power. An Alabama Republican told a congressional investigating committee that the Klan had a powerful appeal to "the uneducated white man, and the man who in his sphere of life is brought nearer to competition with the Negro..." As a matter of fact, poor whites were rising in the social scale—they had never been so well off. But black people were also rising, and the differences between poor blacks and poor whites were rapidly disappearing. More and more whites were being forced into sharecropping and tenancy. More and more whites were working in the fields alongside black people. Poor whites reacted to all this with hysteria. Instead of demanding schools for themselves, they demanded the destruction of black schools. Instead of demanding additional benefits for themselves, they demanded fewer benefits for blacks. Traveling in North Carolina at this time, Nordhoff was struck by the rising hysteria in poor white ranks. The North Carolina Republican party, he said, was composed largely of black people and "the large mass of poor whites in the western or mountain districts." But, he said, "these small white farmers dislike the Negro, whom they know little about, and are easily alarmed at the thought of social equality with him. The Democratic politicians very naturally worked upon their fears on this point..."

The incentives for organizing hate in the disorganized and wretchedly poor South were enormous, and the land was soon blanketed with terrorist organizations. By 1868, according to Grand Wizard Forrest, there were more than a half-million men enrolled in the Klan alone. Most of these men were former Confederate soldiers, and most of the leaders were future U.S. senators and governors like John B. Gordon of Georgia, John T. Morgan of Alabama, and James Z. George of Mississippi. The Klan included, of course, adventurers and sadists who embraced the lost cause for ends of their own. But it also included many prosperous and educated Southerners who believed the organization was the best protector of their interests. In testimony before the Ku Klux Klan investigating committee, John B. Gordon, the rich Atlanta insurance man and railroad lawyer, implied that the organization was supported by "some of the very best citizens of the State — some of the most peaceable, law-abiding men, men of large property...." In fact, Gordon called the organization "a brotherhood of the property owners."

Big property owners and poor whites were initiated into the

underground organizations at secret rites which consecrated them to the pursuit of white supremacy by fair means and foul. "History and physiology were called upon," Walter F. Fleming wrote, "to show that the Caucasian race had always been superior to, and had always exercised dominion over, inferior races. No human laws could permanently change the great laws of nature. The white race alone had achieved enduring civilization, and of all subordinate races, the most imperfect was the African. The government of the Republic was established by white men for white men. It was never intended by its founders that it should fall into the hands of an inferior race. Consequently, any attempt to transfer the government to the blacks was an invasion of the sacred rights guaranteed by the Constitution, as well as a violation of the laws established by God himself, and no member of the white race could submit, without humiliation and shame, to the subversion of the established institutions of the Republic. It was the duty of white men to resist attempts against their natural and legal rights in order to maintain the supremacy of the Caucasian race and restrain the African race to that condition of social and political inferiority for which God has destined it."

Terrorists were prepared for this Christian duty at initiation ceremonies where men swore on Bibles to disregard civil obligations and to clear each other in court by lies and alibis. They swore to God that they would never vote for a black man. Thus fortified, they were assigned to cells which pyramided to the leader of the state organization. The rank and file didn't know the names of the top leaders who gave orders to the leaders of the subordinate cells.

Tightly organized into cells, grotesquely masked, sworn to secrecy and pledged to kill or maim on orders, the paramilitary shock troops rode across the South, guns across their saddle bows, halters around their pummels. Anticipating the tactics of modern totalitarianism, they swooped down on isolated cabins in thunderous cavalry charges, dragging protesting men and women to the woods where they were whipped and lynched. Black and white men were whipped and murdered for voting, attending political meetings, or offering themselves for public office. White women were whipped for dating black men, and black women were whipped for dating white men. Thousands of black people were flogged for trying to buy land or for asking for higher wages. White terrorists also searched cabins for firearms and gradually disarmed the black population. As soon as the black people were disarmed, white terrorists provoked "riots" and massacred thousands.

Men and women, black and white, Northerners and Southerners, Jews, Italians, and Irishmen were among the victims. In South Carolina, for instance, James Martin, an Irish immigrant who was serving in the legislature, was shot down in front of the Abbeville courthouse. During the same period, Samuel Fleishman, a Jewish merchant, was ordered to leave Marianna, Florida, for expressing opinions contrary to "white supremacy." Fleishman had lived in Marianna for twenty years, but a "committee" of white citizens gave him two hours to arrange his affairs and get out of town. "I told them," Fleishman reported, "that if I had committed a crime I was willing to be tried and punished for it...but that I would rather die than leave. They informed me that they would take me off at sundown, willing or unwilling." At sundown, a band of armed men took Fleishman off. A week later, he was found dead on a public road about twenty miles from Marianna.

Throughout this period, white terrorists concentrated on Loyal Leagues, Republican party organizations and other instruments of black assertion. Loyal League leaders were shot down in the streets or driven out of town. Party headquarters were raided and destroyed, and churches and other meeting places were torched. Terrorists also burned down schools and lashed teachers, black and white, male and female. A congressional committee reported that Klan activity in Mississippi in 1870-71 was "marked by the development of the most decided hostility to all free schools, and especially to free schools for colored citizens."

The political history of this time was a history of crime without parallel in American history. Consider, for example, the following political notes, which were typical of the period:

●Alexander Boyd, white solicitor, Greene County, Alabama, shot dead in his hotel after he announced that he had evidence against the Klan.

●M. T. Crossland, white Alabama legislator, assassinated.

●Klan-instigated riot, Eutaw, Alabama. Five Negroes killed, forty-five wounded.

●Dr. J. L. Finlayson, white county clerk, assassinated, and W. J. Purman, white state senator, seriously wounded in Marianna, Jackson County, Florida. By 1871, 153 persons had been assassinated in Jackson County.

●Some three hundred black men killed in massacre at Opelousas, St. Landry Parish, Louisiana.

●More than one hundred black Republicans executed at political massacre in Colfax, Louisiana, on Easter Sunday. Ebenezer R. Hoar said: "This deed was without palliation or justification; it was deliberate, barbarous, cold-blooded murder. It must stand like the massacre of Glencoe, or St. Bartholomew, a foul blot of the pages of history."

●General P. H. Sheridan reported waves of political assassinations in Texas. Political conditions were so bad that Sheridan said if he owned both Texas and Hell he would rent out Texas and live in Hell.

Speaking on the floor of the Senate in 1871, Senator Adelbert Ames of Mississippi detailed the consequences of the first reign of terror which rolled over the South in 1868-70. "It must not be forgotten," he said, "that, as a general thing, it is the prominent Republican who is killed, and not the obscure or insignificant. Now, I would ask, what political party at the North can retain its vigor and lose yearly in each State by murder eight hundred of its best and most reliable workers? It is not so much in the diminution of their numbers by so many that the great political harm is done as in the demoralization consequent thereto. Whole counties become paralyzed, and inaction falls on recognized leaders, who, there, because of the want of universal education, are much more depended upon than in the North. It can very easily be understood how cities, counties, and whole states change their political complexion under such opposition as this."

By 1870, as a direct result of the campaign of violence, black political organizations had been smashed on the local level in most states. By that time, white terrorists and their agents had effectively circumvented reconstruction in Virginia and were well on the way to capturing complete control in North Carolina, Georgia, and Tennessee.

What were Republicans doing all this time?

They were debating—which is, all things considered, the worst possible tactic when men are shooting at you. From first to last, Radical Republicanism was hampered by moderate white governors who wanted to rule but were afraid to govern. In almost every case, these governors acted with so little energy that they seemed to doubt their rights and their cause. As the fires of crisis leaped higher and higher, these governors declaimed and postured but failed to act. And, failing to act, failing to meet force with force, they necessarily informed their adversaries that they would submit to superior force if it were imposed.

It was clear to Charles Caldwell and other black leaders that the Republican governors had to crush the underground organization or go to the wall. Caldwell and other Negro leaders in every Southern state repeatedly and frantically called for arming of the militia and a humane ruthlessness in suppressing

The First White Backlash

the white terror. But this policy was vetoed by the conservative governors who never adequately utilized the arsenal of weapons at their disposal. These weapons ranged from state militia or National Guard forces to anticonspiracy laws of varying severity. Arkansas' Ku Klux Klan law, for example, prohibited all secret organizations and declared members "infamous public enemies" who could be arrested at any time by any citizen, without a warrant. Alabama had a similar law which authorized anyone to kill a person who was in disguise. Alabama and other states also enacted legislation authorizing any justice of the peace to issue warrants running in any part of the state. Under these statutes and others, Republican governors were empowered to authorize any sheriff to go into any county to make arrests. In some cases, as in Mississippi, the governor was empowered to change the place of trial of persons accused of violence "when it shall appear that owing to prejudice or other causes an impartial petit or grand jury cannot be impanelled in such cases." An additional deterrent was an Alabama law, passed in 1868, which authorized the widow or next of kin of victims of mob violence to recover the sum of $5,000 from the county in which the killing occurred." In this same class was a South Carolina law which provided for payment to the widows or orphans of persons killed for their political opinion. In South Carolina, too, it was against the law to eject a person from a rented house or to discharge him from employment for political reasons. South Carolina and other states also passed measures to prevent the intimidation of black voters.

In addition to these measures, which were the strongest ever passed on the state level for the protection of black citizens, Republican governors were empowered to organize and mobilize state militia. In some states, the governor was also empowered to declare martial law and seize railroads, telegraph offices, and other vital installations. With few exceptions, Republican governors shrank from these harsh measures. In the face of repeated requests from their legislatures, the Republican governors of Alabama, Mississippi, and Florida refused to organize militia units. Some governors organized militia units but lost their nerve at the last moment and refused to use them. Indeed, some governors carried timidity to the extreme point of refusing to request federal troops in the face of violent provocations.

At the height of the conflict, in almost every Southern state a strange paralysis seized Republican governors, who waited stoically in their offices for the fires of violence to consume them. A notable exception to this general rule was William G. Brownlow of Tennessee who mobilized his militia and announced that the situation required "a large amount of hanging." Another governor who saw things this way was Powell Clayton of Arkansas who mobilized his militia and declared martial law in the fall of 1868. Clayton divided the state into four military districts under the command of militia generals. The First Arkansas Cavalry, a predominantly white unit, thundered into southwestern Arkansas and pacified the population by hanging several men. Military operations in the southwest were dominated by black infantrymen, who restored law and order in Drew and Ashely Counties. By Christmas, another unit of black infantrymen was re-establishing government control in Crittenden County which was "in complete control," the governor said, "of desperadoes." The black troops hanged several white and black men and executed others before a firing squad.

By draconian measures, Clayton restored law and order in Arkansas and extended the life of the democratic regime of his state. In the process, he won the respect, if not the love, of his enemies. Charles Nordhoff, a conservative foe of Reconstruction, said other Republican governors could have profited by Clayton's example. Nordhoff said "there were in Arkansas a few men — notably Governor Clayton, I think — who held society in an iron grip, and by main force produced peace. They put down with a stern and unflinching, and almost a cruel, hand the disorders which they found; they made laws terrible to read, and they executed these laws with a rigor which saved society, and gave peace to the State by encouraging the orderly people of all parties to take public affairs into their own hands, and by discouraging and terrifying the lawless class."

Prodded by Clayton's actions and by black men in their own states who held him up as an example, Republican governors moved belatedly to contain the spreading insurrection. In the spring of 1870, more than seventy thousand men were enrolled in the South Carolina militia. In the same year, Governor William W. Holden of North Carolina deployed his black and white militiamen in an unsuccessful attempt to quell uprisings in white counties. But Holden had dallied too long. A federal court freed his prisoners and the newly elected Democratic legislature impeached him.

Holden's fate reinforced the ingrained timorousness of some governors. But others, forewarned by the blitzkrieg tactics of North Carolina Democrats, turned with new enthusiasms to the task of building a reliable state police force. By the end of 1870, tens of thousands of black men were marching and drilling the South. Black and white men served in these units, although most of the foot soldiers and many of the company officers were black. Some of the top black officers like Robert Smalls of South Carolina, Sam Mallory of Arkansas, and William Gray of Mississippi rose to the top rank of general.

Because of the Hamlet-like indecision of state governors, who said they feared an all-out race war, the state militia fought with one arm tied by red tape and official fear. Having taken the first step, most governors could not bring themselves to make the strategic commitment which would have permitted an effective and coordinated use of their forces. Instead of figuring out ways to use the militia, most governors spent most of their time detailing reasons why it was inopportune to use it at all. Even worse, they failed to make the administrative and logistic decisions that would have permitted the militia to mount and sustain large-scale campaigns. Despite these handicaps, the poorly equipped and poorly organized militia fought several land and water battles in the South. In several cases, they proved to be the difference between life and death for the Republican regimes.

With the organization of the state militia, the social war in the South assumed a new and menacing aspect. White conservatives, recognizing the power potential of the militia, launched an open attack on the foundations of the state, assassinating individual officers and crossing state lines to fight pitched battles with militia units. In this second wave of violence, which wracked the South in 1871, the federal government was forced to intervene repeatedly to insure republican forms of government in the South.

It was in this climate and against this background that Congress passed three Enforcement bills which put federal elections under the control of federal officers and authorized the President to suspend the writ of habeas corpus and to take other drastic measures to suppress conspiracies against the rights of citizens. Under these measures, the strongest civil rights legislation ever passed on the federal level in America, troops and federal marshals were sent into the South to protect the rights of black citizens, and federal courts assumed new powers in the field of civil rights. On one occasion, in the fall of 1871, President Grant suspended the writ of habeas corpus in nine South Carolina counties.

In South Carolina and other Southern states, thousands of white citizens, including leading doctors, lawyers, ministers, and presidents of colleges, were arrested for Ku Klux Klan activity. Of the 5,172 tried in the South in 1871-72, 1,432 were found guilty and sentenced to prison. Most, however, were released after serving a few months. Before sentencing seventeen Klansmen who pleaded guilty, the presiding judge of the United States District Court in South Carolina said: "What is quite as appalling to the court as the horrible nature of these offenses is the utter absence on your part, and on the part of others who have made confessions here, of any sense or feeling that you have done anything wrong. Some of your comrades recited the circumstances of a brutal, unprovoked murder, done by themselves, with as little apparent horror as they would relate the incidents of a picnic."

Although President Grant used the new remedies sparingly, the mere threat of federal action blunted the force of the Southern counterrevolution and changed its direction. Foiled on one front, Southern conservatives mounted a comprehensive propaganda campaign which struck a responsive chord in the North, which was growing tired of "the eternal nigger." This campaign followed the formula of a White League organizer who told his colleagues that the white men of the South must appeal to the white men of the North as "a wretched, down-trodden and impoverished people." This theme was taken up by a crew of talented propagandists who fanned out over the North, preaching the gospel of a new and repentant South. Throughout this period, Northern reporters and Northern opinion-makers were shrewdly and effectively cultivated by Southerners who dangled the bait of profit, telling Northern industrialists that nothing stood between them and maximum exploitation of the rich resources of the South except "Negro governments." Eschewing frills, the Southern propagandists took their stand on the props of color and property. The South, they said, was being Africanized; and property was being despoiled in a riotous carnival of corruption and radicalism. Northerners were told—with a straight face—that it was time to take up once again the mantle of the great Lincoln and emancipate the white people.

All of this, as can be imagined, was extremely effective. Southerners' insistence that their enemies were the enemies of property won them, first, the interest and then the sympathy of Northern power holders who were engaged just then in a bitter struggle against the restless workers of the North and the rebellious farmers of the West. Their insistence that the claims of color were higher than the claims of the Constitution won them the support and the votes of poor white workers, who had nothing else to defend except their color, and America First nationalists, who were planning just then further aggression against the American Indian and the colored peoples of Latin America and the Caribbean.

The South had a lot working for it, and it adroitly exploited events, manufacturing the myths of corruption and inefficiency which were accepted, almost without question, by later historians who relied almost totally on the memoirs and the newspapers of men who organized a seditious conspiracy against established state governments. The Democratic myth-makers charged, first, that black politicians were throwing away millions of dollars on "bad" white women and amassing astronomical state debts. As for the tax system, they said it was punitive, confiscatory, and Communistic. Hammering away at blackness and corruption, the myth-makers managed to make the two words synonymous, a feat that was not too difficult considering the fact that most white Americans had been preconditioned to make that connection by Webster and the symbolism incarnated in the White House.

There was nothing unusual about all this. The Democrats were revolutionaries who let no consideration of truth or morality stay them in their drive to restore white supremacy. What was unusual was that this propaganda was accepted at face value by Northern whites who certainly knew better. With a little energy and a little good faith, the white men of that day could have established, as white and black historians later established, that there was only a negligible amount of corruption in some states and that the corruption in other states was magnified and distorted out of all measure for partisan purposes. The record was available, and the record clearly indicated that there was no difference in the level of honesty and efficiency in states dominated by black people and states dominated by white people. Nor was there any difference in black-dominated and white-dominated counties in the same states. Since the corruption that existed led to the panelled offices of Wall Street and the business community, since white Democrats and their white agents got most of whatever there was to get, since the same kind of corruption was pandemic in the U.S. Congress, the White House, and the legislatures of Pennsylvania and other states, Northern opinion-makers knew that corruption was neither black nor Southern. They knew that the South was responding to the same forces — social disorganization, economic expansion, and the normal corruption inherent in any system based on the acquisitive principle — as the North. The knew that more money was stolen in New York City by white Democrats than by all the black and white Republicans in the South combined. All this was known, could not help being known, was a matter of public debate and record. It was of record, too, that the Republicans had to pay more, in depreciated currency, to provide schools and other social services the old South had never provided; and that they had to bear the additional expense of absorbing four million new citizens into the fabric of the state.

Northern whites didn't overlook these facts — they simply ignored them. One can see this clearly in the works of the white reporters whose dispatches on life in the reconstructed South helped to turn the tide of public opinion against the Radical Republicans. Foremost among these reporters were James S. Pike (*The Prostrate State*), Edward King (*The Great South*), Robert Somers (*The Southern States Since the War, 1870-71*), Charles Nordhoff (*The Cotton States in the Spring and Summer of 1875*). Somers was an Englishman, and Pike, King, and Nordhoff were Northern-born journalists with the conventional ideological equipment of the day. All were open white supremacists. Even Somers, who is sometimes spoken of as a model of responsible journalism, said that black people were "more like children than grown people." He spoke repeatedly of "darkeys" with "wool-clad brains" and frankly admitted his interest in the "return of the white people of the South to a *rightful* and much-needed influence." (My italics.) Somers and his colleagues saw black people solely in terms decided by white men. They relied almost entirely on anti-Negro Democratic sources. Unable to conceive of events in terms of development and historical continuity, they compared the first phases of an embattled regime with the mature achievements of states under little or no social pressure. Unable to conceive of black people as human beings, they spoke of the "public opinion" of predominantly black states and communities when they obviously meant "white public opinion."

The white reporters who colored the North's view of Reconstruction were, for the most part, talented white men who meant well, according to their lights. Their reports are not without interest, especially since all of them made damaging admissions, consciously or unconsciously, which destroyed the anti-Negro case they were building. But race and class value-judgments are so intertwined with "facts" in their reports as to make them worthless as a faithful reflection of Reconstruction reality.

Value-judgments apart, the white observers were not above the willful distortion of fact. It was James S. Pike, for example, who laid the basis for the oft-repeated story that the South Carolina legislature voted Franklin J. Moses Jr. one thousand dollars after he lost one thousand dollars to W. J. Whipper in a horse race. Having reported, accurately, that one event followed the other, Pike went on to suggest, in the manner of the dishonest propagandist, that one event was the cause of the other. Basing his report on a charge of the Democratic members of a congressional committee, Pike said that the South Carolina house voted one thousand dollars to Moses "by way of gratuity, to reimburse his losses on a horse-race." Pike doubtless knew better, which is more than can be said for the thousands who have carelessly repeated the story. It is a matter of fact that Moses lost one thousand dollars to Whipper at a

horse race run just before the adjournment of the legislature of
1872. It is also a fact that Whipper rose in the house on the last
day of the session and moved that "a gratuity of $1,000 be
voted to the Speaker of this House, *for the dignity and ability
with which he has presided over its deliberations. . .*" (My italics.) Event
B did follow event A, but event A did not cause event B. In
fact, as anyone can verify, it was the custom of the South
Carolina house to vote a gratuity to the speaker on the last day
of the session. Speaker Moses was voted five hundred dollars in
1870, one thousand dollars in 1871 and one thousand dollars in
1872. Speaker Samuel Lee, a Negro, was voted one thousand
dollars in 1873, the year of Pike's visit, and five hundred dollars
in 1874. Robert Brown Elliott, another Negro, received gratui-
ties of one thousand and twelve hundred dollars in 1875 and
1876, respectively. By suppressing these facts and by taking
advantage of the old *post hoc, ergo propter hoc* fallacy — B followed
A, therefore A caused B — Pike manufactured a myth which has
enlivened thousands of history classrooms.

Another sleight of hand, equally forced, was carried off by
Charles Nordhoff who reported, historians say, that Jack
Agery, a black contractor, charged the state of Arkansas nine
thousand dollars to repair a bridge which cost only five hundred dollars. The only trouble with the story is that Nordhoff
didn't say that. What Nordhoff said was that Agery charged
nine hundred dollars, that "scrip was then worth ten cents,
and he received his pay in it, *amounting* to nine thousand
dollars." (My italics.) Accepting Nordhoff's Democratic-derived
facts at face value and discounting his motives, it is obvious
that Agery charged only nine hundred dollars and that he only
received nine hundred dollars, whatever the sum "amounted
to" in depreciated scrip. And since Nordhoff neglected to state
what year the bridge was built and the value of five hundred
dollars at that time, it is impossible to say whether Agery's
bill was excessive or not.

It was of such stories, endlessly repeated in the North, that the downfall of Reconstruction was made. And it is difficult to avoid the impression that the Reconstruction myth-makers wrote with that purpose in mind. Not only Nordhoff but Somers and King and Pike wrote consciously or unconsciously to prove how much money could be made in the South if only the North would help the South get rid of the troublesome black politicians. In Nordhoff in particular, but also in Somers, King, and Pike, seven themes predominate.

1. The "great body of the white people" had learned "a terribly severe lesson." They had learned "to respect the rights of the Negro." There was no hostility to the Union or the government, and there was "no remote wish" to re-enslave the Negro. "Slavery is now seen, all over the South, to have been a huge economical blunder, and a proposition to re-establish it would not get fifty thousand votes in the whole South."

2. It was a mistake to enfranchise the black man. Ignorance and illiteracy could not rule. It was wrong and injurious to the black man to create conditions that placed him in opposition to "the natural ruling element" of the South.

3. The Reconstruction acts had destroyed the good relations heretofore existing between blacks and whites and had "seriously injured the Negro, by making him irresponsible to the opinion of his neighbors, and submitting him, in his ignorance, to the mischievous and corrupt rule of black and white demagogues."

4. The Reconstruction acts had created the color-line in politics. "While the white vote, or the greater part of it, is massed on one side, and the black vote, or the greater part of it, on the other, as is still the case in Louisiana, Mississippi, Alabama, and Georgia, it is impossible to get settled good government; for the political issues will, of necessity, be false, and will have no relation to any real question of administration, but only to questions of race."

5. The "only sure remedy" was "in the absolute noninterference of the Federal power."

6. The Ku Klux Klan was a myth. There were, to be sure, isolated outrages but "no one pretends that murder is practiced for political purposes."

7. A satisfactory settlement—satisfactory, that is, to the "natural ruling element" of the South—would open the natural wealth of the South to the exploitation of Northern and European capital.

At least one reporter, James S. Pike, believed "a satisfactory settlement" required and justified open revolution. Appalled by the reticence and the apathy of white South Carolinians, Pike appealed to the "unconquerable revolutionary forces" of "the superior race." It was necessary, he said, "for the whites to rely mainly upon themselves, and mainly upon action quite outside and independent of politics, to redeem the State, if it is to be redeemed." He said it would be "a violent presumption against the manliness, the courage, and the energy of South Carolina white men, to allow the State to remain in the permanent keeping of her present rulers." Pike added: "Does anybody suppose that such a condition of things as exists to-day in South Carolina is to last? Such a supposition is to ignore the history and the character of mankind. Suppose the men, or a larger portion of the white men, of South Carolina who have gone through the War of the Rebellion are cowed and demoralized by its results; how is it with the individuals of the rising generation who are fast taking their places? Is not the hot blood of the South in their veins? They have the ardor of youth. They have the stimulus of young ambition; they have the pride of ancestry; they have the inherited valor of successive generations. Have they no part to play in the future? We may rest assured that no depressing circumstances of the present are going to destroy or repress the natural development that comes of race and blood. Opportunity alone is wanting; and that, we know, is always found by the bold and aspiring."

Anger, outrage, contempt, scorn: these were the emotions aroused in white observers by the spectacle of the South in travail; and their reports, amplified by the conservative white press, enabled Northerners to view the emergence of the Ku Klux Klan movement with tolerence if not enthusiasm.

The South shrewdly exploited the emerging mood, dexterously fanning the flames of the first of many white backlashes. At that juncture, the Northern middle class was disenchanted by graft and corruption in New York City and Washington, the excesses of the "Robber Barons," and the rising power of the Irish and other immigrant groups. Threatened by the poor (but white) at home and the great faceless forces of the Industrial Revolution, the middle class found it easy to sympathize with those who felt threatened by the poor and different in the South. They saw the claims of the masses as a threat to traditional values. The revolutionary turbulence of the black masses sharpened their fears. By 1874, the *Nation*, speaking of South Carolina, said: "This is . . . socialism."

At the same time, the poor laborers and immigrants of the North saw a potential threat to their wages and homes in the rising black cloud of the South. Labor therefore turned on labor, joining hands with the big landholders of the South to eliminate certain alternatives not only for labor in the South but for labor in America.

Another dimension to this surrealistic picture was the changing requirements of the white power structure, which used force in the first years of Reconstruction because its interests—solidification of national unity, supremacy of Northern fiscal policy, high tariffs, etc.—paralleled the interests of black people, the supremacy of the Republican party, and the consolidation of the party's Reconstruction program. By 1872, however, the Northern victory had been solidified beyond recall, and the Northern power structure had a first mortgage on the rising class of New South bankers, planter-merchants and corporation lawyers. As a result, the Republican party began to change. There were demands for a political settlement from business-oriented politicians who said the political troubles in the South were impeding the establishment of a national domestic market.

For different and, indeed, contradictory reasons, powerful groups in the North adopted the point of view of the South on the questions of "Negro domination," "Negro corruption," and the rule of the propertied by the poor and propertyless. Among the concrete manifestations of the waning influence of Northern idealism were the 1872 revolt of the liberal middle-class Republicans and the passage, again in 1872, of the Amnesty Act which lifted the political disabilities of most former Confederates. More ominous was the drift of the Supreme Court which signalled the abandonment of the black man in a series of decisions limiting the power of the federal government to enforce the Fourteenth and Fifteenth Amendments. The final nail in the coffin of black power was the Great Depression of 1873 which plunged the nation into social turmoil and doomed the democratic experiment in the South. Election returns told the story. In 1872, almost all Northern states went Republican. In 1874, almost all Northern states, including the abolitionist stronghold of Massachusetts, went Democratic. For the first time since 1861, Democrats won a majority in the House of Representatives. And this meant that it was all over, except the shooting.

No one knew this better than white conservatives who emerged from underground and mounted a full-scale revolutionary attack against the six Southern states with Republican and republican forms of government. General John McEnery, the Democratic candidate for governor in Louisiana, said: "We shall carry the next election if we have to ride saddle-deep in blood to do it." A white Alabama editor said: "We must render this either a white man's government or convert the land into a Negro man's cemetery."

The white population was whipped into a frenzy by a campaign that blamed all the ills of the South on black politicians. All black politicians were denounced as "shameless,

heartless, vile, grasping, deceitful, creeping, crawling, wallow-
ing, slimy, slippery, hideous, loathsome, political pirates." All
black people were denounced as barbarians incapable of com-
prehending Christianity or white culture.

White men who continued to associate with black Republicans were read out of the white race and their names were
ostentatiously and publicly enrolled in "death books." It
became a matter of policy for white Democrats to sever all
social and business ties with white Republicans. Nordhoff, who
witnessed the preparations for the brutal Mississippi campaign
without altering his general conclusions, said it was extremely
effective. "Now," he wrote, "to be a lawyer, and meet, as you
enter the court, only a stony glance of hatred or repulsion; to
be a merchant, and know that your neighbors will go a block or
two further rather than trade with you; to be conscious as you
walk the streets that men are cursing you for being a Northern man, and asking themselves, 'What the——makes him
stay here?'—this is not pleasant for honorable men, who pay
their taxes, do all their duty as citizens, and add materially to the
prosperity of the State...."

It was not pleasant—nor was it safe. When all else failed, the
white insurrectionists maimed or killed white men in order to
keep them white. The victims were not only Northern white
men but also Southern white men and Southern white women.

In a well-organized and generally successful campaign to
disengage poor whites from the economic and social promises
of the Republican regimes, the insurrectionists used both sticks
and carrots: frightening poor whites with the specter of black
men taking all their women and entrapping them with the
promise of economic gain. In Louisiana, in 1874, white merchants and landowners were urged to give preference to white
laborers over black laborers. This policy was adopted by many
businessmen and landowners. A steamboat company replaced
its black crewmen with whites. And in Mississippi, in the same
period, white porters replaced black porters in Vicksburg, and

the Vicksburg & Meridian Railroad fired its black mail agents and hired whites.

The white insurrectionists offered black men a choice between death or humiliation. The choice, as a Mississippi newspaper put it, was between bread or no bread. *Blacklists* of defiant black Republicans were circulated among big landowners and printed in public newspapers; and thousands were fired for refusing to vote Democratic. Thousands more were whipped and murdered for supporting the Republican cause.

With the open support of conservative white newspapers in the North, the insurrectionists whipped the white population into line and formed statewide White Leagues which seized courthouses and forced Republican officials to resign. The White Leaguers were dangerously adept in disrupting the electoral process and breaking up campaign meetings. One of their favorite tactics was to attend Republican campaign meetings and sit on the front row with cocked pistols on their knees. In this atmosphere, all meaningful political activity ceased, and many white Republicans fled to the North.

As the pressure increased, the Republican coalition cracked under the strain of its internal contradictions. Native whites—poor and prosperous—were the first to withdraw. They deserted out of fear of the struggle, out of fatigue, out of private hopes and fears. "Thousands," John R. Lynch wrote, "who had not taken an open stand, but who were suspected of being inclined to the Republican party, denied that there had ever been any justifiable grounds for such suspicions. Many who had taken an open stand on that side returned to the fold of the Democracy in sackcloth and ashes,—upon bended knees, pleading for mercy, forgiveness and for charitable forbearance. They had seen a new light; and they were ready to confess that they had made a grave mistake, but, since their motives were good and their intentions were honest, they hoped that they would not be rashly treated nor harshly judged." More damaging to the Republican cause was the defection of leading

Republicans. When the showdown came, former Governor Scott of South Carolina, former Governor Warmoth of Louisiana, former Governor Alcorn of Mississippi and former Governor Reed of Florida were either on the sidelines or in the enemy camp.

Black Republicans, without means, without a common plan, and, for the most part, lacking weapons, fought back with bravery and ingenuity, organizing extra-legal state guards and, in some cases, whipping backbone into wavering colleagues. Particularly courageous in this effort were black women who banded together and refused to associate with husbands or boy friends who abandoned the Republican cause. In some cases, it is reported, black women ripped the clothes off black men who switched, under pressure, to the Democratic banner. Standing side by side with these women were brave men like Charles Caldwell who stiffened the spines of black and white Republicans. In Monticello, Florida, and other cities, black men vindicated, with arms in hands, their right to vote. When whites tried to push black men away from the polls in Monticello, "angry words ensued, and in about ten minutes," one black participant testified, "the voting places were closed on account of the excitement. Then you could see any number of white men coming up with arms. I suppose in about ten or fifteen minutes there were about 1,000 colored men on the ground with arms, but not near so many whites. I suppose there were nearly 1,000 shots fired off in the air, but no one was hurt."

Black men also formed vigilante units to protect black and white leaders. Throughout this period, politicians like Albert T. Morgan and William J. Purman were guarded and protected by armed black men. Morgan tells us in his memoirs that at the beginning of this period black men guarded his house day and night. A similar experience was reported by Purman, the Florida Radical. After an unsuccessful attempt on his life, "a committee of a dozen, or perhaps more, black men" visited Purman. "They were armed," he said, "to the teeth, and said that there were six or eight hundred armed men around the town, and that they were going to come in and sack the town that night on account of the murder of their friends.... I begged of those men, for God's sake, not to do any such thing ... and made them hold up their right hands and swear to me to go and call off their friends and return home. Had I not done it there would have been a terrible calamity right at that time." At that time and later, black men contested the encroachments of the White League movement. In Alabama, King reported, black men, discharged by white employers, formed a "bread or blood populace whose presence in the country was in the highest degree embarrassing." Faced by foes with superior resources, black men also resorted to the torch. The papers at the time were filled with reports of burnings of farms and other buildings by unknown persons.

There was no lack of militancy on the part of black men. But their struggle was unorganized, and there was never any doubt as to the outcome. With the federal government looking the other way, Republican governments began to topple like dominoes. The first to fall in this second period of struggle was Texas, where Governor E. J. Davis refused to recognize an election characterized by violence and fraud and called on his predominantly black militia to hold the state capitol in Austin. With the Democrats in control of the upper floors of the building and the governor and the black militia in control of the lower floors, Texas teetered on the brink of a total racial war. Governor Davis appealed to the federal government for support, but President Grant refused to intervene and Texas became, in January, 1874, a white Democratic state.

In the spring of 1874, the predominantly black militia of Arkansas waged a similar struggle, fighting pitched battles in the streets of Little Rock and a naval engagement on the Arkansas River. The military struggle was a stand-off, but the Democrats triumphed by fraud and internal subversion, and Washington again refused to intervene.

Events hurried on now at an ever dizzier pace. A coordinated attempt to topple the governments of Louisiana and Alabama was launched in the fall of 1874. The Louisiana attempt failed, but White Leaguers carried Alabama in a canvass punctuated by violence, economic intimidation, and fraud. Despite repeated pleas, the Republican governor of Alabama refused to organize the militia, and black men organized their own state guard. With the help of this unit, black men staved off complete collapse, carrying the Black Belt and sending thirty-five legislators to the predominantly Democratic legislature.

In the meantime, the Reconstruction drama was lumbering to a bizarre climax on the national level. In 1874, in the midst of the bloody skirmishes in the South, the Freedmen's Bank failed, sending seismic shocks of despair through the black communities of America. The bank had been chartered by Congress in 1865 to encourage thrift among the freedmen, and it had branches in major black communities in the North and South. But the Freedmen's Bank, like so many institutions founded ostensibly for freedmen, had fallen under the control of dubious white financiers and speculators who had recklessly squandered the funds in high-risk ventures. The failure of the bank seared the consciousness of African-Americans and checked the growth of black initiative and enterprise. Even more disheartening was the failure of Congress to authorize full payment to the black men and women who had more than two million dollars on deposit when the bank closed its doors.

Another ripple on the surface of events was caused by the passage of the Civil Rights Act of 1875. Passage of this legislative landmark capped a five-year fight which began in 1870 with the introduction by Charles Sumner of a civil rights bill which would have banned segregation on all common carriers, in hotels, inns, theatres and other places of public amusement, churches, cemeteries, schools and other public institutions. The sweeping provisions of the original bill were opposed by Republican and Democratic strategists, but

Sumner refused to compromise, keeping the measure before Congress until his death on March 10, 1874. On his death bed, surrounded by distinguished public figures, including Frederick Douglass, Sumner delivered his last public message, saying: "You must take care of the civil rights bill—my bill, the civil rights bill—don't let it fail." Black congressman, especially Robert Brown Elliott, zealously supported Sumner's bill, and the measure was passed finally on March 1, 1875, after provisions barring segregation in schools and churches had been eliminated. Paradoxically, the Civil Rights Act of 1875, like the Civil Rights Act of 1965, signalled the last gasp of Northern idealism and the beginning of a period of white hysteria and reaction.

When President Grant signed the Civil Rights Act, Mississippi whites were organizing the notorious Mississippi Plan which would bring the carnival of violence in the South to a gory climax. Faced with a Republican majority of thirty thousand in a state with a black majority and a sound reform movement, Mississippi White Leaguers devised a three-pronged attack of economic intimidation, political chicanery, and military force. Every Democratic organization in the state became a military unit armed with cannons supplied in at least one instance by sympathetic federal troops. Heavily armed and skillfully organized, the White Leaguers destroyed the foundations of the Mississippi Republican party with a series of massacres and lighting-like *coups d'etat*. Having gained complete control on the local level, the Democrats confidently awaited the November, 1875, elections for the legislature.

Rapid and decisive action was necessary at this point, but Governor Adelbert Ames drifted. He was an excellent governor and a brave man, but he was not made for revolutions. Moreover, he demonstrated at this crucial moment one of the central weaknesses of white leaders of black men. He was the leader of the black people of Mississippi, but he was not in the situation of Mississippi black people. He didn't have to take the abuse of Mississippi black men and the white men allied with them. They had to win or go to the wall; but he was white and he could return to the North and live a very comfortable life there as a white man. Ames' private letters prove that he had, indeed, come to this conclusion. He had already decided that struggle was futile. And he was seized at this terrible moment by a great passion for his pretty wife, Blanche, and the joys of domesticity. To Blanche, he wrote:

Four years since our lives were united as one. It hardly seems possible that the time is so long. They have been happy, peaceful years. Though the first seemed full of love, they each in succession grow more and more so. We learn from year to year how great love can grow, and how dependent a mutual love is. I miss you greatly. It is true my time is much occupied but when alone in my room, and before going to sleep and after waking, you are in my thoughts. This house does not seem a natural place for you and the children. It almost requires an effort to locate you and them in the rooms. It seems more like a hotel where we stayed, but for a day. This is not home and never can be.... I feel that the days we are separated are days lost — and that is a misfortune which multiplies such days. I know of no such true happiness and contentment as comes from being with you and our babies, and as you see I am disposed to quarrel with the fates which take me from you even for a day. Need I repeat again — my beautiful Wife, and as good as beautiful — that I love you? I do love you and send you kisses enough to envelop you as a cloud."

And again:

Why is it, beloved, I dwell so much on a different occupation than that I am now devoting myself to? It is because I love you so much and find so little contentment away from you — or is it the fact that our own latitude is the best for us. — Slavery blighted this people — then the war — the reconstruction — all piled upon such a basis destroyed their minds — at least impaired their judgment and consciousness to that extent we cannot live among them ..."

It was an ill-chosen moment for Ames to meditate on the bliss of love. From Clinton, from Vicksburg, from Friars Point, from all over the state, came long lists of casualties and atrocities and anguished pleas for action. The governor's mansion, Ames reported, was "crowded all day long with Republi-

"White Backlash" of 1870's was guided by propagandists who said it was necessary to sacrifice Negro voters in order to bring about a reconciliation of North and South.

Leading forces in white counterrevolution which destroyed Negro's black power base in Reconstruction period were Ku Klux Klan and White League terrorist organizations.

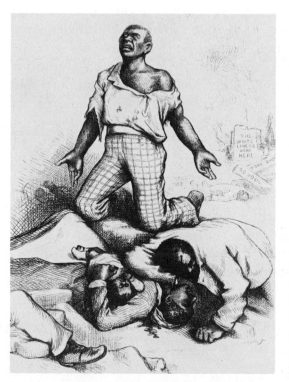

Victims of white terror are shown in this nineteenth century drawing with the caption: "Is *This* a Republican form of government? Is This protecting life, liberty, or property? . . ."

can friends and Negroes from the field of battle.... There has
also been a crowd at the front gate all day long. The town is
full of Negroes from the country who come to escape
harm...."

What was Ames going to do about all this?

Ames didn't know. He turned first to the U.S. government
and was told by the President that the "whole public is tired of
these annual autumnal outbreaks." Then, late in the autumn,
when the game was already lost, Ames finally organized a
handful of militiamen and called on the brave Charles Caldwell
to undertake the dangerous task of transporting arms and
ammunition to outlying districts. Caldwell led a forced militia
march through Hinds County, and for this act was marked for
death. During this same period, James Lusk Alcorn, the first
Republican governor of Mississippi, led a force of White
Leaguers and Klansmen who deposed the black sheriff of
Coahoma County. Hardly less revealing was the course of Hiram
Rhodes Revels, the first black U.S. senator, who had quarrel-
led with Ames over some trifling political issue and was now
supporting the White Leaguers and Klan-oriented Democrats.
In public statements and public letters, Revels supported the
Democrats and expressed the opinion that Democratic rule was
best for his people. If Revels misjudged the import of the
Democratic onslaught, it was not the Democrats' fault. The
Democrats said frankly that they intended to re-establish white
supremacy. And they told Mississippi blacks and Northern
whites that they intended to do it with violence. "The Republican journals of the North," the *Aberdeen Examiner* said, "make
a great mistake in regarding the present campaign in Mississippi in the light of a political contest.... The present contest is
rather a revolution than a political campaign."

So it was.

With black and white men marching, with cannons booming
and the air sultry with the heat of an imminent confrontation,
all the fire went out of the good Ames. When White Leaguers

demanded that he disband the militia, he meekly complied, signing "a peace agreement" which virtually handed the state to his adversaries. Under the terms of the agreement, which was signed on October 13, White Leaguers promised to disarm and permit a free election. Ames, on his part, agreed to disband the state militia and silence his more militant supporters. Ames signed the agreement with reluctance. He knew that his supporters would accuse him of selling out. But he explained to Blanche that there was no alternative: "We began too late to organize," he said, "and have too little means to accomplish much with the militia." He went on to say: "Yes, a *revolution* has taken place—by force of arms—and a race are disfranchised—they are to be returned to a condition of serfdom—an era of second slavery. It is their fault (not mine, personally) that this fate is before them. They refused to prepare for war when in time of peace, when they could have done so. Now it is too late. The nation should have acted but it was 'tired of the annual autumnal outbreaks in the South.'... The political death of the Negro will forever release the nation from the weariness from such 'political outbreaks.' You may think I exaggerate. Time will show you how accurate my statements are.... Last night I made up my mind to resign after the election when this revolution shall have been completed. Why should I fight on a hopeless battle for two years more, when no possible good to the Negro or anybody else would result? Why?"

Why, indeed?

That Ames should ask himself such a question at such a critical moment in the struggle is commentary enough on the limitations of his leadership. Ames kept his part of the controversial agreement, but the White Leaguers, to no one's surprise, continued to kill and maim. With Ames preparing his alibi and blaming the black people of Mississippi for his own defeatism and timorousness, and with the federal government stonily looking the other way, the White Leaguers ruthlessly suppressed the black voter, and Mississippi ceased to be a free state. In the process, hundreds of black men were killed and thousands were injured. By election day, November 2, Mississippi was a state become a prison. Thousands of black men were sleeping in the woods and swamps, and thousands more were barricaded in their homes.

In most counties, armed White Leaguers, supported by artillery and imported cavalrymen from Alabama and Louisiana, guarded the polls and drove away intrepid black voters. In Meridian, black voters, barred from the polls, gathered in a group across the street and stood there for hours "sullen and morose." In Scott County, Democratic "squirrel hunters accidentally" fired on Republican party workers. In Forrest, men with whips dispersed a large crowd of black voters. In Okalona, a Democrat "army" fired "by accident" on a group of black voters who had gathered in a black church. A U.S. Senate committee said later that "in several of the counties the Republican leaders were so overawed and intimidated, both white and black, that they were compelled to withdraw from the canvass those who had been nominated, and to substitute others who were named by the Democratic leaders, and that finally they were compelled to vote for the ticket so nominated, under threats that their lives would be taken if they did not do it". This was noticeably the case in Warren County, where the Democratic nomination of one Flanigan for sheriff was ratified at the Republican county convention, held in Vicksburg, the members acting under threats that if it were not done they should not leave the building alive. Similar proceedings occurred in other counties." The committee also found that "on the day of the election, at several voting-places, armed men assembled, sometimes not organized and in other cases organized; that they controlled the elections, intimidated Republican voters, and, in fine, deprived them of the opportunity to vote the Republican ticket. The most notable instance of this form of outrage occurred at Aberdeen, the shire town of the county of Monroe. At half past nine o'clock on the day of the election a cannon in charge of four or five cannoneers, and supported by ten or twelve men, a portion of the military company of the town, was trained upon the voting-place and kept in that position during the day, while the street was traversed by a body of mounted, armed men under the command of Capt. E. O. Sykes, of Aberdeen. . . ."

These tactics were undeniably effective. In the overwhelmingly black county of Yazoo, Republican candidates got seven votes. Republicans got four votes in Kemper and only twelve at Tishomingo. There was a similar Democratic landslide in Columbus where the Democratic mayor reported that the election was as "quiet as a funeral."

It was the funeral of democracy. President Grant, who did nothing to prevent that calamity, said later: "Mississippi is governed today by officials chosen through fraud and violence, such as would scarcely be accredited to savages, much less to a civilized and Christian people." And a U.S. Senate committee, which did nothing to reverse the results, said that post-Reconstruction Mississippi was an illegal society. It called the election "one of the darkest chapters in American history."

In the wake of that event, the predominantly Democratic legislature threatened to impeach Governor Ames and he resigned. Alexander K. Davis, the black lieutenant governor, was impeached, but he was subsequently cleared of the charges by a Mississippi court. During this same period, as we have seen, Charles Caldwell was assassinated for his part in organizing the state militia.

With Mississippi again in the white column, only three states—South Carolina, Louisiana, and Florida—remained in the orbit of Radical Republicanism. As America turned the corner of 1875 and headed into the centennial celebration of the Declaration of Independence, white men with guns turned their attention to the three hold-outs and vowed in the name of Jefferson and the first Revolution to make a new revolution in support of the theory that all white men were endowed by their Creator with certain inalienable rights over all black men.

9

America at the Crossroads

A PLAYWRIGHT COULD NOT have arranged a better scenario. From the Rockies to the Catskills, the great stage of America was festooned with flags and Revolutionary props in honor of the one hundredth anniversary of the Declaration of Independence. In Centennial Hall in Philadelphia and in auditoriums and schools across the country, amateur actors, bewigged and powdered, lumbered up imaginary Bunker Hills; and professional orators, armed with manuscripts, asked once again for Liberty or Death.

Onto this great stage, peopled with phantoms and patriotic ghosts, came an onrush of real people who demanded that the actors become real by deciding in 1876 in their own name whether they really believed what was said and done in 1776. Attempts were made to shush the intruders, to push them into the wings. But the intruders, some of whom were covered with real blood, forced their way to center stage and all Americans were soon embroiled in a real revolutionary struggle that overshadowed the centennial of the Declaration of Independence as the Black Revolution of 1963 overshadowed the centennial of the Emancipation Proclamation.

In 1876, as in 1963, the central questions were the unresolved issues of the original American Revolution.

Did all mean All?

Was America a government of white people for white people or a government of all the people for all the people?

Long before the opening of the Centennial Exposition in Philadelphia, these questions forced their way into the minds of Americans who had been evading them for years, *who had always been evading them.* The capture of the state of Mississippi by an armed white minority and the suppression of the black majority dramatized this issue and made it clear to most Americans that America was approaching a dangerous fork in the road.

America had been approaching that fork for ten years.

Black Reconstruction had reopened the whole question of the meaning of America. Faced with the principle made black flesh, many Americans had already repudiated the Declaration of Independence in their hearts. And now, in 1876, men in the North and South were organizing an interstate conspiracy that would lead most men to openly renounce the Declaration of Independence on the centennial of the Declaration of Independence. By singular coincidence, this conspiracy coincided with a massive wave of racism in America. In March of that year, the Supreme Court gutted the Fourteenth and Fifteenth Amendments by limiting the power of the federal government to protect black voters in the South. In April, the governor of California spoke at a mammoth anti-Chinese mass meeting in San Francisco. And in June, the white man's remorseless aggression against the red man was temporarily stymied by the massacre of Custer at Little Big Horn.

It was in this setting and against this background of blatant racism that Southern insurrectionists conceived and carried out a conspiracy against South Carolina, Florida, and Louisiana, the last strongholds of black power. By 1876, Democrats held commanding positions in both Louisiana (Democratic house) and Florida (Democratic senate), but South Carolina was still

solidly Republican. Encouraged by the wave of reaction in the
North, insurrectionists in the South called for an open attack
against these three states based on the notorious Mississippi
Plan. In December, barely a month after the fall of the
Republican government of Mississippi, the *Charleston News
and Observer* ran a bold headline: "ORGANIZE! ORGANIZE!
ORGANIZE!" The paper went on to say: "Next year is
centennial year. [The] special task of South Carolina white men
is to redeem, regenerate and disenthrall their people and give
them a new natal day from which shall date, a second time, the
freedom and independence of South Carolina."

    South Carolina *was* free—it would never be so free again.
The state contained, at that juncture, 415,000 black people and
289,000 white people. There were seventy-seven black men in
the state legislature, four of the eight state cabinet members
were black, and one of the two most powerful men in the state
was the young (thirty-four) Robert Brown Elliott, who was
speaker of the house and chairman of the Repubican state
executive committee. The state administration was headed by
Daniel H. Chamberlain, a cold, brilliant, tragic figure. With the
help of Elliott and other black leaders, Chamberlain had
reformed the administrative apparatus and had drastically
reduced state expenditures. But Chamberlain was playing a
dangerous game that alarmed the Republican leaders of the state.
Desperately anxious for white acceptance, he was playing to
the white conservative galleries. In fact, as his private letters
show, he was close to outright collaboration with the enemies
of the Republican regime. And national Republican leaders like
Senator Oliver P. Morton were openly saying that he had
already given up "the State to the opposition" and that his
attitude was "a practical identification with the Democrats." At
the last moment, Chamberlain pulled back from the conservative embrace and was nominated for a second term as governor.
By that time, however, he had wittingly or unwittingly given
Democrats enough ammunition to destroy the Republican
regime.

In the election of 1876, Chamberlain headed a Republican ticket of four black men and four white men, including Robert Brown Elliott, the nominee for attorney-general. He was opposed by Wade Hampton, who emerged as the leader of the revitalized Democratic party. For a time, the Democrats toyed with the idea of making a fight for the legislature and conceding the gubernatorial race to Chamberlain. But a "straight-out" faction of Democrats proposed and pushed through a revolutionary campaign based on the Mississippi Plan.

There was a similar realignment of forces in Louisiana, where Republican Stephen B. Packard faced F. T. Nichols, and in Florida, where Governor M. L. Stearns was opposed by G. F. Drew. The cast of characters for the 1876 drama was completed in the summer of 1876 when the national Republican party nominated Rutherford B. Hayes, the drab, unimaginative governor of Ohio, and the national Democratic party nominated Samuel J. Tilden, the drab, unimaginative governor of New York.

These events unfolded on the surface. But beneath moved darker currents. Throughout this period, there was consultation between the leaders of insurrectionary movements in South Carolina, Louisiana, and Florida, and the leaders of the states that had been "redeemed" for white supremacy. In the spring of 1876, General M. W. Gary, the arrogant, hot-tempered leader of South Carolina "straightouts," wrote a letter to Mississippi and asked for additional information on the campaign plan which won that state for white supremacy. Based on the information received, Gary drew up a plan which was adopted and refined by the South Carolina "Red Shirts." Here are some excerpts from the South Carolina battle plan:

"Every Democrat must feel honor bound to control the vote of at least one Negro, by intimidation, purchase, keeping him away or as each individual may determine, how he may best accomplish it."

"Never threaten a man individually. If he deserves to be threatened, the necessities of the time require that he should

National Capitol of 1877 was the scene of the historic
compromise which ended Black Reconstruction and paved
the way for inauguration of Rutherford B. Hayes as
U.S. President.

Contemporary drawing attacked methods of the "White Redeemers" of the Southern states. Democrats also limited black power by gerrymandering and fraud.

"IN SELF-DEFENSE."

die. A dead Radical is very harmless — a threatened Radical or one driven off by threats from the scene of his operations is often very troublesome, sometimes dangerous, always vindictive."

Gary's plan was followed in Florida and Louisiana as well as South Carolina. Democratic organizations shifted to a war footing and issued canvassers Winchester rifles and dirks. The whole white population was armed and organized, and organized pressure was brought to bear on black and white Republicans. Democratic organizations in Florida were told that Republican voters were not to be employed, rented land, or given credit. A black leader said: "All colored people that voted the Republican ticket were to be starved out the next year."

The key state in this conspiracy was South Carolina, which set the tone for the 1876 uprising. According to a white reporter, the state in 1876 resembled a military camp. All able-bodied white men were enrolled in rifle clubs, and thousands of whites, wearing flaming red shirts, were kept constantly parading. Perhaps the best description of South Carolina at that moment was penned by a white native whose letter was published in the *New York Tribune.*

The air [he wrote] is filled with reports of outrages and murders which never appear in print. No prominent Republican of either color can safely leave a town. Let a hint that he intends to ride out into the country get wind and he is sure to be ambuscaded. But more than this. The whites regard a Republican of their color with tenfold the vindictiveness with which they look upon the Negro. Scores of white Republicans are hurrying in alarm to the newspaper offices to insert cards in which they renounce their party and profess conversion to Democracy. If these men hang back and refuse or neglect to join the precinct club or the nearest military company, their conduct is reported to the township meeting. A committee is appointed to request an explanation. They call on the suspected man at their earliest convenience. If he is sensible, he will submit profuse apologies and regrets, and hurriedly take up his rifle and follow them to the drill room.

During the course of the campaign, armed Democrats disrupted Republican meetings, assassinated black officials and lynched black voters. There were repeated outbursts of violence and massacres at Hamburg (five Negroes killed) and Ellerton (thirty-nine Negroes killed).

Although their adversaries controlled most of the resources, the black people of South Carolina counterattacked with skill and boldness. Of immense importance in this connection is the fact that many black men were enrolled in the state militia. Black men without access to official arms bought guns and ammunition and prepared to carry the fight to the enemy; still others burned down houses and barns and lashed timid Republicans. In Charleston in September, black Republicans attacked black and white Democrats, torched buildings, and smashed store windows. The next month at Cainhoy, near Charleston, black Republicans hid their guns in the bushes. When Democrats barged in and started a fracas, the black Republicans dashed to the bushes, retrieved their guns, and opened fire. Five white Democrats were killed.

Alarmed by the escalation of the conflict, Governor Chamberlain appealed to President Grant, who called the Hamburg massacre "a cruel, blood-thirsty, wanton, unprovoked and uncalled for" attack, "a repetition of the course that has been pursued in other Southern states in the past few years." On October 17, Grant issued a proclamation commanding the rifle clubs of South Carolina to disband. Instead of disbanding, the rifle clubs adopted new names: Allendale Mounted Baseball Club (150 members), First Baptist Church Sewing Circle, Mother's Little Helpers. Nine days later, Grant dispatched federal troops to South Carolina. Most of these troops sided with white Southerners who invited them into their homes and showered them with hospitality.

With terror and fraud in the air, Americans went to the polls on Tuesday, November 7, to elect a President and federal and state officials. "The election in South Carolina," according to the white South Carolinian previously cited, "was one of the greatest farces ever seen. In counties where the Negroes had terrorized affairs, streams of colored Republicans poured from poll to poll all day, voting everywhere.... In counties terrorized by the whites, white bravoes rode from poll to poll, and voted time and again. Hundreds of Georgians and North Carolinians crossed the borders and joined in the work. In Edgefield County the influx of Georgians and the repeating were simply tremendous. The total number of voters in that county, according to the recent state census ... is 7,122, and the county has always, hitherto, gone Republican by one thousand votes; yet, although a thousand Negroes certainly, and an unknown number above that, were induced by money or fear of starvation to refrain from voting, the total number of votes cast was 9,289, and the Democrats carried the county by the astounding and tell-tale majority of 3,225! Similarly startling in most of the counties were the changes as compared with the census or past elections."

The first returns indicated a smashing Democratic victory on the local and federal level, and white Southerners poured into the streets, cursing, praying, and shouting. Meeting a group of black people, a white Tennesseean shouted: "Glory to God! We've got you. Glory! Glory! Glory! Glory!"

As it turned out, the Tennesseean's cry was a bit premature. A closer inspection of the returns indicated that Tilden had won 184 electoral votes, one shy of the necessary majority, and that Hayes had won 169 electoral votes. If Hayes had indeed carried Florida, South Carolina, and Louisiana, as Republicans claimed, then he was the next President of the United States. The ultimate electoral authority in the disputed states was the state returning board which was empowered to go behind the returns and throw out ballots stained with blood and fraud. Exercising this function, the returning boards of South Carolina, Louisiana, and Florida, with black men playing leading roles, certified the election of Republican slates and Hayes electors. White Southerners refused to accept the results and for several months there were two governors and two legislatures in South Carolina and Louisiana. It seemed for a time that there would also be two U.S. Presidents. When Congress convened in December, there was wild talk of civil war and a *coup d'état* by the U.S. Army. Fearing a disintegration of the Republic, Democrats and Republicans stitched together a compromise Electoral Commission which awarded the disputed electoral votes and the Presidency to Hayes. But the Democrats were far from mollified, and they mounted a filibuster which prevented the orderly counting of the electoral votes in the House of Representatives. This posed a problem of the first magnitude. For if the filibuster continued until inauguration day, America would be without a President. And massive disorder, perhaps war, would be inevitable.

In this volatile situation, the business community and large sectors of the Northern public panicked. From the big Northern newspapers, from the boards of trade and chambers of commerce of New York, Pittsburgh, and Chicago came one unanimous cry: "Peace, peace at any price." Congressman Lucien Bonaparte Casswell of Wisconsin summed up the spirit of the hour. "The members of Congress," he said, "are of the impression that the people wish to revive business at any political sacrifice." And what this meant in plain English was that the people demanded the sacrifice of the black man and the letter and spirit of the Declaration of Independence.

The sacrifice was prepared at a series of meetings that began in December, 1876, and continued through the spring of 1877. The climax came on Monday, February 26, 1877, in three meetings between representatives of Hayes and white Southerners. The first two meetings were held in House and Senate committee rooms. The third meeting was held that night in the room of W. M. Evarts in the Wormley House, a posh D.C. hotel, owned, ironically, by a wealthy black businessman. At these meetings, Southerners promised to call off the filibuster, and Hayes' representatives promised the South "Home Rule," withdrawal of federal troops, and an increased allocation of economic resources. Incredible as it may seem now, this private agreement, which changed the course of American democracy, was reduced to writing. On Tuesday, February 27, Hayes' representatives drafted the following letter:

GENTLEMEN: Referring to the conversation had with you yesterday in which Governor Hayes' policy as to the status of certain Southern states was discussed, we desire to say in reply that we can assure you in the strongest possible manner of our great desire to have adopted such a policy as will give to the people of the States of South Carolina and Louisiana the right to control their own affairs in their own way; and to say further that we feel authorized, from an acquaintance with and knowledge of Governor Hayes and his views on this question, to pledge ourselves to you that such will be his policy.

The agreement was signed and delivered, the filibuster was called off, and Rutherford B. Hayes was inaugurated as the nineteenth President of the United States on March 5, 1877.

On April 10, President Hayes withdrew the token federal force in Columbia, South Carolina, and the government of Daniel H. Chamberlain fell.

Fourteen days later, on April 24, President Hayes pulled the rug from under Republican Governor S. B. Packard of Louisiana.

Radical Republicans and black leaders denounced Hayes for his "betrayal" of black voters. J. G. Blaine pointed out in Congress that Hayes' title to the Presidency rested on the same foundation as the titles of the Republican claimants of the South. "If Packard is not the legal governor of Louisiana," Blaine argued, "Hayes has no title to the office of President." B. F. Wade dwelt at length on the irony of the situation, pointing out that the President had betrayed the black men who had risked their lives to make him President.

Daniel Chamberlain, the deposed governor of South Carolina, said President Hayes' Southern policy amounted to "a proclamation to the country and the world that the will of the majority of the voters of a state, lawfully and regularly expressed, is no longer the ruling power in our states, and that the constitutional guaranty to every state in this Union of a republican form of goverment and of protection against violence, is henceforth ineffectual and worthless."

The immediate effect of the overthrow of Black Reconstruction was the installation in the South of conservative New South regimes dominated by planter-merchants, railroad chieftains and corporation lawyers. Ignoring the needs of poor whites and poor Negroes, these governments drastically slashed state services and devised tax programs that soaked the poor. Traveling in Georgia after the redemption of that state, Charles Nordhoff said that free schools were unknown outside the large cities and towns. The U.S. commissioner of education reported that Alabama Democrats had crippled the educational system. There was a similar development in South Carolina where the Democratic government closed the integrated state university, abolished the system of state scholarships and reduced the liberal appropriations for state schools.

In most states, new constitutions were drafted with anti-Democratic features that severely limited the power potential of both poor Negroes and poor whites. As C. Vann Woodward has pointed out, the so-called Redeemers evinced a decided hostility to all modes of democracy and attempted to make the new governments naked instruments of the rich and powerful.

All this was in marked contrast to the legacy of the Reconstructionists who had done many astonishingly good things despite mistakes and blemishes which were, in large part, inevitable under the circumstances. During their days of power, black politicians and their white allies had enormously extended the social capital of the South and had created a base for industrialization by building roads, levees, dams, and public buildings. Most importantly, they had created a free public school system in a region hostile to both schools and positive government effort.

Defenders of the Compromise of 1877 say that
abandoning the Negro voters of the
South was the only way to reconcile the
North and South.

Rutherford B. Hayes, nineteenth President of the United States, played a central role in the Compromise of 1877 which paved the way for white control of the South.

George H. White of North Carolina was the last black man to sit in Congress in post-Reconstruction period. His Congressional term ended in 1901.

Speaking on the floor of the South Carolina constitutional convention of 1895, in response to the taunts of "Pitchfork" Ben Tillman of Edgefield County, Thomas Miller defended the legacy of Reconstruction. "The gentleman from Edgefield," he said, "speaks of the piling up of the state debt; of jobbery and peculation during the period between 1869 and 1873 in South Carolina, but he has not found voice eloquent enough, nor pen exact enough to mention those imperishable gifts bestowed upon South Carolina between 1873 and 1876 by Negro legislators—the laws relative to finance, the building of penal and charitable institutions, and, greatest of all, the establishment of the public school system." Miller added: "We were eight years in power. We had built schoolhouses, established charitable institutions, built and maintained the penitentiary system, provided for the education of the deaf and dumb, rebuilt the jails and courthouses, rebuilt the bridges and reestablished the ferries. In short, we had reconstructed that State and placed it upon the road to prosperity."

A similar epitaph was offered by Albion Tourgee, the white Radical, who said: "[The Radical Republicans] instituted a public school system in a realm where public schools had been unknown. They opened the ballot-box and jury box to thousands of white men who had been barred from them by a lack of earthly possessions. They introduced home rule in the South. They abolished the whipping post, the branding iron, the stock and other barbarous forms of punishment which had up to that time prevailed. They reduced capital felonies from about twenty to two or three. In an age of extravagance they were extravagant in the sums appropriated for public works. In all that time no man's rights of person were invaded under the forms of law."

All this was achieved by men who were condemned by history to make bricks without straws. This was particularly true of the black men of power. Pulled from the faceless masses and flung into the breach between advancing industrialism and a declining planter aristocracy, they were condemned to labor with inadequate tools on ground that had not been adequately prepared. They never received proper backing from their Northern supporters, and they were betrayed repeatedly by their allies. History—the historic fears of poor whites and the historic greed of rich whites—stood between them and success. History, in fine, provided the opportunity, but cleverly withheld the raw materials. It may be true, as some contend, that they were condemned, no matter what they did. Still, what they did was important. Within the limits of the time and the Revolution, and with the resources at their disposal, they served man well. Because of them and through them, America grew, adopting the Fourteenth and Fifteenth Amendments, which would never have been adopted had they not been adopted then. More than that—these men established, beyond question, the right of black men to participate in power, and they created political instruments that would revolutionize America and the South if made concrete today.

The first order of business for every Democratic administration was the discrediting of these men. The investigative process in South Carolina has been analyzed with great subtlety and perception by Joel Williamson, who wrote: "Using the power of official office, Democrats proceeded publicly to smear charges of corruption across the face of Republicanism in the state, unqualifiedly damning every Republican officeholder and every man—excluding themselves of course—who had ever voted for a Republican candidate. The strategy was to establish guilt by accusation. The method has since become familiar." That this was, indeed, the strategy is proven by the private letters of James Conner, the South Carolina attorney general, who wrote W. D. Simpson, the lieutenant governor, in the summer of 1877: "Briefly & all this in confidence," he wrote, "I think our course is to get the Inditments [sic] & not issue requisitions [for extraditions], but publish in Shape of a Report, the testimony the Committee has taken: an immense deal of it, & the most captivating parts are historical & would not stand test as legal evidence, but the moral evidence would be crushing." Prophetically reading the minds of most white historians of the Reconstruction, Conner added: "The press would revel in it, & we would politically guillotine every man of them."

By this method and by a reign of white terror, the Republican party was destroyed in the South. But individual Republicans managed to hold onto pockets of power in several states. Black voters sent representatives to Southern legislatures and congressmen to Washington until the dawn of the twentieth century. In Mississippi, the powerful Republican machine of Jackson retained control of that city for thirteen years after the counterrevolution, and Jim Hill, the powerful black politician, served as secretary of state for three years under an otherwise all-white Democratic administration. In Republican strongholds like Beaufort, South Carolina, black men continued to hold offices as county clerks and sheriffs. Throughout this period, there were black policemen in the South. And scores of black Republicans were appointed to the federal posts of postmaster and internal revenue collector.

As the years wore on, the area of black expressiveness narrowed, and by World War I it was considered subversive for black men to hold public office. By that time, the whole black population had been reduced to a form of group servitude and the South, with the approval of the Supreme Court and every structure of power in the North, was grinding out Jim Crow laws of increasing severity.

The long-term effects of this turn-about were disastrous, not only to the black men, but to the South and to America. Having lost their power, black men soon lost the power of their being. Using the state apparatus, white men pushed black men out of skilled trades and shamelessly appropriated their surplus funds in fraudulent sharecropper transactions. Even worse, the state deliberately fostered ignorance and multiplied black criminals who were fed into the maw of the enormously profitable convict system. A totalitarian system came into being in the heart of America, and America, in sanctioning that system, became less than a democracy. As a solid bloc of reaction, the South stood athwart every impulse of reform and renovation. And this solid bloc of reaction changed the whole tone and temper of American life. Racism enveloped the whole country and poked neo-colonial fingers into Latin America and the Caribbean. Black people protested. They got up meetings and called on the President. But nobody was listening and nobody seemed to care.

THE DREAM DIED.

And the dreamers wandered restlessly across the face of the country, trying to find a place where man did not hunt man. They went, carrying with them the memories of days in the sun, the memories of pomp and majesty and processions of power and of the time when poor black men and poor white men bowed down together and tried to lift the earth with their bare hands — memories so fantastic, so incredible that there would come a time when people would no longer believe them. But dreams, however inspiring, are not nutritive. And so the dreamers went, burdened down with old documents and outlawed hopes. The brilliant Robert Brown Elliott, not yet forty and with a career of black power behind him still unmatched, held on in South Carolina for several years and then migrated to Louisiana where he died at the age of forty-two. P. B. S. Pinchback went back to school, got a law degree and migrated to Washington, D. C., where many of the old power brokers gathered to reminisce, no doubt, about the good old days. Francis Louis Cardozo also settled in Washington where he became principal of a black high school which still bears his name. Richard Cain, the former South Carolina congressman, abandoned politics and was elected bishop of the A.M.E. Church. J. T. Walls, the former Florida congressman, became superintendent of the farm at Tallahassee State College where he died in 1905. Hiram Revels, the first black senator, became president of Alcorn College, and Blanche K. Bruce, the second U.S. senator, was appointed registrar of the U.S. Treasury.

The newly-weds were also in transit. Albert Morgan and his black bride, Carrie Highgate Morgan, left Mississippi and joined the long list of Republican refugees in Washington, D. C. With the aid of Senator Bruce, Morgan got a job as a clerk in the pension office. But when the Democrats returned to power in 1885 he was peremptorily dismissed. With his wife, four daughters, and two sons, Morgan migrated to Kansas where he operated several businesses. In 1890, he left his family and moved to Colorado where he prospected for gold and operated a "School for Money." In the meantime, the Morgan girls, who were spectacularly beautiful, became actresses. One of them said later: "We went on stage, and Mamma was our chaperon...then she lived with Angela—as she has with one of us, ever since—mostly with Angela.... For twenty-seven years her home was in New York City. She never remarried.... Mother became a mental healer, Christian Science lecturer and dramatic reader. These are her professions, but she is wonderfully equipped in all phases of literature, art, and religion....." Morgan apparently never saw his wife and family again. Author Frank E. Smith wrote: "The bright shaft of the young idealist, who rewrote the statute books to marry Carrie, who wanted to remold an entire regional culture in a day, had been blunted beyond repair in the Reconstruction politics of Yazoo County and the confining pressures of raising a family as a pension-office clerk."

Jeremiah Haralson, the last black congressman from Ala bama, was a metaphor of an age of unemployed black power. Black as an ace of spades, shrewd, forceful, persistent, Haralson maneuvered frantically in an abortive attempt to find a weak spot in the thick white curtain white men were lowering between black Americans and the sun. Haralson ran for several offices in Alabama and was defeated by fraud and violence. He then served as a clerk in the Interior Department and the Pension Bureau before wandering across Louisiana and Arkansas. In 1912, he returned to Selma and found the fruit rotten on the vine. In despair, he moved again, going to Texas and later to Oklahoma and Colorado. Haralson didn't find what he was looking for. And one day in 1916, while wandering near Denver, he was attacked and killed by wild beasts.

It was over.

The curtain that lifted for a moment dropped, perhaps forever.

The road not taken, the road of a color-blind and class-blind Constitution, the road of responsible participation by all in a government for all, was forgotten. And a chorus of vilification was organized to dissuade men from examining too closely the forces and phobias that pushed America down a one-way street of racism and reaction when it came, at a fateful moment in the nineteenth century, to a fateful fork in the road.

The dream died.

And the reconstruction of that dream, when it comes, if it comes, must go back, as Du Bois has said, to the fundamental principles of that first Reconstruction—Economic Security, Political Liberty, and Light for all the bondsmen of America, black and white.

Selected Bibliography

Allen, James S. *Reconstruction: The Battle for Democracy, 1865–1876*. New York, 1937.

Ames, Blanche. *Adelbert Ames, 1835–1933*. New York, 1964.

Appletons' Annual Cyclopedia, 1865–1878.

Aptheker, Herbert (ed.). *A Documentary History of the Negro People in the United States*. New York, 1951.

Bernstein, Leonard. "The Participation of Negro Delegates in the Constitutional Convention of 1868 in North Carolina," *Journal of Negro History*, XXIV (1949).

Bond, Horace Mann. "Social and Economic Forces in Alabama Reconstruction," *Journal of Negro History*, XXIII (1938).

Brodie, Fawn M. *Thaddeus Stevens: Scourge of the South*. New York, 1959.

Buck, Paul H. *The Road to Reunion*. Boston, 1937.

Campbell, George. *White and Black*. New York, 1889.

Conway, Alan. *The Reconstruction of Georgia*. Minneapolis, 1966.

Current, Richard N. (ed.). *Reconstruction, 1865–1877*. Englewood Cliffs, 1965.

Donald, David. *Lincoln Reconsidered*. New York, 1956.

——. *The Politics of Reconstruction, 1863–1867*. Baton Rouge, 1965.

——. "The Scalawag in Mississippi Reconstruction," *Journal of Southern History*, X (1944).

Douglass, Frederick. *The Life and Times of Frederick Douglass.* Hartford, 1881.

Du Bois, W. E. B. *Black Reconstruction in America, 1860–1880.* New York, 1935.

Foner, Phillip S. *The Life and Writings of Frederick Douglass.* 4 vols. New York, 1950.

Franklin, John Hope. *Reconstruction after the Civil War.* Chicago, 1961.

Harlan, Louis R. "Desegregation in New Orleans Public Schools During Reconstruction," *American Historical Review*, LXVII (1962).

Hirshon, Stanley P. *Farewell to the Bloody Shirt.* Bloomington, 1962.

Hyman, Harold M. *New Frontiers of the American Reconstruction.* Urbana, 1966.

King, Edward. *The Great South.* Hartford, 1875.

Korngold, Ralph. *Thaddeus Stevens.* New York, 1955.

The Ku Klux Conspiracy. Testimony Taken by the Joint Select Committee to Inquire into the Condition of Affairs in the Late Insurrectionary States. 13 vols. Washington; Government Printing Office, 1872.

Lynch, John R. *The Facts of Reconstruction.* New York, 1913.

McPherson, James M. *The Struggle for Equality: Abolitionists and the Negro in the Civil War and Reconstruction.* Princeton, 1964.

Morgan, Albert T. *Yazoo.* Washington, 1884.

Nordhoff, Charles. *The Cotton States in the Spring and Summer of 1875.* New York, 1876.

Perkins, A. E. "Oscar James Dunn," *Phylon*, IV (1943).

Pike, James S. *The Prostrate State.* New York, 1874.

Quarles, Benjamin. *Lincoln and the Negro.* New York, 1962.

Richardson, Joe M. *The Negro in the Reconstruction of Florida, 1865–1877.* Tallahassee, 1965.

Riddleberger, Patrick W. "The Radicals' Abandonment of the Negro During Reconstruction," *Journal of Negro History*," XLV (1960).

Russ, William A. Jr. "Registration and Disfranchisement under Radical Reconstruction," *Mississippi Valley Historical Review,* XXI (1934).

Shenton, James P. (ed.). *The Reconstruction: A Documentary History of the South after the War, 1865–1877.* New York, 1963.

Shugg, Roger W. *Origins of Class Struggle in Louisiana.* Baton Rouge, 1939.

Simkins, Francis B., and Woody, Robert H. *South Carolina During Reconstruction.* Chapel Hill, 1932.

Simmons, William J. *Men of Mark.* Cleveland, 1887.

Singletary, Otis. *Negro Militia and Reconstruction.* Austin, 1957.

Smith, S. D. *The Negro in Congress.* Chapel Hill, 1940.

Somers, Robert. *The Southern States since the War, 1870–1871.* New York, 1871.

Sweat, Edward F. "Francis L. Cardozo: Profile of Integrity in Reconstruction Politics," *Journal of Negro History,* XLVI (1961).

Taylor, A. A. *The Negro in South Carolina During Reconstruction.* Washington, 1924.

Tourgee, Albion. *The Negro in Reconstruction in Virginia.* Washington, 1926

———. *A Fool's Errand.* New York, 1879

Warmoth, Henry C. *War, Politics and Reconstruction.* New York, 1930.

Weisberger, Bernard. "The Dark and Bloody Ground of Reconstruction Historiography," *Journal of Southern History,* XXV (1959).

Wharton, Vernon Lane. *The Negro in Mississippi, 1865–1890.* Chapel Hill, 1947.

Williamson, Joel. *After Slavery: The Negro in South Carolina During Reconstruction, 1861–1877.* Chapel Hill, 1965.

Wish, Harvey (ed.). *Reconstruction in the South, 1865–1877.* New York, 1965.

Woodburn, James A. *The Life of Thaddeus Stevens.* Indianapolis, 1913.

Woodson, Carter G. (ed.). *Negro Orators and Their Orations.* Washington, 1925.

Woodward, C. Vann. *Origins of the New South, 1877–1913.* Baton Rouge, 1951.

——. *Reunion and Reaction: The Compromise of 1877 and the End of Reconstruction.* Boston, 1951.

Woody, Robert H. "Jonathan Jasper Wright," *Journal of Negro History,* V (1920).

Wynes, Charles E. (ed.). *The Negro in the South Since 1865.* University, Alabama, 1965.

Index

in politics, 84, 88, 125, 132, 133, 137–39, 142–46, 161, 164–68, 171–73, 181–87, 190–91, 386, Northern whites in, 146–50, 170; politics, 72, 74, 76, 128, 166–68, 171–72, 177–78, 373, 378–80; Southern whites in politics, 146–47, 168; taxation and public finance, 114, 152–55, 163, 174–75, 176–77; and white terrorist campaign, 163–64, 168, 169, 373, 376–78
Springer, T. W., 86
Stearns, M. L., 373
Stevens, Thaddeus, 15, 29, 33, 35–36, 38–44, 53, 57–59, 88, 132–33, 162
Strother, Alfred, 110
Sumner, Charles, 15, 17, 19, 22–23, 28, 29, 31, 33–35, 40, 44, 57, 88, 361–62
Swails, Stephen, 133, 138, 173, 178, 184, 191

Taliaferro, J. C., 125, 239, 250
Taylor, A. A., 281–82, 313, 316–17
Tennessee, 17, 131
Texas, 60, 131, 279, 280, 281, 282, 296, 342, 360
Thirteenth Amendment, 28, 29, 35
Tilden, Samuel J., 373, 378
Tomlinson, Reuben, 172, 303
Tourgee, Albion W., 44, 92, 96, 312, 329–30, 384
Toynbee, Arnold, 60
Turner, Benjamin, 289
Turner, Henry McNeal, 86, 278, 286, 294–295

U. S. Army, 26, 31, 56, 100–101, 106, 112, 197
U. S. Congress, 15, 17–18, 45, 50, 53–54, 57, 80; Negroes in, 126, 128, 142, 146, 168, 212–14, 269–71, 285
U. S. Supreme Court, 278, 356, 371

Vesey, Denmark, 5
Virginia, 60, 70, 131, 279, 280, 281, 282, 296

Wade, Benjamin F., 17, 380
Walker, Donald S., 105
Wallace, John, 106
Walls, Josiah T., 285, 286, 388
Warmoth, Henry Clay, 125, 128, 235, 237–38, 239, 243, 246–47, 250–52, 253–57, 260–53, 359
Washington, D.C., 41, 61
Wells, J. M., 92
Wharton, Vernon 82, 96, 216–17, 229, 232
Whipper, William J., 86, 138, 152, 159, 165, 172, 178, 317, 322, 351–52
White, George H., 383
White, James T., 119, 296
White League, the, 356–69
Whites, Northern, 7, 9, 46, 66–67, 93–94, 332
Whites, poor, 7, 21, 48, 60, 64–66, 83–84, 95–96, 196; and Negroes, 28–29, 33, 57, 207
Whites, Southern, 7, 8, 9, 10, 11, 21, 44, 62, 65, 66, 69, 74–76, 83–84, 91–92, 94–95, 160–63, 232–33, 289, 323–25, 332
Wilder, C. M., 180, 182
Williamson, Joel, 324, 385–86
Wilson, Henry, 72, 98, 260
Wood, Robert H., 194, 228
Woodson, Carter G., 145
Woodward, C. Vann, 381
Woody, Robert H., 187
Wright, Elizur, 52–53
Wright, Jonathan Jasper, 68, 109, 138, 144, 189, 190

Yulee, David L., 105